Price Setting

Price Setting

Truman F. Bewley

polity

Copyright © Truman F. Bewley 2025

The right of Truman F. Bewley to be identified as Author of this Work has been asserted in accordance with the UK Copyright, Designs and Patents Act 1988.

First published in 2025 by Polity Press

Polity Press
65 Bridge Street
Cambridge CB2 1UR, UK

Polity Press
111 River Street
Hoboken, NJ 07030, USA

All rights reserved. Except for the quotation of short passages for the purpose of criticism and review, no part of this publication may be reproduced, stored in a retrieval system or transmitted, in any form or by any means, electronic, mechanical, photocopying, recording or otherwise, without the prior permission of the publisher.

ISBN-13: 978-1-5095-6576-4

A catalogue record for this book is available from the British Library.

Library of Congress Control Number: 2024946664

Typeset in 10.5 on 12 pt Times New Roman
by Fakenham Prepress Solutions, Fakenham, Norfolk NR21 8NL
Printed and bound in Great Britain by CPI Group (UK) Ltd, Croydon

The publisher has used its best endeavors to ensure that the URLs for external websites referred to in this book are correct and active at the time of going to press. However, the publisher has no responsibility for the websites and can make no guarantee that a site will remain live or that the content is or will remain appropriate.

Every effort has been made to trace all copyright holders, but if any have been overlooked the publisher will be pleased to include any necessary credits in any subsequent reprint or edition.

For further information on Polity, visit our website:
politybooks.com

Contents

Acknowledgments vi

1. Introduction — 1
2. The Pricing of Manufactured Goods — 22
3. Retail Pricing — 87
4. Restaurant Pricing — 117
5. Pricing by Contract Manufacturers — 144
6. Pricing in the Construction Industry — 152
7. The Pricing of Cement — 161
8. The Pricing of Commodity Lumber, Plywood, and Oriented Strand Board — 174
9. The Pricing of Midwestern Food and Feed Grains — 183
10. Conclusion — 205

Appendix — 206

Notes — 210
References — 215
Index — 220

Acknowledgments

I gratefully acknowledge support from Sloan Foundation Grant B2000–69 and very generous support from the Cowles Foundation at Yale University. I owe a great deal to my colleague, Professor William Brainard, who did some of the interviews with me, helped arrange some of them, encouraged me, and spent a good deal of time reading and criticizing versions of the manuscript. His suggestions were invaluable. I am grateful to Professors Garry Brewer, James Robinson, and Timothy Guinnane for comments on the manuscript. I thank my research assistant Jorge Colmenares Miralles for his help with locating references. I am grateful to Michael Aronson for comments, advice, and encouragement. He was the editor of my book *Why Wages Don't Fall During a Recession*, Cambridge, MA: Harvard University Press, 1999.

1
Introduction

Why do the prices of some products fall little or even rise during business downturns while the prices of others fall dramatically and rebound during economic booms? It is not surprising that in highly competitive industries prices fluctuate with shifts in demand and supply, but what explains the dearth of price declines in markets where firms have more direct control of prices? This question is central to an understanding of business cycles. Although economists have proposed many explanations of downward price rigidity, no widely applicable theory has firm empirical support. Perhaps this is so because such support requires knowledge that is difficult to obtain, such as understanding the objectives of price setters and the constraints they face.

Hoping to find insight into price formation and rigidity, I imitated Alan Blinder and his coauthors (Blinder et al., 1998) by interviewing businesspeople who participate in price setting.[1]

Blinder and his associates used interviews to evaluate empirically twelve theories of price stickiness. The interviewers asked many questions, but their core approach was to describe each of the theories to respondents and ask them to assess its applicability to their company. On the basis of the answers, the authors rated on a numerical scale the importance of each theory as an explanation of price stickiness at that firm. The average of all the scores from all the interviews is a measure of the overall relevance of the theory. Blinder and his coauthors randomly chose the companies to be solicited for interviews, where the probability that a company was chosen was proportional to its value added.

Although I found the work of Blinder and his coauthors to be useful, I did not follow them by asking respondents to comment on the relevance of particular theories of price rigidity. Instead, when arranging interviews I explained that I hoped respondents would tell me what I needed to know to understand pricing in their company and industry. Before interviews, I emailed respondents a list of questions designed to make clear what topics interested me. During interviews, I used what respondents came up with as a basis for further questioning. A disadvantage of this approach was that not all respondents dealt with the same topics, so that the incidence of responses of a given type may not be a reliable gauge of its importance. Interpretation must rely on learning how respondents think, on the logic in the responses, and on circumstances described in them. An advantage of the approach is that I learned things I would not have thought to ask about. One reason I avoided the approach of Blinder and his coauthors is that economists may have overlooked correct theories of price rigidity. In fact, Blinder and his coauthors did not ask about the explanation of price rigidity that I found to be the most widely applicable.[2] Another reason for not asking about theories is that in my experience such questions can cause respondents subtly to stop cooperating, if they think a theory is silly or if they feel they are being drawn into intellectual competition with a professor.

Because of my interviewing method, I could not select respondents randomly. Businesspeople are reluctant to participate in loosely structured interviews, because they worry that they might inadvertently reveal confidential information or say something that would embarrass their company. So, I had to gain trust, which I did by using what is called the snowball sampling method. I started by interviewing friends and acquaintances and, at the end of every interview, I asked for referrals to other possible respondents, while indicating what kinds of companies and people interested me. I promised full confidentiality to everyone I asked for interviews. This approach was for the most part successful, though slow. Sometimes, more than a year passed before a company's lawyers agreed to let me interview in their firm. I had disappointments. For instance, I never penetrated the Internet commerce industry and I never had an interview with a plate-glass manufacturer. In requesting referrals, I sought variety in the types of businesses but also strove adequately to cover the main industries in the American economy and the most important companies within each. I did not record the number of interview requests that were refused, but believe I talked to key people in most of the categories of businesses I studied. Interviews usually took place in the respondent's office, or in a restaurant, and lasted about ninety minutes. Most interviews were tape-recorded and later transcribed, though some respondents refused to be recorded. I checked for accuracy all the transcriptions that I did not do myself.

One might expect in a study like this to read about negative productivity shocks and Federal Reserve Bank inflation targeting or forward guidance, because these topics are much discussed in macroeconomics. Neither topic ever came up spontaneously, except when a few respondents mentioned the effects of drought on agriculture and of low water levels on river and lake shipping. I occasionally brought the topics up, but eventually desisted, because respondents implied they were irrelevant to pricing. They may have reacted this way regarding Federal Reserve Bank policy, because there was little inflation at the time.

I came up with three main findings, each of which is a phenomenon, together with explanations of why it occurs. The phenomenon in one finding is that the prices of highly differentiated products seldom decline and tend to increase only sluggishly in response to changes in demand or supply, whereas the prices of undifferentiated products respond so quickly to such shifts that many are volatile. By a highly differentiated product I mean one produced by only one firm and that is not a good substitute for any other product. A strong brand, for instance, makes a product highly differentiated.

The phenomenon in another main finding is that marginal variable costs of manufacturing firms tend to remain constant or to decline as a function of output until capacity is reached, at which point marginal variable costs rise abruptly. This assertion may seem counterintuitive, since, presumably, as output increases in the short-run more labor is used with a fixed amount of capital equipment. The proposition that marginal variable costs may be constant over a wide range of outputs is not new. For instance, Robert Hall suggests this idea (Hall, 1986), and Blinder and his coauthors present empirical evidence supporting it (Blinder et al., 1998, ch. 12).

The impact of declining or constant marginal variable costs on the ability of manufacturing firms to make money creates a link between the behavior of marginal variable costs and product differentiation. Firms with constant or declining marginal variable costs lose money if they set price equal to marginal variable cost, unless they produce at a level so close to capacity that marginal variable costs exceed average variable costs. This predicament no doubt helps explain the drive of many firms to differentiate their products, because differentiation normally enables firms to charge more than marginal variable cost and hence perhaps to cover fixed costs and earn a profit.

Constancy of marginal variable costs suggests an explanation of price stickiness that should be considered. The explanation is that if a product's price equals a constant markup over marginal variable costs, then constancy of marginal variable costs implies price rigidity. The rigidity to be explained is the lack of response of price to the business cycle. If we assume that a firm's marginal variable costs are roughly proportional to the average wages and salaries it pays, then it is reasonable to assume that nominal marginal variable costs do not fall during recessions, since economy-wide averages of nominal wages and salaries seldom fall.[3] The proportionality between the price of labor and marginal variable costs is, however, questionable, since variable costs in manufacturing are often dominated by the costs of variable factors other than labor, costs that may have little to do with labor costs. The assumption that prices are a constant markup over marginal variable costs should also be questioned, because profit margins often decline during hard times. A weaker form of this assumption may be approximately valid, however, because many manufacturing firms set the price of each of their products to be roughly equal to a markup over the sum of average variable costs, and an assignment to the product of a share of the firm's average overhead and fixed costs. Costs including this assignment are known as fully absorbing costs. If price is a markup over fully absorbing costs, then the markup of price over average variable costs is positive, even if no additional margin is added for profits. If we add the assumption that average variable costs are constant, then this line of thinking leads to a weak form of downward price rigidity; namely, that in a recession prices will not fall below some level that exceeds the constant level of average variable costs. This reasoning does not imply upward price rigidity, because wages and salaries are not upwardly rigid. A weakness of the theory is that some firms reduce the markup of price over average variable costs when demand slumps, by using what is called contribution margin pricing. A contribution margin price is one between average variable costs and fully absorbing costs.

The views of businesspeople do not support the attribution of downward price rigidity to cost-based pricing and constancy of marginal variable costs. None of my respondents came up with this idea as an explanation of price stickiness, and Blinder and his coauthors had a similar experience. Cost-based pricing, together with constant marginal variable costs, was one of the theories they asked about, and it did badly.[4] My view is that though the mechanism described in the theory may contribute to downward price rigidity, much more information is needed to assess the mechanism's importance.

The phenomenon in a third main finding is the widespread use of formula-based pricing in long-term contracts governing trade in commodities between firms, where, in business jargon, prices are "formula-based" if they are indexed to some publicly available statistics, and the word "commodity" refers to an undifferentiated product sold on a reasonably competitive market. I will use the words in these senses. By commodity, I do not mean something bought and sold, which is the normal usage in economics.

It should not be imagined that all products are either commodities or highly differentiated, since there are many degrees of differentiation. For instance, airline travel is somewhat differentiated and yet has fairly flexible pricing. The processes that create its prices have little in common with those generating the prices of commodities or of highly differentiated products. Most goods sold in stores seem to be either commodities or highly differentiated.

It is well known that most commodities have volatile prices. Respondents attributed the volatility to factors that varied with the product. Respondents said that supply fluctuations caused the prices of meat and fresh fruits and vegetables to be volatile. Extreme changes in the prices for natural gas and wholesale electricity were attributed to demand. Fluctuations in the prices of fresh fish and of petroleum and its products were said to be due to changes in both supply and demand. In discussions of the prices of lumber, commodity plywood, and oriented strand board, I heard about price-inventory cycles. When prices rise, expectations of further increases motivate market participants to buy and store products, driving prices higher. The reverse was said to occur when prices decline.

In most commodity markets, there is a volume of spot[5] transactions between individual buyers and sellers who negotiate the prices. Because of the volatility of commodity prices, traders need guidance as to what to bid and ask. This need is filled by market-reporting companies, consulting companies, trade journals, and government agencies that make anonymous surveys of negotiated prices in specific markets and publish summaries of the findings. The negotiated prices surveyed are usually for spot transactions. The summaries of surveys by private organizations are available only to those who purchase them, and these sales pay for the surveys.

The published summaries not only guide traders, but form the basis for formula-based prices. The formulas specify prices as mathematical functions of survey results. The formulas are usually defined in long-term contracts between buying and selling companies. Trading at formula-based contract prices is common in many commodities, and in some the volume of trade at formula-based prices far exceeds that at negotiated prices. An attraction of formula-based prices is that they reduce the risk of disruption of the buyer–seller relationship caused by an impasse in price negotiations or by a buyer or seller reneging on a long-term fixed price contract. If spot prices are volatile, either the buyer or seller in a long-term fixed price contract is likely at some time to want to cheat and buy spot rather than according to the contract. If there were no contract the price would have to be renegotiated frequently, risking an impasse. The buying and selling companies cannot just agree to trade with each other at the current spot price, because that price is usually not clearly defined. Spot transactions typically are arranged privately at prices that are not made public. Buyer and seller need negotiate a formula only once in a while, and formula-based contracts can safely be made long term, if the formula-based price stays close to spot market prices for the same product. Such indexed contracts are common in, for instance, the chemical, food, petroleum, steel, scrap steel, lumber, and natural gas industries.

Much of this book is devoted to supporting the three main findings, but the book also contains descriptive material on pricing. The hope is that such information stimulates thinking about theoretical issues by providing concrete contexts.

1.1 Rigidity of the Prices of Highly Differentiated Products

A key question is why the prices of highly differentiated products do not fall sharply during recessions. Comparison with competitive commodity markets suggests a superficial answer. There are many sellers of a commodity, and the seller with the lowest price can steal as much in sales from higher priced sellers as it can handle. As a result, the demand faced by each seller is extremely elastic, so that when market demand declines, every seller believes it can increase its profits by reducing its price. This mechanism is weaker when products are highly differentiated, because there is only one producer of each good, and the different goods are not good substitutes for each other. Because the goods are not good substitutes, a price reduction by a producer would probably have to be large just to be noticed by those more interested in buying competing products. Nevertheless, it is puzzling that producers of highly differentiated goods reduce prices so little during recessions. There must be some substitutability even among highly differentiated goods, and low sales impose costs on firms that could be reduced by increasing sales. An example of such costs is the loss of skilled employees through layoffs.

Part of the explanation of the dearth of price cuts during slow times may have to do with producers' attitudes. Producers of highly differentiated products know that because differentiation is a source of market power it is a source of wealth. One of their preoccupations is to protect the differentiation, and one way to do so is to keep customers' attention focused on a product's qualities. Producers say that for this reason they try to avoid price change, because price volatility attracts attention to a product's price rather than its characteristics. Those who choose prices for differentiated products say that price change commoditizes products, where by commoditize they mean attract attention to price and away from a product's properties. Typically price setters choose prices that seem unlikely to attract attention, then keep the prices constant for a fairly long time, and use a product's qualities to sell it. This way of choosing prices leads price setters to associate price with product quality, and respondents claim that customers tend to make the same association. A fairly common argument against price reduction is that it can diminish potential buyers' perceptions of a product's quality.

One reason producers may wish to avoid price fluctuation is that the administrative process of changing price may be expensive for the seller and for customers as well. I asked about such costs and, with some exceptions, they were said to be insignificant impediments to price change.

When I asked producers of highly differentiated products why they did not reduce prices during recessions, the most common answer was that the quantity sold would not increase or would do so by only a small amount. The second most common answer was that price increases meet such strong opposition that it would be difficult to reverse a price reduction after demand recovered.

If a price reduction would hardly affect the quantity sold, it is natural to assume that a price increase would also hardly do so. Hence we are left with the need to explain why firms do not increase prices during recessions. The explanation, I believe, is that buyer opposition to price increases discourages them.

Respondents offered explanations of why the demand for highly differentiated productive inputs reacts little to price reduction. These explanations form a coherent story, especially when substitution among inputs involves switching costs. These costs inhibit firms from reacting to a decline in the price of an input by substituting it for one or more other inputs. Hence, switching costs tend to make inputs nearly proportional to outputs. Reducing the price of an input is not likely to have much effect on the demand for the output, unless the output has a high elasticity of demand and the input's cost is a large fraction of the cost of the output. Example 1 in the Appendix illustrates this story. Since the story requires that the output's elasticity of demand not be high, a full explanation of the lack of response of input demands to price reduction in a recession requires an explanation of modest response of final demands to price reduction, where by final demands I mean demand for consumption goods and capital equipment.

Respondents who set prices for highly differentiated products did not explain clearly why final demands respond little to price reduction during periods of low demand. A possible explanation is the superficial answer mentioned at the beginning of this section. Example 2 in the Appendix is, I believe, a natural formalization of this story. In the example, demand is inelastic at every price, and I encountered no evidence of such wide-ranging inelasticity. The lack of realism of this implication indicates that the story is at best an incomplete explanation.

One could accept provisionally as an empirical regularity price setters' belief that final demands for highly differentiated products respond little to price reduction, especially during periods of low demand. To go beyond this disappointing stance, one needs more empirical information. One needs to verify that price setters' beliefs are accurate, that final demands do respond little to price reduction. If it is true that final demands are unresponsive, one needs to know why. More empirical information might eliminate many of the possible explanations that come to mind and open the way to an understanding of the lack of response. A rough summary of what price setters say and imply is that they select a price from a range of prices they believe buyers will find appropriate, hoping the choice will encourage buyers to focus on the product's qualities. Within the range, demand responds little to price reduction, because the product fills buyers' specific needs that are quickly saturated. It cannot be said, however, that demand is inelastic, because a price increase might so offend buyers as to reduce demand sharply.

A common response of sellers of all types to demand decline is to increase the use of temporary promotional discounts. When such discounts are applied to highly differentiated goods, normally the price returns after the promotion to its level before the promotion, which in retail trade is called the regular price. This is done in order to convince customers that the discount is indeed a discount that should be taken advantage of while it lasts. Promotions for a particular product are held sufficiently infrequently and the discounts are usually large enough to inspire in customers the impression that the promotion is an unusual opportunity. Vendors believe the discounts increase demand more than would a permanent price reduction of the same size. Temporary discounts are common though not universal in retail trade and in some industrial markets, such as the markets for machine tools. Temporary promotional discounts are a merchandising tool used in good times and bad and should not be confused with reductions in regular or list prices. The responsiveness of demand to temporary promotional discounts does not necessarily contradict a lack of response of demand to reductions in regular or list prices, because a large part of the effect of promotions on demand probably results from shifting purchases through time and concentrating them in a short period.

Opposition to price increases comes from final buyers and from intermediaries, such as wholesalers or distributors and large retailers. Opposition from final buyers comes only when high frequency of purchase makes them aware of price increases. The opposition of final buyers is expressed by complaints, reduced purchases, and switching to substitute products. Large retailers and distributors sometimes refuse to pay price increases, threatening to drop the product. Consumer opposition to price increases is pronounced in the restaurant industry, where consumers are especially apt to notice price increases. In the major household appliance industry, where customers buy too infrequently to be aware of price increases, the opposition to increases comes from large retailers and seems to be effective. In the automobile industry price increases occur even during recessions. This may be so because in this industry most customers buy too infrequently to notice price increases and intermediaries are not in a position to oppose them. It seems that where opposition to price increases exists it does discourage them. A recurrent theme in the interviews was that a strong deterrent to price reductions during a period of slack demand is the anticipated opposition to future price increases made to reverse the reduction.

Manufacturers of highly differentiated products strive to find a hook that will tie a clientele of customers to their product. The hook can be brand loyalty or a customer's habit of eating a certain food. It can be that a customer knows how to use only certain kinds of computer programs. It can be that a customer's industrial process requires a certain proprietary chemical. In industrial settings, some manufacturers use an approach to pricing called value pricing, where the seller claims that its product saves the buyer money in its production processes relative to any available alternative and that the product's price is set so as to share the savings between buyer and seller. Although canny buyers resist such sales pitches, they are nevertheless effective in tieing buyers to certain products. If a manufacturer adheres to a value pricing story, then its price is not affected by product demand.

A somewhat different reason for price rigidity exists when a manufacturer sells a flow of a differentiated product to another company, such as a retailer or another manufacturer. The product might be a component of one of the buyer's products or it could be a branded good purchased by a retailer to sell to the public. In many such cases, the price is held fixed in part in order to avoid frequent negotiations of price changes, which could disrupt the relationship between buyer and seller if the negotiations failed. Both sides would normally regret such a disruption, the buyer because it needs the product and the seller because of the loss of sales.

Since buyers and sellers of commodities often negotiate prices, one wonders why the difficulty of these negotiations does not make commodity prices rigid. One answer may be that in a commodity market, since all buyers and sellers deal in the same good, it is normally easy to change trading partners if a negotiation stalls. Another answer is that when a buyer and seller are too closely linked to change trading partners easily, they tend to trade at flexible formula-based contract prices rather than rigid prices. Formula-based contract prices often have nearly the same function in commodity trading as can rigid prices in the buying and selling of highly differentiated goods. Both help preserve the relationship between buyer and seller by neutralizing the price adjustment process.

Since product differentiation gives sellers market power, one might conclude that it is market power alone that generates price rigidity. One might imagine that because the producer of a highly differentiated product has a monopoly on the sale of its product, the way to test whether it is market power alone that causes price rigidity is to examine pricing by companies that are the sole producers of an undifferentiated product. Such a test would not be valid, because a product produced by only one firm is by definition differentiated. A test would have to involve an undifferentiated product manufactured by oligopolists with market power. There are nearly undifferentiated products, such as cement, gypsum wallboard, and some kinds of paper and steel that are produced by oligopolists who clearly have market power. The prices of these goods are fairly flexible, though not as volatile as the prices of many commodities. The lack of differentiation can make it so easy for producers of these products to increase profits temporarily by undercutting competitors' prices, that it is hard for the producers to resist doing so. This is evidence that market power may not be able to create price rigidity unless the seller's ability to control price is reinforced by product differentiation.

There are large numbers of companies that produce closely related but differentiated products and that compete on product attributes as well as on price. Examples are restaurants, contract manufacturers that produce goods designed by their customers, and contractors in the building trades. Consideration of such companies supports the connection between product differentiation and price rigidity.

Restaurateurs explain that their industry relies on regular customers who eat at favorite restaurants fairly often and in each usually order one of a few dishes. Such customers are likely to notice price increases and to react badly to them. In order to avoid antagonizing and maybe losing some of these customers, restaurateurs hesitate to raise prices and are reluctant to reduce them because of the difficulty of reversing the declines later. In many restaurants, the resistance to price change is due in part to the cost of changing menus or menu boards, but the main concern seems to be the anticipated reaction of customers.

Contract manufacturers bid for work, and awards of work are normally based on the bid and reputation for good service and product quality. The world of contract manufacturers seems to be divided between those who compete mainly by bidding low and those who rely on a reputation for quality work. Those who rely on bidding low seem to react to recessions by reducing bids. Those who emphasize quality use the same arguments for not reducing bids in slow times that producers of highly differentiated goods use for not reducing prices, namely, that price reductions would do little to increase sales and would be hard to reverse after demand recovered.

So much of the pricing in the construction industry is the result of competitive bidding that it is hard to imagine that any downward price rigidity could exist there. Nevertheless, I found a few examples of price stickiness, linked to materials pricing. Those who do not reduce prices in slow times justify their inaction using arguments similar to those used by producers of highly differentiated products.

It is interesting to compare bargaining over commodity prices with that over prices of highly differentiated goods. When manufacturers of highly differentiated goods sell to large companies, such as retail chains, wholesalers, or large manufacturers, customers normally can use their buying power to depress prices. But large buyers usually have trouble holding down the prices of commodities. A large buyer could certainly depress a commodity's market price by reducing purchases, but then it would buy less product and large buyers typically want to pay a lower price for more product not less. Furthermore, many commodity markets are so large that large reductions in purchases would be required to achieve significant price reductions. Some large buyers of commodities use forward contracting to protect themselves against price increases. For instance, restaurant chains and manufacturers of prepared foods make contracts with food producers that fix prices before the beginning of the growing season. Farmers accept such contracts as protection against price declines.

I came upon two exceptions to stickiness of the prices of highly differentiated products. These are the prices of branded building products manufactured from materials that are commodities with volatile prices. Because the cost of the commodity inputs dominates the cost of the branded products, and contracts with formula-based prices tie the prices of the branded products to the prices of the commodity inputs.

The contrast between the price behavior of undifferentiated products and of highly differentiated products is similar to the contrast between the behavior of wages and salaries of temporary and regular employees. The market for temporary employees is almost an auction market and has fairly flexible wages. The close relationship between employer and regular employees makes it difficult to reduce their pay, because employees expect loyal service to be rewarded by pay increases and so are likely to consider pay reduction to be a betrayal. The parallel between labor and product markets weakens when one compares the consequences of price increases and pay reduction. The main concern about increasing the price of a highly differentiated product is that buyers find substitute products and stop buying. The main concern about reducing the pay of regular employees is that they become less productive, though there is also concern that they may quit.[6]

1.1.1 Macroeconomic Implications

An interview study of pricing ought to give insights into the inflation process. Unfortunately, I have nothing to say about this matter, because there was little inflation when I was interviewing and few respondents were in positions of responsibility during earlier inflationary periods.

An important theme in the interviews was that vendors of highly differentiated products often encounter strong resistance from customers to price increases. The resistance is to be expected since buyers can usually identify the vendor as responsible for a price increase. The resistance was described with such vehemence that one wonders that there could ever be inflation of the prices of such products. The recent inflation shows that the resistance can be overwhelmed. Probably inflation weakens the resistance by diffusing responsibility for increases. Highly differentiated products are so widespread that the resulting upward stickiness of their prices is probably enough to explain why nominal increases in aggregate demand can have real effects, even during periods of inflation. Similarly, employers' reluctance to cut pay and the reluctance of vendors and manufacturers of highly differentiated products to reduce prices should be enough to explain how reductions in nominal aggregate demand can have real effects.

1.1.2 Related Literature

There is an interesting theoretical literature on switching costs that deals mainly with issues in industrial organization: see von Weizsäcker (1984); Klemperer (1987a, 1987b, 1987c, 1989, 1995); and Beggs and Klemperer (1992). These authors capture part of the intuition of how switching costs can contribute to price inflexibility. They point out that in markets with switching costs a firm's price reduction may attract few new customers, because the costs discourage customers of rival firms from taking advantage of the reduced price: see von Weizsäcker (1984, p. 1103); and Klemperer (1987b, p. 386).

A well-known theory of price rigidity is the kinked demand curve theory of Hall and Hitch (1939); Sweezy (1939); and Abreu, Pearce, and Stacchetti (1986). According to this theory, oligopolists who all produce the same product, or close substitutes, refrain from reducing prices, because rival firms will match reductions. Similarly such oligopolists refrain from raising prices, because no competitor will match increases. Some respondents mentioned that they had to be cautious about cutting prices, because rivals might match the reductions. Such concerns no doubt inhibit price cutting.

Strictly speaking, the kinked demand curve theory does not apply to producers of highly differentiated products, since such products by definition have no close substitutes. When a producer of a highly differentiated product lowers its price, the concern is not that rivals will reduce their prices too but that, even if they don't, their customers will not leave them to take advantage of the lower price. When a producer of a highly differentiated product raises its price, the concern is not that rivals will not raise their prices but that, even if they do, the price increase will provoke the producer's customers to look for an alternative product and perhaps shift patronage to it.

The logic of the kinked demand curve argument applies no matter how many sellers there are. Kinked demand curve behavior, however, requires that different sellers coordinate their price setting, which may be difficult if the sellers are numerous. The wild behavior of many commodity prices indicates that the coordination normally does not occur when there are many sellers of a commodity. Thus, it seems appropriate to assume that the kinked demand curve theory applies only when there are few sellers of the same product or of close substitutes.

An argument against the kinked demand curve theory is that the prices of nearly undifferentiated goods do seem to be somewhat flexible, even when there are so few sellers that the kinked demand curve theory ought to apply. I have alluded to the cement and gypsum wallboard industries as examples of such flexibility.

Arthur Okun provides an explanation of price rigidity in some ways similar to that presented here. His explanation is inspired by consideration of retail trade (Okun, 1981, ch. 4). He focuses on the search costs of consumers who shop at different retailers looking for the lowest prices. He observes that retailers can reduce consumers' search costs by always having low prices that consumers can count on. He asserts that some retailers attract and retain loyal customers by having consistently low prices. He interprets the commitment to steady low pricing as part of an implicit contract between buyer and seller. Okun argues that there are customers throughout the economy, not just in retail trade, that favor certain sellers for similar reasons. He calls markets with such attachments customer markets. He reasons that prices in customer markets do not fluctuate much, because sellers wish to attract regular buyers by reducing their costs of searching for the seller with the lowest price. He contrasts customer markets with what he calls auction markets, which are competitive markets where prices fluctuate in response to changes in supply and demand.

The steady low pricing that Okun attributes to some retailers is the marketing strategy used by what are called everyday low price supermarket chains. They have few promotional discounts, though they usually do pass on to consumers fluctuations in the wholesale prices of fresh foods. There are many successful grocery chains, however, that use an opposite pricing strategy, called high-low, which uses heavily advertised temporary promotional discounts to attract customers. Many vendors of all kinds use similar pricing strategies successfully to entice customers. Okun is correct, I believe, in pointing out that some of the price rigidity in the economy is a consequence of alliances between buyers and their suppliers. My conclusion is that those alliances stem not from reduction of buyers' costs of searching for the lowest price, but from investments made by buyer and seller that make trade between them possible or from switching costs that make it difficult for a customer firm to replace an input purchased regularly from another firm.

1.2 The Behavior of Marginal and Average Variable Costs as a Function of Output

For many manufacturing processes, the behavior of marginal and average variable costs as a function of output is governed by technology. For instance, if the production equipment is designed to operate at one speed, labor and material costs are nearly proportional to output. In some businesses, respondents could not speak sensibly of the relation between output and marginal or average variable costs, because their plants' equipment runs around the clock at a nearly constant speed and shutting or slowing it down can damage it and incur startup costs. Iron and aluminum smelters, cement kilns, petroleum refineries, and paper mills face such constraints.

A technological issue is one of the explanations given for decreasing marginal and average variable costs. Many factories use the same equipment to produce a variety of products, and manufacturers count as variable the setup cost of changing a production line from one product to another. Usually the larger are orders for a product, the longer are its production runs and hence the lower are changeover costs per item produced and the lower are marginal and average variable costs of production.

The other common explanations for decreasing marginal and average variable costs have to do with attitudes of the work force. When activity in a workplace declines, workers are likely to slow down in the hope of preserving their jobs. A high production rate also creates a sense of urgency that inspires employees to work hard and imaginatively.

Initially, I asked about marginal variable costs, but found that few respondents fully grasped the concept. I therefore switched to asking about average variable costs, except when I learned that the respondent understood marginal cost. All respondents seemed to be familiar with average variable costs. The switch does not weaken the import of the basic finding, because if average variable costs remain constant or decline as output increases, then the product of output and marginal variable costs is less than or equal to total variable costs. Hence a firm that sets price equal to marginal variable cost earns no more than its total variable cost and so earns no margin to pay for fixed costs and profit. This is the conclusion of interest. A reason for thinking of the findings as applying to marginal as well as average variable costs is that the reasons respondents gave for constant or declining average variable costs imply constant or declining marginal variable costs as well.

In a firm with more than one production line for each product, marginal variable costs may increase with the firm's output, even if the marginal variable cost of each line does not do so. This is so, because the firm may use its most efficient lines when output is low and use older less efficient lines as output increases. Although it is true that even some small manufacturing companies have multiple lines for producing a product, I conclude from respondents' emphasis on the increase in productivity with output that the effects of increased use of less efficient lines in good times is normally more than offset by other productivity enhancing effects of increased output.

The assertions regarding marginal variable costs are supported by the findings of Blinder et al. (1998, p. 102). These authors estimate that about half of the U.S. gross national product is produced by firms with constant marginal costs and another forty percent is produced by firms with declining marginal costs. Blinder and coauthors found, as I did, that some respondents were not comfortable with the concept of marginal costs.

1.3 The Treatment of Fixed Costs by Manufacturers of Products that Are Not Commodities[7]

Some of the evidence for constant or declining marginal variable costs has to do with how manufacturers of goods that are not commodities treat fixed costs. If manufacturers' marginal variable costs increased with output, then those who both produce for competitive markets and set their own prices might be able to set prices equal to marginal variable cost, cover fixed costs, and make a profit. This is so, because marginal variable costs would exceed average variable costs. Although many of the 246 manufacturing firms where I interviewed both faced stiff competition and could set their own prices, few were in this happy situation, and many had to charge more than marginal variable cost just to break even. Many firms arrange to charge more than marginal variable cost by basing price on fully absorbing cost systems. Although manufacturers use these cost systems flexibly, the results seem not to be marginal cost pricing, which some respondents frowned on. They were concerned that it would cause their factories to be very busy producing low margin products at a loss.

1.4 The Treatment of Fixed Costs by Commodity Manufacturers

Another test of assertions regarding marginal variable costs is to see if commodity producers treat fixed costs in a way consistent with marginal costs' being constant or declining up to a capacity limit. Commodity producers with constant or decreasing marginal costs should operate production facilities at full capacity or not at all, provided the companies are sufficiently small relative to their market that the output of each alone does not significantly influence market prices. Commodity producers' use of capacity supports the assumption that their marginal variable costs remain constant or decline as output increases, though the support is clearest in the lumber industry and the agricultural and fishing industries. The other commodity industries where I interviewed are those that produce hogs, pork, cattle, beef, chicken, turkey, aluminum, chemicals, petroleum, and natural gas. Because of space limitations, I present evidence only for the lumber industry. The farmers I interviewed operated farms at full capacity or within the limits imposed by output control programs organized by governments or agricultural cooperatives. Similar remarks apply to the domestic U.S. fishing industry. The lumber industry has many small companies, which produce at full capacity or not at all, and some even increase output when lumber prices fall. Large lumber companies tend to reduce output when lumber prices are low, and do so with the openly expressed goal of supporting prices. Only one respondent said they operated with partial shifts, because operating at a higher level would not be profitable. This is what one would expect to hear if marginal variable costs on each production line increased with output and if the elasticity of demand for each producer's output was high. I interpret these observations as supporting indirectly the assertion that marginal variable costs on each production line remain constant or decline as output increases up to capacity. I do so cautiously, however, because I did not press questions about operating with partial shifts as often as I should have.

1.5 Formula-based Pricing

During the period of this study, there was a marked increase in the use of contracts with formula-based pricing of commodities. This was fortunate, because respondents could explain to me why they were adopting this form of pricing. Two factors seem to explain its increased popularity since the mid 1990s. One factor is the increased volatility of commodity spot prices, which makes long-term contracts with formula-based prices more practical than those with fixed prices. The other factor explaining the increased use of formula-based pricing is increased consolidation of American business, which creates corporations that build large factories whose function is to supply another corporation with a commodity. These organizations cannot afford to allow disagreement over price to disrupt their relationship, so instead of frequently negotiating prices they negotiate a formula that adjusts the contract price automatically as spot prices or production costs change. There is a long history of contracts that adjust prices to government indices of production costs, as in the railroad and coal mining industries. What seems to be new is the increased use in contracts of indices of spot market prices.

1.6 Organization of Commodity Pricing

Because of space limitations, I report in detail on only two of the commodity producing industries where I interviewed, the lumber and feed and food grain industries. Nevertheless, I say a few words about the pricing methods used in each of the commodity industries I covered. Pricing in the lumber, steel, steel scrap, meat, hogs, and cattle industries is dominated by negotiated spot prices and formula-based prices derived from spot prices, though the hog and cattle industries use futures markets as well, and the cattle industry makes some use of auctions. Pricing in the natural gas industry is dominated by short-term contracts with fixed prices and by formula prices based on surveys of these short-term fixed prices. The short-term contract prices are fixed prices for gas delivered during a day or month. In the commodity chemical industries, spot market prices play an important role, but so do longer term contracts with varying pricing systems. Among the many systems used are formula prices based on surveys of spot prices, formula prices based on published surveys of what are called posted contract prices, and open market terms, where the seller sets the price and can change it at any time. Posted contract prices are established by bargaining among a few large manufacturers. The dominant pricing method in the paper industry is to use open market terms; producers announce prices separately. The U.S. seafood industry relies on spot pricing, formula prices based on surveys of spot prices, and long-term contracts, where price is renegotiated when change seems to be called for. There are also port auctions for fresh seafood. The pricing of aluminum is dominated by prices for aluminum futures and differentials to these prices, where the differentials are established by dickering among traders and by formulas based on surveys of negotiated differentials. In the petroleum and petroleum products industry, prices are typically a futures price plus a differential, where the futures price is often a price not of the commodity traded but of a related commodity called a marker commodity. Only a few commodities are used as markers. The differentials are established by negotiations between buyer and seller or by formulas based on surveys of negotiated differentials. Although the prices of dairy products are highly regulated, they are essentially formula prices based on market prices of a few dairy commodities.

1.7 Plan of the Book

Chapter 2 summarizes information gathered from interviews with respondents from manufacturing firms. Topics include the reasons for price rigidity, the impact of administrative costs of price change, the relation between output and the average and marginal variable cost of production, fully absorbing cost accounting and pricing based on it, and the reasons for using formula-based pricing. Chapter 3 deals with non-restaurant retail firms that sell from stores. I discuss reasons for variation in the markups on individual products, the use of temporary promotional discounting, the pronounced differences between the behavior of retail prices of commodities and differentiated products, and large retailers' resistance to increases in manufacturers' prices of differentiated products. Chapter 4 covers restaurant pricing. Key themes are restaurant antipathy to increasing menu prices and the use by large restaurant chains of long-term contracting and of futures markets to control fluctuations in the wholesale prices the restaurant chains pay for food ingredients. Chapter 5 contains material on pricing by contract manufacturers and, in Chapter 6, I describe briefly pricing in the construction industry. The companies discussed in these last two chapters usually bid for work, which makes their pricing competitive and flexible. Their pricing is of interest here, in part because the companies usually treat fixed costs in ways that resemble fully absorbing cost systems. This practice suggests that the companies may experience pressure on their profit margins caused by constant or declining marginal and average variable costs. Another reason for interest in contract manufacturers is that the pricing of some companies tends to be downwardly rigid. Chapter 7 contains a description of pricing in the cement industry, which is an oligopolistic industry with somewhat flexible pricing. I present this industry as evidence that price rigidity of highly differentiated goods should probably not be attributed to market power alone, but requires some product differentiation. Chapters 8 and 9 contain descriptions of pricing of lumber and food and feed grains, respectively. Pricing in these industries illustrate most of the methods used to price commodities and contrasts with the pricing of highly differentiated products. Chapter 9 contains a brief description of futures markets.

In presenting the findings, I include quotations from interviews, since respondents' words usually express their thoughts better than paraphrases. In order to respect confidentiality, I do not mention the names of respondents, their companies, companies they refer to, or brands. When quoting a respondent, I identify the respondent by a short description rather than a name. There is a one-to-one correspondence between short descriptions and respondents. My own words and those of Professor William Brainard are enclosed in square brackets. The quotations from tape-recorded interviews are verbatim, except that I omit irrelevant phrases and personal, company, and brand names. I insert brief explanations in parentheses. I do not correct grammatical errors, including my own. The quotations are chosen to show the range of views on a topic, not the relative numbers of respondents with particular opinions. I favor quotations from respondents that express clearly views of a significant group of respondents.

1.8 Related Literature

Many authors have noted the contrast between industries with flexible and sticky prices. Early works on the topic are: Okun (1981, ch. 4), whose work I have discussed; and Means (1935, 1962, 1972). Means classifies industries as atomistic or concentrated. Atomistic industries have competitive market prices. Concentrated industries have what he termed administered prices. Administered prices are set by sellers, held constant for months or years, and seldom decline during periods of slack demand. Prices in atomistic industries, such as agriculture, are set by markets rather than by sellers and adjust constantly to set supply equal to demand. Means does not explain why administered prices are rigid. The main thrust of his discussion of the topic is that there is an association between industrial concentration and price inflexibility.

Before the work of Blinder et al. (1998), several studies of pricing appeared that were based on questionnaires and interviews. One may group together the studies of Lanzillotti (1958, 1959, 1964) and Kaplan, Dirham, and Lanzillotti (1958). They are based on information obtained from company managers. These studies describe the pricing process and also deal with company pricing goals and whether companies seek to maximize profits. I have avoided the last topic, judging that it is obvious that businesspeople want to make money. Furthermore, the precise meaning of profit maximization is not clear, given the uncertainty in business environments and ambiguity in the definition of profit. Robert Lanzillotti, in particular, was heavily criticized for questioning the profit motive: see Adelman (1959); Kahn

(1959); and Lanzillotti (1959). Barback (1964) has questioned the descriptive accuracy of the profit motive in a book based on seven case studies of businesses.

Other interview studies of pricing are: Fog (1960); Hague (1971); and Haynes (1973). The first study is based on interviews in 139 Danish companies and is remarkably thorough. The book by Haynes is based on interviews in 88 American companies. The book by Hague is based on case studies of thirteen British companies. All three of these books question whether firms can make effective use of marginal calculations. Haynes (p. 43) asserts that few firms measure their cost and revenue functions accurately, so that they cannot make marginal calculations. Furthermore, he did not encounter much evidence of the use of marginalist thinking (p. 78). Fog (p. 40) asserts that though manufacturing firms have some idea of how demand changes with price, only a few were able to give definite figures on the effect of price change on sales. Hague (pp. 123–126) asserts that the firms he studied did not know the elasticity of demand for their products. The question of whether firms do or can make marginal calculations is the subject of an old controversy: see Lester (1946); Machlup (1946); and Gordon (1948). I do not contribute to this discussion, since it deals with how pricing problems are analyzed, not the nature of the problems. I cannot resist, however, expressing mistrust of the argument that businesspeople do not use marginal arguments because they don't know calculus. It struck me when interviewing that companies find the appropriate mathematics and mathematical talent to deal with problems that have clear objectives and constraints, such as calculating optimal bids in reverse auctions for electricity, the most profitable mix of crude oils for an oil refinery, or the most effective use of futures for hedging.

The books of Fog and Haynes contain some information on the relevance of the kinked demand curve theory of price rigidity. Fog (1960, pp. 130–131) finds evidence supporting the theory. Haynes (1973, pp. 69–70) is inconclusive as to the relevance of the theory.

2
The Pricing of Manufactured Goods

This chapter contains much of the evidence for this book's three main findings, evidence from 290 interviews with officials of 246 manufacturing firms. Recall that the main findings have to do with an association between product differentiation and downward price rigidity, the relation between output and manufacturers' marginal variable costs, and the widespread use of formula-based pricing of commodities. In Section 2.1, I discuss manufacturers' choice of prices of highly differentiated goods. Section 2.2 contains evidence on causes of the downward price rigidity of highly differentiated products. Section 2.3 contains graphs showing that price indices of motor vehicles and major home appliances in the U.S. are fairly stable in comparison with the quantities sold of these two classes of products. The pictured price fluctuations seem minor in comparison with those in graphs of the prices of many commodities, such as those of lettuce, lumber, wheat, and flour shown in Figures 3.4.1, 8.5.1 to 8.5.3, 9.2.1, and 9.2.2, respectively. In Section 2.4, I present evidence on the impact of the administrative costs of price change. In Section 2.5, I discuss the behavior of the marginal and average variable costs of production as output changes. Section 2.6 contains material on the use of fully absorbing cost systems in manufacturing. In Section 2.7, I discuss manufacturing firms' formula-based pricing of commodities.

2.1 Methods for Pricing Highly Differentiated Products

Since producers of highly differentiated products wish to compete primarily on the basis of product characteristics, they choose prices intended to discourage customers from treating price as a decisive factor in the purchase decision. An approach used when pricing capital equipment and branded consumer goods is to look at the prices of related products, to estimate from this information the relation of market price to product features, and to choose the price that best reflects the product's total value given the estimated market evaluations of its features. The goal is to choose a price that is normal by market standards. Often, production costs are adapted to the prices arrived at in this way. The President of a northeastern lumber distributor[1] said:

"I can say there is no (price) volatility on highly value added products . . . [So highly value added means less competition?] Absolutely. [Then you can hold the price?] Absolutely. The more that we can value add, and value add includes not only making it a proprietary product but also having a brand name recognized, the less volatility we have. [Do you prefer not having volatility?] We prefer not having volatility. [Why is that?] Because then it does not draw attention to the price. It draws attention to the product. The minute you have volatility, then price becomes the determinant of the value. If you don't have volatility, then you have to focus on what it is that you are selling. Volatility makes price a selling issue. [And then you have to reduce your price to compete?] You have to reduce it, but then you have to go through arguing raising it when the price goes up, and it becomes a contentious issue between you and the client always, and that contentious nature is something that does not breed trust and it does not breed credibility. If I miss the market by a day, and you find out before I do, then you think I am trying to jam you with a price, even though I may have no intention of doing that at all . . . I want the primary judgment of value to be the product and its performance."

The Controller of Consumer Products for manufacturer 4 said:

"The initial pricing for us is really very critical and we do spend a fair amount of time in determining what that introduction price is going to be . . . We are developing a product for the marketplace . . . We look at, of course, the cost of the product and we know what type of margin we need to achieve on the product in order to justify being in the product, but then we also have to look at where it is going to be positioned against the competition. And then the third thing is that certain price points – I mean, in our product ... there is like certain price points that do really well ... We have to look at what the price point is, where it is going to fit within the competition and also utilizing these certain price points that seem to be established for flashlights. So then, from that price point we look at what the retailer's margin is going to need to be ... They will say, 'Okay, in our flashlight category we need to achieve on an average a 40 percent margin.' [So if you want their price to be $8.49, you work backwards to what your price will be?] Yeah. Exactly."

The General Manager of Pricing for manufacturer B of major household appliances said:

"The way the pricing works ... it is really market back pricing – starting with retail price points ... For example, in top mount or side-by-side refrigerators, $999 is a key price point ... On a $999 refrigerator, there is a certain feature pack that – you know, filtration and automatic ice maker and spill proof shelves and slide out shelves and clear door bins and humidity controls ... For almost all of our customers (retailers), they dictate to us a certain margin requirement that they have at retail, and a lot of our pricing is mathematically back from the margin."

A Vice President of Finance for manufacturer A of marine engines said:

"We have got to stay pretty close within ranges of our competitors ... A good share of our dealers are what we call dual. They will handle more than one line of outboard engines ... If you get out of whack with your competitor on that price (of one model), they just start to shift their sales to the other one ... That is why you have got to be so super sensitive to what is happening with all of the competitors ... If you had the ability to just price off of costs, then you would expect that (the profit margin as a percent of sales) to be pretty uniform, and it is not uniform at all. We have to price much more to the competition in the marketplace, and so that number will vary widely."

A high official of automobile manufacturer B said:

"[What about setting this initial price? Is there some danger in charging too low a price that you will get retaliation or damage the image of the product?] It is the same issue around, sort of, the product image is in many parts built on the price. How customers view your product is, to some degree, and how they, sort of, fix it in the universe of similar products, is in large degree based on price. [So you can really hurt your product – ?] By not positioning it appropriately. [You can even make them think so badly of it that it would hurt the sales, if you charge too low?] Yeah, because people will think, 'Well, if it is priced this way, then this is not my segment' or this is not – you know, 'though the features of the vehicle may seem to appeal to me, I have some questions about whether this vehicle is really' – [Is what it seems to be?] Yeah."

In considering sales to businesses, it helps to distinguish sales of capital equipment and software, which are usually discrete, from sales of flows of inputs into production. In the first case, prices are often negotiated, with the negotiations sometimes guided by a notion of the product's market value. The Chief Engineer of manufacturer C of injection molding machines said:

"On large machines, large machines would be a machine over 2,000 tons (of clamp pressure) and above, there is really not a list price . . . A 2,000 ton machine would go for a million and a half, two million dollars . . . We have a predetermined cost and price, but there is not a published price . . . On the smaller machines, there is a published price list that is not publicly published, but all the salespeople work from the same price list, and then depending on the situation the sales managers or the Vice President of Sales have certain latitude to get discounts. Pretty much every order, the price is negotiated . . . If we have a design project, there is a list price and then there is what we would call the street price and that is the number that if you could sell the machine at that price, price is no longer the deciding factor. It is some other area, technology or the relationship (of salespeople with the customer) or something . . . We try and design and then we establish a minimal acceptable margin at that street price and that street price is just by talking to salesmen and sales managers and their gut feel . . . [And then, you design backwards from that to get the cost to give you a proper margin?] We try to."

In the case of input flows, prices are normally governed by formal or informal long-term negotiated contracts. Sellers may buttress their position by appealing to value pricing arguments. The Director of

Marketing, Research, and Pricing Administration for manufacturer of specialty materials B said:

> "It was priced to value, so that we understood what it cost a manufacturer to use the thousands of (fasteners) he uses every year to produce his machinery or to produce whatever he is making and so we knew the cost of the (fasteners) and we said we will price our products (which are glues that replace fasteners) somewhat less than that so that, on a per application basis, we are saving him money. I mean whatever it might be, 10 to 20 percent or whatever, saving him money versus what he is doing, but pricing the product so that it is not priced to the cost. It is priced to the value. The first bottles of (glue) were probably four or five dollars a bottle . . . It may have cost 35¢ to produce."

The Chief Financial Officer of a manufacturer of parts for recreational vehicles said:

> "[How do you come up with a price on these parts?] It is an engineering function. Once it has been decided what is going to be built, then we have manufacturing engineers who can figure out how much material it is going to require, how much labor it is going to require, put in overhead factors. So we come up with an estimated cost before we make the sales decision, before we arrive at the price, and we put our margin on that. [So you just decide the price, or it is negotiated with them?] Oh, it is negotiated . . . [During the recession . . . it was not going to increase your volume lowering the price?] No, no. That doesn't have anything to do with volume. Most of our customers on LTAs (long-term agreements) live up to their word. [They are not going to say, 'I can get it cheaper somewhere else.' There is just too much invested in the relationship?] Too much invested in the relationship."

The competition for business is often deliberately based on product characteristics as much as price, and doing so helps avoid price wars. The President and CEO of a manufacturer of synthetic rubber seals and gaskets said:

> "We have a case right now with a filter customer who is aggressively saying that he has a price from one of our competitors that beats our price . . . We have a different product that we are going to offer for these people . . . We are going to counter with that

new product, which also has some manufacturing economies. It can run faster. We are going to pass that into it and offer the new product at a slightly lower price, which has a slightly better margin . . . I will lose a customer before I destroy my market in that area. [If you gave too low a price to him, you think that would mean other customers would demand it?] Oh, it would get out . . . That looks good on the absorption of overhead, but what happens when your competitor does the same thing? Then you have predator pricing and you destroy the marketplace. [What you do is start a price war then?] Oh, yeah. That goes on all the time. You just have to be careful of that."

2.2 Downward Rigidity of Highly Differentiated Product Prices

Most producers of highly differentiated products were against reducing prices under any circumstances. The retired President of manufacturer of specialty materials A said:

"I can't think of any instance where I can remember that somebody made a price cut voluntarily. Why would you do that?"

As I have mentioned, the most common explanations for the resistance to price reduction were that price reduction would not increase the quantity purchased enough to be profitable, especially during a recession, and that price cuts would be unwise, because customers so resist price increases that it would be difficult later to reverse the price reduction. The kinked demand curve theory received some support from the interviews, though that theory does not really apply to truly differentiated goods. Other factors were pertinent because of particular circumstances of the respondent's firm. One such factor was use of value pricing. Another factor was use of temporary promotional discounts, which motivates firms to stabilize list prices, not selling prices.

2.2.1 Incidence of Product Differentiation and of Explanations for Downward Price Rigidity of Highly Differentiated Products

In order to assess the impact of product differentiation, I identified the manufacturing firms that produced highly differentiated products. I did so by removing from consideration firms that produced primarily commodities and those that as contract manufacturers produced goods for customer companies that used or marketed the products and owned their designs. For firms that sold both commodities and differentiated goods, I ignored the parts of the interview that referred to commodities. Of the 246 interviews in manufacturing firms, 48 were concerned almost exclusively with the pricing of commodities. Of the remaining 198 interviews, 36 were in 35 contract manufacturing firms. Exclusion of these 36 interviews left 162 interviews in manufacturing firms that sold highly differentiated products. Because I occasionally interviewed separately more than one person from a particular company, the 162 interviews apply to 160 companies.

In 82 of the 162 interviews that apply to highly differentiated products, respondents said their companies resisted cutting price during recessions, and these interviews were in 81 companies.[2] In 34 of the 162 interviews, respondents explained why they had reduced one or more product prices during an economic slowdown. There is some overlap between the group of 82 and the group of 34, because the same company had cut the prices of some goods and did not reduce the prices of other goods.

The tables below show the frequency of various explanations given in the groups of 82 and 34 interviews just mentioned. The responses are not weighted by firm size, which varies from a few million dollars to billions of dollars in annual sales. Hence the table does not show the economic importance of the various explanations. Nevertheless, a few stand out. Among the reasons for not reducing price in a recession, the two most prominent are that price cuts do little to increase sales and that once a price is reduced it is hard later to undo the cut because of resistance to price increases. These two explanations were given in 45 and 27, respectively, of the 82 interviews. Respondents mentioned many other explanations, but none came up in more than ten interviews. Among these were concern that a price cut would damage a product's quality image or could lead to demands for floor stock protection, which I will describe presently. Some mentioned concern that a price cut would inspire competitors to reduce their prices as well, a concern that is central to the kinked demand curve theory. See Table 2.2.1.

In the 34 interviews where respondents explained why their companies had reduced prices, the most popular explanation of why price was cut was to increase sales, which indicates that manufacturers of highly differentiated products do reduce price if the reduction seems likely to increase sales significantly. This explanation was given in twelve interviews (in twelve different companies). Three other explanations received significant attention, each being mentioned in six or seven of the 34 interviews. These explanations were that a customer

Table 2.2.1

Reasons for Not Reducing the Prices of Highly Differentiated Products	Number of Interviews and Firms
Inadequate Increase in Sales	45
Hard to Undo the Price Cut Later	27
Competitors Would Also Reduce Price	9
Floor Stock Protection	10
Hurt Reputation for Product Quality	7
Total Number of Interviews and Firms	82

Table 2.2.2

Reasons for Reducing the Prices of Highly Differentiated Products	Number of Interviews and Firms
To Increase Sales	12
Customer Request	6
A Competitor Cut Its Price	6
The Cut Was a Promotional Discount	7
Total Number of Interviews and Firms	34

had requested a price reduction to help it cope with a recession, that a competitor had reduced its price, and that the price reduction referred to a temporary promotional price reduction. See Table 2.2.2.

2.2.2 Price Reductions of Highly Differentiated Products during Recessions Do Not Increase Sales Enough to be Profitable

Respondents gave diverse reasons for believing that price cuts do little to increase sales especially during a recession. The Senior Vice President of Manufacturing for a men's clothing retail chain said (in 1999):

"Probably about six or seven years ago, we brought our first product (dress shirts) in from the Far East, and we dropped the price to $42 from at the time it was probably about 46, 47, and sales did not increase at all. In fact, they dropped off. For me, it was a desperate disappointment. I could not understand what was happening, and the feedback from the sales force was, they are asking, 'You have cheapened the product. It is not made in the USA anymore. It is made in Hong Kong. It is cheap. We don't want to buy it.'"

The next two quotations are from an interview with several people from one company. The Director of Marketing of a large apparel manufacturer said:

> "[It would make sense to almost cut the price of the elastic ones and raise the price of the inelastic.] Oh, gosh. That sounds like (a cigarette company) . . . Remember when they went out and cut the price of cigarettes? It was all based on price then. I am like who wants to get into that."

A Marketing Director of a large apparel manufacturer then said:

> "[And everybody else starts cutting price?] Right. And we don't want to commoditize the market any more than it is."

The Controller of consumer products manufacturer 4 said:

> "I think there will be a slowdown. Whether it is really going to create a lot of pricing pressures for us, I really don't think it will. What it will affect in us is movement off the shelf, because we are dependent on the number of people that walk down an aisle (in a store), and as consumers shop less, our product is going to be impacted, because like I said for the most part, it is not the type of product where you wake up in the morning and say, 'Buy one.' . . . From the studies that we have done and from our knowledge, it is still very impulsive . . . [Why don't you think that it (a recession) would bring any change in price?] Because I think as the number of people dwindle going through the stores, the fact that this light is 50 cents less is still not going to increase the volume. I don't think somebody is walking up to a flashlight and saying, '5.99 is too much,' because if 5.99 was too much, then they would buy another model that was 4.99, but they wouldn't just suddenly say, 'Well Jee, this is a better value now that it is 4.99 and it used to be 5.99.' . . . The price points are all out there. So I think for the consumer, if he has a price point in mind for what a flashlight is worth to him, he is going to find that price point."

The President of a company that manufactures security devices said:

> "My experience has been whenever we have dropped prices there hasn't been a corresponding increase in sales . . . People don't get up in the morning and say, 'I have got to buy a bike lock.'"

The Pricing of Manufactured Goods 31

The President of machine shop A[3] said:

"We make specialty hand tools for both industry and consumers . . . We have never cut prices in a global sense because the economy was bad. We cut prices only on a particular set of products for a particular account in order to beat out competition . . . In our business, there is little relation between price and demand. Our products are relatively unique . . . There will be few competitors in the store. They are unusual products. Most of our business is retail."

The CEO of a recreational power boat building company said:

"[You can't attract customers away from other manufacturers?] You can and that is always a goal anytime you can increase market share, but that was part of the theory of how we redid our pricing. Making these changes that I have described to you actually allowed us to lower our prices this year from last. We are the only boat manufacturer in the world that did that. [And has that increased your market share?] It has but at wholesale not retail . . . It has attracted new dealers . . . which is a form of market share . . . This is a very difficult market to attract new dealers and we have. [But the dealers aren't selling boats?] Nobody is selling boats right now, and anybody who tells you they are is a liar. Period. It is that bad. [That is terrible.] Welcome to the marine industry."

The President of a manufacturer of marine accessories said:

"[So did that affect pricing, the downturn in sales (in the early 1990s)?] No, it really didn't, because at that time dropping price wasn't going to help anything. There just wasn't any business. I mean, if I went to (a boat builder) and said, 'Hey, that switch instead of being $50 is now $25,' they would say, 'That's nice. I am not building any boats.' So there was no elasticity. So no, we didn't change price. [And the same with your competitors?] Pretty much. [So there was no competitive pressure from them, they were reasoning the same way?] Pretty much."

The last lines of the next quotation are reminiscent of Okun's theory (Okun, 1981) of an implicit contract between buyer and seller firms that calls for stable pricing. Notice, however, that the bond that gives rise to the implicit contract stems not from reduction of the buyer's cost of searching for the lowest price but from the buyer's cost of switching suppliers. The President of rerolling company B said:

"[What happens when you have an overall slump in demand?] . . . Typically the ingot price (of aluminum) goes down during that time, so our margins tend to be better, but our volume is less . . . [Do you price lower to try to recapture some sales?] There is an expression in this business . . . 'There is no use chumming in an empty lake.' . . . (Another expression is) 'Cutting the price of coffins to increase demand.' . . . There is no more demand there. The question is whether you hold your share and whether you keep your relationships. First of all, it is hard for people to switch (suppliers). There are switching costs. So in a short recession, they have to do trials. They have to feel comfortable with you."

The Director of Marketing, Research, and Pricing Administration for manufacturer of specialty materials B said:

"I don't think we would gain in sales (from a price cut). I mean, when you are dealing with industrial accounts, they can only use what they can use. I mean, if he is not producing as many cars, you can't sell him more adhesives no matter what price you sell it at. I mean, he doesn't produce any more cars. And so – if we are on every car made in America – if they reduce the number by a million or two million – we could give it away and they are not going to use more than what they are using, so it doesn't make sense to do it."

The President of a company that manufactures small parts and fasteners for the electronic and aerospace industries said:

"A price reduction at (our company) might or might not increase demand. Service, which is availability, is more important. Print position is important too. If the (our company's) part number is on the customer's manufacturing drawings, then that manufacturer has to use that part . . . We are now in a downturn. Price is an issue, but there is not a lot of business out there. There are real limits as to how much you can expand sales by cutting price."[4]

2.2.3 Sellers of Highly Differentiated Products Do Not Want to Reduce Prices during Recessions because Reductions Are Hard to Reverse

Many respondents said that a reason for not reducing the price of a differentiated product is that it would be difficult to raise it back up later. The President of machine shop A[5] said:

"About 70 percent of our business is with (a company), an industrial and retail distributor. They are a branded distributor ... Pricing is renegotiated every year ... It is a dogfight back and forth ... We will say we need a 2 percent increase. They say they can't raise prices without losing business ... If you reduce a price, it is hard to get it up later. If we are making brass parts, where a large part of the cost is in materials, you can get your price back up again ... Everywhere else, price changes are very hard, and this influences our thinking about pricing. This is an additional reason not to cut prices in a recession."

The President for North America of a manufacturer of specialized paints said:

"We will try to be really wary of taking our existing products and lowering the price even for one time deals, because we find it is pretty hard then to get the price back to where it was."

The Vice President and General Manager of ball bearing manufacturer B said:

"[What is against lowering the price?] ... Because you will never get it back again. [It is just too hard to get the price back up?] Impossible. [Explain why that is true.] Because they simply won't pay it ... Price increases have been out of the question in the bearing business for the last ten years ... In most OEMs'[6] business, they probably have 75 percent of their cost in goods and services that they purchase and only 25 percent or less probably in direct labor. So they immediately go out and attack where they can get the biggest bang for their buck."

A Marketing Official for tire manufacturer B said:

"[Is there a reason for not lowering the price (in a recession)?] Yeah. Once you lower the price, it is awfully hard to get it back up. [Oh, it is? Why is that?] Well, your customer (i.e. distributor or dealer) thinks if you could afford that margin at that point in time, why can't you afford it now?"

The Chief Engineer of manufacturer C of injection molding machines said:

"I would say, when a customer buys a lot of machines on a regular basis, there is resistance to lowering the price with that customer, because once you give him a discount it is there forever for that customer, unless there is some new machine or something where you can regain your footing . . . There is always a resistance by sales and marketing to reduce the price, because you will never get it back."

2.2.4 It is Difficult in General to Increase the Prices of Highly Differentiated Products

Manufacturers' claims that price cuts are difficult to reverse are reinforced by the fact that the difficulty of raising prices came up often in contexts other than price cutting. The difficulty of increasing price came up in 91 interviews with manufacturers, which is many more than the 27 interviews in which the topic came up in the context of price reduction. Vice President 1 of a huge producer of branded and unbranded foods said:

"(A brand of vegetable) oil, let's say the price of vegetable oil goes up. Well we will stop our trade spend (for advertising and promotions) on that . . . So we will say, 'The cost of the inputs have gone up. We don't want to change the price at the store level, but we are going to apply less monetary resources behind that to move that product,' . . . [Why don't you want to raise price to the store?] Well the consumers are pretty resistant to that. [It is not that the stores resist?] The stores don't like it . . . They don't want to be known as the store that is carrying the higher priced brands."

The Vice President of Strategy and Business Development for a large tool manufacturer said:

"[My next question was resistance to price increase. So you get that from all your retailers, from all your buyers?] . . . They just say, 'No.' . . . 'We will drop the product.' . . . It is a very tough effort to get large (retail) customers to agree to price increases, right now. It has been for a while, very very difficult . . . Their view is that they are always trying to figure out ways to get prices down. There is no such thing as a price increase . . . That is their stance. That is their culture. People who take price increases don't keep their jobs."

The Chairman of a manufacturer of telecommunications equipment said:

> "[Is there any reason not to change your prices when you set these end user prices?] Unfortunately yes. It is impossible to raise the price . . . Because the market does not understand that. I don't think ever I have seen it happen . . . I think the way to raise the price is to bring out product with more features, that you raise the price there . . . If you get involved in long-term relationships with other companies . . . as customers or as OEMs or resellers, the bigger ones, the price is fixed there, and they will not accept raising price. [What they are selling is fixed in price too?] Right. [So it comes back to you?] Right. Not only that. They simply will not accept. That is it. It is unacceptable."

2.2.5 Price Rigidity in the Major Household Appliance, Automobile, and Machine Tool Industries

I consider three industries where final customers' purchases tend to be so widely spaced in time that the customers might not be aware of price changes.

Pricing of Major Household Appliances

In the major household appliance industry, respondents said that the infrequency of purchase reduced consumers' awareness of prices and diminished the strength of brand. A Merchandise Manager for a large consumer electronics and appliance retail chain said:

> "[Do your customers resist price increases?] I think it would depend on the product, the frequency of the shopping pattern. I mean, in appliances, when somebody buys an appliance once every ten to fifteen years, when you are back in the market place, I am not sure that they even understand what the price is before they go out."

A Marketing Manager for manufacturer A of major household appliances said:

> "[So you were telling me that first of all that you don't have many repeat customers, only about 40 percent.] When you talk about appliances and you look at the life of them, because of

the extended life of the product, what happens is people tend to believe that they have been out of the industry or out of the purchase cycle for so long that regardless of how satisfied they are – and again we get great marks for customer satisfaction, in the high 90s, and yet when we go back and ask those same customers when it is time to buy another appliance will you buy another (an appliance brand), the answer typically is, "Well, we haven't been in the appliance market as a buyer for such a long period of time. We are going to go out and shop. So we will go look at what is new." So we end up with only about 40 percent customer loyalty."

There is strong opposition in the industry to price increases, but it comes not from consumers but from large retailers. A Marketing Manager for manufacturer A of major household appliances said:

"The last thing they (the major appliance retailers) want is a price increase. It is written in bold letters in Buyer 101, 'You will not accept a price increase from your vendors.' . . . If you bring them a new feature or something that nobody has and you can get it, you can get a $50 premium at retail. They will let you take a $35 premium in cost . . . [Well, what about general inflation?] . . . They resist those prices. They don't give a shit what the economy is doing . . . Truman, they look you in the eye and go, 'Do you want to sell this stuff or not?' Here is the basic premise of selling appliances . . . 'There are two blanks on the purchase order. There is one blank here for the price, and there is one blank in here for the quantity. You Mr. Seller' – they are looking at me – 'get to fill in one of those two numbers, but only one of those numbers. If you fill in the price, I fill in the quantity. So if you want $599, I will buy ten of them from you. If you want 10,000 of them, I will fill in the price.'"

The industry seems to have some downward price flexibility. In order to understand the next quotation, one needs to know what the Minimum Advertised Price or MAP is. This is a price chosen by a manufacturer and, if the manufacturer subsidizes a retailer's promotional advertising, the retailer is legally forbidden to advertise the product for a price less than the MAP. The MAP increases the manufacturer's influence on the retail price of its products. Despite the MAP, in the markets for major household appliances, promotional price competition can be so ferocious that it depresses non-promotional prices, so that selling prices do not always return to a regular level after a promotion. This glimmer of downward price flexibility may be due to brand weakness in the industry. A Marketing Manager for manufacturer A of major household appliances said:

> "Now we start to jockey. Well, the retail price starts to come down, squeezes the manufacturer's margin – [Even though the MAP is up there?] And then ultimately if the actual sell starts to come down far enough, then we will end up having to lower the MAP ... There is about 5 or 8 points, which is a lot of volume, 5 or 8 percent of total market share of this millions of unit industry that moves with promotion ... The only way you keep from having to drop the price on that piece, now that everyone else is competing with it, is to come with something new. I mean, you have got to bring new features, new configuration, new aesthetics, something new. That drives the price up, because during the course of the year the game plan for that market share that moves between vendors based on promotion is what continually pulls it down. So you bring new stuff again. [Even in good times, it gets dragged down?] Yes ... And in bad times even faster."

Since the previous quotation alludes to a process by which competing manufacturers undercut each other's prices charged to retailers, I say a few words about how this works. According to an antitrust statute, the Robinson–Patman Act of 1936, it is illegal for a manufacturer to charge two different retailers different prices for the same good if the retailers compete in the same market. I heard a great deal about this statute from respondents and try to explain their interpretation of the law rather than the law itself. The law applies to a situation in which a firm A sells a product α to firms B and C and in which firms B and C either both resell α in the same market or use α to produce products β and γ, respectively, where products β and γ are close substitutes and are sold in the same market. In these situations, the Act forbids firm A to charge firms B and C different prices for product α, with some exceptions. One exception occurs if it is cheaper for firm A to deliver product α to one firm than the other. It could be cheaper because of lower transport costs or because one of firms B and C buys larger quantities of product α than the other and the larger quantity reduces the unit cost of producing or delivering the product. The other exception occurs if a fourth firm D offers to sell to one of firms B or C, say to firm B, the product α or a close substitute for it at a price lower than what firm A charges for product α. This circumstance is known as a competitive situation, and in it firm A can legally match firm D's price to firm B, while not reducing its price for sales to firm C. In this case, firm A is said to meet competition, and this exception is called the meet comp exception. A Marketing Manager for manufacturer A of major household appliances said:

> "If you (a retailer) say to me off of this price sheet, 'You know, that is fine for 80 percent of the line, but I have got an offer from (an appliance producer) and I have got an offer from (another appliance producer), and they have offered me a similarly priced featured product and instead of $300, they will sell it to me for $280.' In all businesses, and we utilize it in this business too, we have a vehicle called the meet comp that allows me to sell competing dealers at a different price based on a competitive situation. So if you will give me a letter or a copy of the quote . . . that you have an offer equal to or lower than this, then if I choose to I can drop my price on some core product down to $280 for you."

Automobile Pricing

I heard of no opposition to price increases in the automobile industry other than the possible impact of an increase on consumer demand. Price increases do occur, even in slow times. Respondents implied that temporary promotional discounts stimulate sales more than equivalent reductions in regular prices. A high official of automobile manufacturer B said in February 2001:

> "We are in the midst of an industry that is, if not struggling, at least down off of its record levels of volume from last year, and seeing a definite weakening in the overall economy is causing a lot of concern . . . The response to that is to do a number of things. One is reduce cost. But reducing cost in this industry tends to be a longer-term issue . . . On the revenue side, you just announce a new set of (higher) prices, and again, you have competitive issues and will it really stick and will you have to give it back in rebates and the like. But it is a quicker fix than the reduced costs fix . . . You do have the impact on volume, but not necessarily as predictable and it has to be managed. But the revenue is immediate . . . Longer term do you have to do some sort of incentive in order to get volume back up again if you deteriorate in volume as a result of the pricing action? . . . A lot of times again, the price increase is not all that obvious. A lot of

times, it is tied to equipment or it is tied to some other features that the customer values . . . [Why give incentives rather than just dropping the price back?] That is an interesting question. I think to some degree it is expected. Back to the issue of the customer wants a deal and we are sort of almost on this kind of dope and it is hard to get off kind of thing."

A high official of automobile manufacturer C said in February 2001:

"[Why not reduce the price rather than having all these incentives during the year?] I will tell you, we have done some repositioning,[7] to be competitive on vehicles. It works sometimes. The problem is you have to be careful, because it depends on what the product is. Because what you can do by reducing the price is you can tell the customer that there is no value there, and customers get used to consumer cash. [Oh, they like that.] Oh yeah. [Don't they get the idea that there is no value there if they see a discount, when they see some rebate?] Everyone wants to think they got a great deal . . . In a recession, it is very hard to get people to purchase vehicles, unless there is some compelling reason to act. You have to create something that drives urgency. [Some deal that is going to go away?] When (an American automobile manufacturer) did zero zero (zero interest rate and zero down payment on automobile loans), that drove urgency . . . During the zero zero, we saw (an American automobile manufacturer) actually took some price in there. [Actually increased their sticker price?] Sure. [What was the reason for doing that?] Because if you increase your sticker price, your customers are getting zero zero. Essentially, they are paying for part of it . . . [They don't think people will notice that?] But they don't. They notice it, but they don't really care, because the message, the big message out there is zero zero . . . I take my price up $500, but I still have to have a $1000 incentive . . . because of the call to action that incentives create, that urgency in the market place. [The price reduction on a car doesn't do that? No urgency?] It can. It depends on the customer, but normally no. It is not going to drive traffic. What drives traffic to the showroom is the deal."

Pricing of Standardized Machine Tools

I discuss the pricing of machine tools that are not custom built and are sufficiently standardized to have a recognized price. Although many customers buy such machines infrequently, customers do remember and follow their prices, probably as part of keeping informed about new technological developments. Customers not only follow prices, but also expect them to stay the same or to fall, and tend to react to increases by changing suppliers, delaying purchases, or not buying at all. A consequence of buyer resistance to price increases is seller resistance to price decreases on the grounds that it would be hard to reverse a decrease. The Chief Engineer of manufacturer C of injection molding machines said:

> "When raw material changes on a manufactured product, it is not easy just to change the (list) price. We try to. If you raise the price and nobody else does, then the price doesn't stick and your discounts just go up . . . [Do your customers resist price increases?] They resist price increases . . . By switching (to a new supplier) or negotiating or delaying a purchase or there is also a phenomenon where people aren't buying new machines. The machinery itself, the mechanical components, don't really wear out. So there is a lot of customers, who rather than buying a new machine will remanufacture a machine . . . [Even during boom times, you can't justify a price increase? . . .] It is very difficult . . . People just want to keep their costs constant . . . There is always a resistance by sales and marketing to reduce the (list) price, because you will never get it back . . . It is the same when we buy components. We have a price and when a supplier comes back and wants a price increase we always say no and we keep saying no until they say, 'Well, we are not going to sell any more to you.' . . . [Why take this symbol of the existing price? I mean, is it just a way of negotiating?] No. People don't want to spend more money."

The Director of Sales of machine tool manufacturer E said:

> "Market conditions in Europe have forced us to lower our price . . . because of the exchange rate . . . When the exchange rate recovers . . . I doubt that prices will go back up. We will figure out a way to grind some cost (out) of it. [Why would you not?] It is very difficult to raise prices and make them stick. [Oh people resist.] Oh absolutely. [They get used to it?] Yeah. We have a fifteen-year track record of (our) machines get cheaper. They get better and they get cheaper every year."

The reluctance to change regular prices leads to a preference for manipulating promotional discounts. The Vice President of Finance of machine tool manufacturer D said:

"[Do you ever decrease the (list) price of those standard machines?] Oh, no, we don't decrease some of the list prices, no. [Why not?] Well, it is out there, and we usually discount against them, unless we re-engineer the machine and then we may come out with a different list price . . . [You are not going to try and sell more in slow times by reducing the list price?] No, we would just offer discounts off of that. [Why not reduce the list price and advertise?] Well, we would go out to our agents and either discount it or offer greater commissions, and I think that we want the ability to go back to the – that the list price should be the list price and that the discount – [It is hard to raise the list price?] It is harder to raise or maneuver the list price than it is to maneuver around by the discounts . . . What you get is customers who may have a program and they may be looking at the machine and ask about the machine. And then they won't do anything and in six or nine months they will come back and the whole economic situation may have changed (improved), and so the work to change (reduce) the list price kind of gets you in a problem. I mean, it is easier to say, 'Well, that discount was only good for a certain period of time.'"

2.2.6 Reasons for Cutting the Prices of Highly Differentiated Products in Slow Times

Many of the price cuts I heard about by manufacturers of highly differentiated products were imposed by demands from major customers that were manufacturing firms. The Vice President of a small company that produces and distributes fabric filters to process industries said:

"We just reduced prices to our largest customer, for competitors are hurting them and they were looking for help. We in turn, asked for help from our suppliers, telling them we wanted to keep our customer's plant open."

The Vice President of Distribution for a manufacturer of industrial minerals said:

"Downturns in the economy have typically made competition keener . . . [Do they (customers) ever say, I want to renegotiate my contract?] Absolutely. [Oh, they will?] The car companies are notorious . . . They walk in and say they want 20 percent price cuts every year or a 20 percent price cut in a given year because of problems . . . We will never say no . . . We will work within the framework of the contract and maybe either negotiate an extension or do something, where we offset it."

Even though product differentiation diminishes the negative impact of competition on prices during periods of reduced demand, market forces do act to some extent in the ways predicted by neoclassical economics. For instance, some manufacturers of highly differentiated products cut prices to meet competition. The Chairman of a manufacturer of telecommunications equipment said:

> "We do reduce price when competition comes in. Well, first of all you made a mistake and you came up with a price which is too high and you get a response from the market that tells you so. So that would be one reason to reduce price, and the other one is that more and more competition comes in and you have to reduce your price because again your customer tells you to reduce the price ... You reduce price only when you have to because you are losing an order. You try to be careful not to reduce prices ... You understand that if you reduce price, you have done it forever."

The President of rerolling company B said:

> "On the other hand, I think you do have to keep demand in your plant. You can't opt out. There are times when you just have to have a price war. So if we had a new entry, say, into one of our key markets, and they lowered the price for a year, we might have to do that to stay where we are."

2.2.7 Rigidity of the Prices of Flows of Inputs of Highly Differentiated Goods from One Manufacturing Firm to Another

One reason for the price stickiness of differentiated goods is the existence of a close relationship between a good's producer and a buyer, who uses the good as an input into a manufacturing process. Buyer and seller protect the relationship by avoiding conflict over price. Often the relationship exists because of the buyer's switching costs of adjusting its production methods if it were to replace the input by a substitute input produced by another supplier. The Plywood Sales Manager for western lumber company B said:

> "[Let's start with the commodity plywood and work our way back. How is that priced?] Most of it is based on (a publication

The Pricing of Manufactured Goods

of a wood products market-reporting company) . . . It is so volatile that – I mean, it literally can change by the hour. It usually changes three or four times a week . . . We have, for example (a company's name), where they are a distributor, but they are strictly distributing to boat manufacturers and RV manufacturers and truck body OEMs, those types of people. That type of business, it is more stable . . . There are, say, five other mills that can supply the panels that that particular customer base needs, whereas if you are dealing in commodity sheathing, there is 50 mills in the country that can supply that panel. [So the stuff used for boats and so on, that is so specific. I guess you can't have any hollow parts inside.] Well, for one thing, they are typically specified just for that application. So we will change our lay-up and create an item that is specifically for that application . . . And then the other thing is, a lot of those products are speced out as western plywood. So they need the species of veneer that we get in the West versus like southern pine, where all the southern mills are. It just doesn't have the same strength characteristics . . . So that limits the amount of competitors that can supply into those markets. [And that really makes the pricing easier?] Well, yeah. It makes it more stable, so we are not sort of riding this (market-reporting company's) roller coaster as I call it. [Why is that? . . .] Well, because the customer can't shop around nearly as much . . . [Well, they could just call up another supplier.] True, but when their customer . . . is a manufacturing operation. When they find a panel that they like, they don't want to deviate either, because when you introduce something new into their process, then they have to deal with it. Maybe it is a little different than what they are getting from the other supplier, and there is a lot of brand loyalty when you go into that type of market, which is another reason why it is good for us . . . [You can just play two people off against each other.] True. But we do offer some things that others don't. We have different sizes. So we can produce panels that are larger. So if a shop is cutting them, there might be an optimal panel size where they can get 10 parts out of it instead of 6 parts out, if it is smaller . . . With our distributors, we have agreements . . . where we will try to keep pricing stable for them. They are supplying into industrial markets where they (the customers) are a manufacturer just like we are, so they don't necessarily need the cheapest price. They just want it to be stable. They need to be competitive, of course, but they want it to be stable ... [And really the origin for that is that only a few competitors can do what you do?] Right ... So they could get it from someone else, but typically there is some R&D that has to be done and there is a transition period. Sometimes it might be a few weeks, but sometimes it might be a few months where their production process is interrupted or at least isn't running as smooth as it was, because they have tried a new product. You know, maybe the thickness tolerance isn't as tight or it warps a little bit more or those types of things, and it just takes a while to really dial in a product ... I am sorry if I misled you there. They (industrial plywood prices) are not that stable ... If the commodity price changes everyday, the industrial prices change once a month, let's say. It is just a different level of stability ... [So then on sales there tends to be bargaining every time?] For the commodity items. [And for the industrial items?] For the industrial items, typically it is more of a programmed type business. So we will have a pricing formula or we will just flat out have a fixed price that we say, 'We will hold it for a month,' or 'We will hold it for a quarter' or that type of thing. [And the formula is based on what?] The formula is typically based on (a market-reporting company's publication)."

2.2.8 Downward Price Rigidity of Value Priced Productive Inputs

If value pricing is to be effective, its practitioner must behave in a way consistent with the stance that the product's price is set so that both seller and buyer share the savings resulting from the customer's use of the product. For this reason, the product's price falls only if the price of substitute products fall or if a new more economical substitute product becomes available. Hence an economic slump does not necessarily create pressure to reduce the price of a value-priced product. The practitioners of value pricing I encountered produced computer software or specialty materials and chemicals. The Director of Marketing, Research, and Pricing Administration for manufacturer of specialty materials B said:

> "I can't envision the situation where I would want to lower the price of our product other than to gain market share ... [Not to expand the market by finding new applications?] ... We don't think so because if you have done your homework correctly on price to value, the opportunity you are going after – it is already priced below what it costs that company to do it another way."

The Director of Marketing Expertise for large chemical company B said:

"If I just was preaching value, value, value, and I had convinced you of that and you had agreed to buy from me in that case, and I came in the next week and lowered my price, wouldn't you scratch your head and say, 'What the hell is going on here? . . . There must be something I don't understand.' . . . If I have clearly established my value versus the next best alternative and I am not worried about a generic . . . where is the pressure to lower my price coming from?"

A Marketing Manager for a large air separation and chemical company said:

"We can tell in the lab if our product is superior or not or we ask customers and they tell us if certain products are better. Then we charge more for that product, and the amount of the premium is guesswork . . . [What share do you think the company should get?] . . . The customer gets between 50 and 70 percent . . . [If you actually cut the transactional prices (rather than just the fictional list prices)?] That is really not the goal though. We don't want to cut the prices. You know, the salespeople want to cut prices. The salespeople always say, 'Your delivery times are too long and your price is too high and we don't have enough inventory.' But the people I work with every day are more the marketing people and they want less inventory and higher prices. So the goal is not to cut price. [Even in slow times like now?] Even in slow times. We work very hard to keep pricing stable. [You say prices go up once in a while. Why is that?] Well, we are the market leader; at least we are in some businesses. When our costs go up, that usually triggers a price increase, and the reason we wait until our costs go up is because we can justify it. We can write a nice letter and we can pass the red face test and raise the price. So if energy costs go up or whatever. [Sometimes energy prices go down, though.] We don't lower prices then, but the discounts might change. We might allow larger discounts, particularly if the competition is doing that, but we don't start the fight with the competition . . . We don't want to cut price, because we don't want to compete on price. We want to compete on performance."

2.2.9 Other Factors that Contribute to the Downward Price Rigidity of Highly Differentiated Products

What merchants call floor stock protection can discourage manufacturers of some products from reducing the prices they charge. When a manufacturer reduces the price it charges distributors or retailers, it also reduces the value of their inventories. In order to avoid so enraging such customers that they cease carrying the product, manufacturers may in essence buy back the inventories at the original purchase price and then sell the inventories back at the new lower price. The expense of this procedure can preclude price reduction. The President of a sports rifle manufacturing company said (in 1999):

> "[In the last recession ... Was there any move to cut prices?] No, there was no move to cut prices. One of the problems with doing that is protecting all of the inventory that is out there. If you want to lose customers (distributors), there is no faster way than to cut prices and not to protect his inventory. [How would you protect his inventory?] Well, if you were to embark on that, which is a very expensive thing to do, which is why we don't do it ... what has been done is that your sales people go in and inventory what they have and then you equalize his price to your new price."

A drawback of manufacturers' cutting prices of branded consumer goods is that distributors and dealers may not pass on price reductions to final buyers. This possibility discourages manufacturers from reducing prices. A marketing director for very large manufacturer of branded foods 3 said:

> "[So if you have a (price) decrease to everybody they will – ?] ... Some will margin up. I mean, it is always the argument. If you ever take a price decrease, which is rarely discussed, that the trade (grocery stores) will just margin up on it. They won't change their pricing. They will just keep it where it is and take a higher margin. Whenever I have ever had a discussion about decreasing price, that has been the discussion, since we have never done it."

Some respondents attributed the kinked nature of the demand curve for their company's branded product to buyer behavior rather than to competitors' matching price reductions and not matching price increases. The idea is that a company's regular customers know when the company raises its price and may then buy a substitute product from another source, whereas when the company reduces its price, few customers of competing firms are aware of the price reduction and so do not take advantage of it. This scenario is consistent with a view that highly differentiated products tend to have a clientele of buyers who know about that product and know less about substitute products. The Vice President and CFO of a small manufacturer of dental equipment said:

> "We don't look at the elasticity of demand. We are going to sell just so much. There are only so many dentists out there. If our price is too high, they will go to another product, they will substitute. If we lower the price, they will stock up and take longer to reorder. They won't substitute our products for someone else's just because its price is low, or that is rare. They will flee, but they won't come in . . . We are going to sell more only if we enter a new market. We won't sell more by lowering price. Dentists do little substituting if we lower price, but do do it if we raise price."[8]

2.2.10 Related Literature

Among the company surveys made before the publication of Blinder et al. (1998), the book (Fog, 1960) has material that is pertinent to downward price rigidity. On pages 106–107, Fog talks about the great difficulties companies encounter trying to raise prices, especially of goods sold to industrial buyers. On page 121, he mentions that manufacturing firms are reluctant to reduce prices, because it will be difficult to raise them back up later.

Since the publication of Blinder et al. (1998), and perhaps inspired by it, empirical papers on pricing have appeared that are based on micro data produced by governments or economists' surveys or derived from supermarket scanner data. The papers based on govenment data establish that wholesale and retail prices change often (roughly every four to six months). Some of these papers are: Alvarez, Burriel, and Hernando (2010); Bils and Klenow (2004); Costa Dias, Dias, and Neves (2008); Dhyne et al. (2006); Fabiani et al. (2010); Klenow and Kryvtsov (2008); Nakamura and Steinsson (2008); and Vermeulen et al. (2012). None of these papers explicitly distinguishes the price behavior of commodities from that of differentiated goods. All of the papers note, however, that prices of energy and unprocessed foods vary more than do other prices. The papers: Alvarez, Burriel, and Hernando (2010); Bils and Klenow (2004); and Vermeulen et al. (2012)

note that there is a positive association between the variability of an industry's prices and its competitiveness. The variability of retail prices may be a modern phenomenon. Kackmeister (2007) presents evidence that retail prices were less variable in the years 1889–1899 than in the years 1997–1999.

Some of the papers based on surveys are: Amirault, Kwan, and Wilkinson (2004–2005); Apel, Friberg, and Hallsten (2005); Carlsson and Skans (2012); Carson et al. (1998); Correa, Petrassi, and Santos (2018); Druant et al. (2012); Greenslade and Parker (2012); Hall, Walsh, and Yates (2000); Hoeberichts and Stokman (2010); Kashyap (1995); Kwapil, Scharler, and Baumgartner (2007, 2010); Levy and Young (2004); Loupias and Ricart (2006); Moura and Rossi (2010); and Stahl (2010).[9] Some of these papers, such as Kashyap (1995) and Levy and Young (2004), document particular instances of extreme price rigidity.

Some of the surveys imitate the work of Blinder et al. (1998) by including questions that ask respondents to comment on the relevance to their businesses of particular economic theories.[10] The theories that the Blinder style surveys most strongly support are implicit and explicit contracts, coordination failure, and cost-based rigidity. By coordination failure, the authors mean that though a firm would like to raise some prices, it cannot do so because of concern that rivals will not raise their prices or the industry price leader will not raise its prices. These concerns are, of course, posited in the kinked demand curve theory. Theories of cost-based price rigidity assert that prices are based on costs and that costs change slowly.

Several surveys notice an association between price stickiness and industry concentration. Of particular interest are three papers that note that an important reason for not raising prices is concern that raising them would antagonize customers. These papers are: Amirault, Kwan, and Wilkinson (2004–2005); Kwapil, Scharler, and Baumgartner (2007); and Greenslade and Parker (2012). Nakamura and Steinsson (2013) is a useful survey paper on price rigidity.

2.3 The Price Stability of Two Types of Differentiated Goods

The four graphs that follow show U.S. time series for retail price indices and measures of real output for two classes of durable consumer goods that are highly differentiated. These are vehicles (automobiles and light trucks) and major household appliances, such as refrigerators and dishwashers. The price series are quite stable, whereas the measures of real output fluctuate with the business cycle.[11,12,13,14]

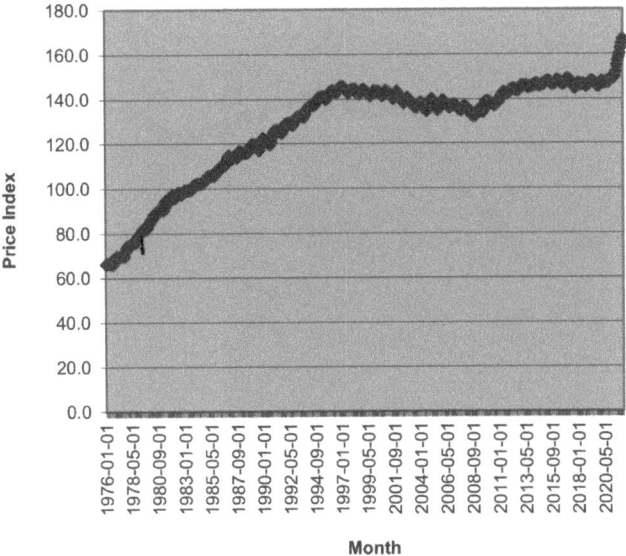

Figure 2.3.1 Consumer Price Index for New Vehicles, Monthly Data, Not Seasonally Adjusted, January 1976–December 2021

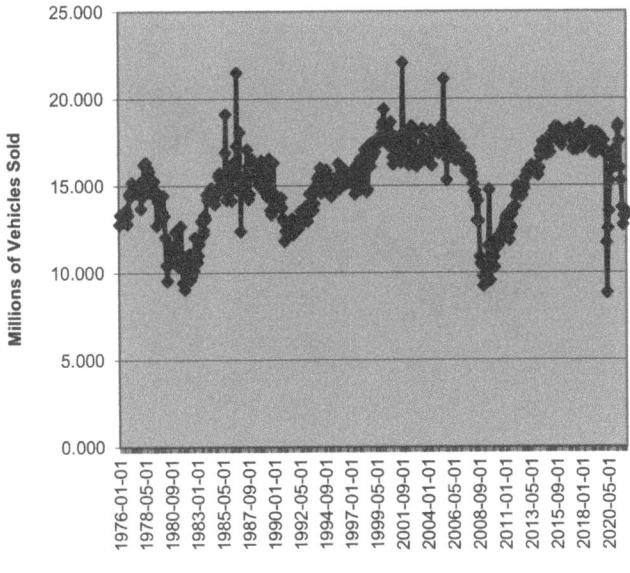

Figure 2.3.2 Total Vehicle Sales, Monthly Data, Seasonally Adjusted, January 1976–December 2021

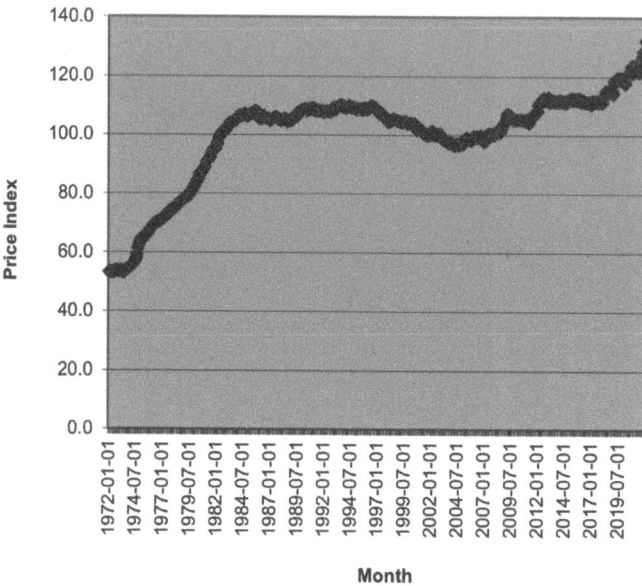

Figure 2.3.3 Producer Price Index for Major Household Appliances, Monthly Data, Not Seasonally Adjusted, January 1972–December 2021

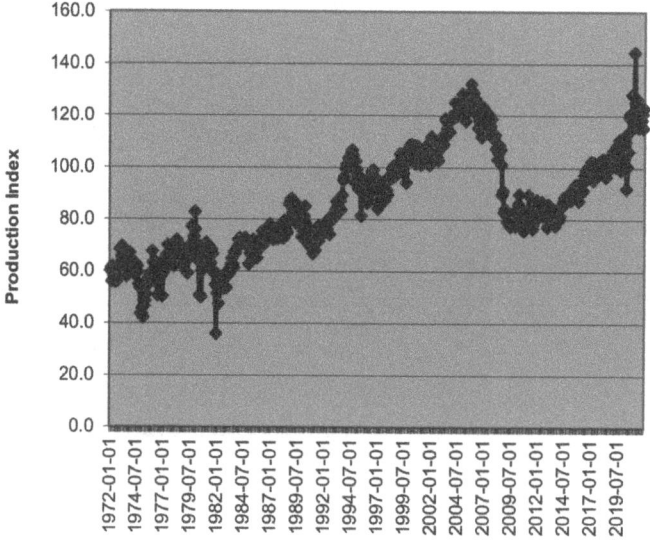

Figure 2.3.4 Industrial Production of Major Household Appliances, Monthly Data, Seasonally Adjusted, January 1972–December 2021

2.4 Effects of the Administrative Costs of Price Change

Respondents discussed the impact of the administrative costs of price change in 79 of the interviews with respondents from manufacturing companies. The conclusions are that the seller's administrative costs are small for many of the firms and have little effect on price change in most firms. Some respondents believed the costs of adjusting to price change could be significant for customers who are retailers or distributors. Table 2.4.1 summarizes the findings.

For many respondents, the administrative cost didn't matter, because the gains from price change were much larger than that cost. The Executive Vice President of a paper-converting company said:

> "So raising a price to your customers, which is what you are about to do, does that require a lot of administrative costs that make you hesitate before doing it?] We don't hesitate at all. We will do whatever . . . [Just because it is so important?] You have to do it, yeah."

Concern for the impact on distributors and retailers was an issue that could slow price adjustment. The Vice President of Marketing for a division of a manufacturer of automobile replacement parts said:

> "[Is it expensive to change prices?] It is, but due to the size and the volume that we have, as little as half a point price change will more than offset all of the costs associated with changing the price. [You mean half a percent?] Half a percent. So if we can get a one percent price increase, it more than offsets. If we get a half a percent of price increase, it will offset our cost, but not enough to bother our customers with doing that. [That is a consideration too, the bother to the customer?] It is. If we are going to take a price increase and we took a half a percent, our customers would

Table 2.4.1

The Administrative Costs of Price Change	Number of Interviews and Firms
Inhibit Price Change	10
Do Not Inhibit Price Change	55
Are Too Small to Matter	47
Are Costly for Customers	23
Total Number of Interviews and Firms	79

call up and say, 'Look it. If you are going to take a price increase, take a price increase. Don't bother us with a half a percent.'"

The President and owner of a company that manufactures lubricants for sporting equipment said:

"We set pricing once a year, and then we go from there. [So you don't allow yourself to change prices during the year?] No. [Why not?] Because of the two-step distribution, it is really cumbersome to change pricing. If you change it on a distributor, they have produced catalogs, they have produced brochures, they have programmed their computers, they have established to some extent retail price points, and you change it. It is all of a sudden what they have published is inaccurate . . . [Is this expensive for you to do this, when you change prices at the end of the year?] Nah, expensive? No, everything is on a computer."

For most of those who did not have to deal with distributors or retailers, the administrative costs of price change were irrelevant. The Vice President of Sales and Marketing for a medium-size manufacturer of webbing said:

"Every single customer is treated differently. I mean, it is a negotiation. It is not like, that is the one you want, that is the price you have got. That is not the case."

The Vice President of Marketing and Sales of machine tool manufacturer A said:

"[Is there any cost to changing the list price that keeps you from changing it all the time?] The only cost would be logistically, just the cost of communicating that change, redoing documents. [Is that expensive?] Not substantial. [So that is not something that is keeping you from changing prices often?] No, not really. And again in this industry it has almost come to the point where your list price is pretty irrelevant anyway. [So you are constantly on the phone?] You are trying to figure out where that market price is going to be, where that individual transaction price needs to be."

The Vice President of Sales for a medium-size manufacturer of control hydraulics said:

"[Do the administrative expenses of changing prices reduce the frequency of price change?] No. It has nothing to do with it. It is all computerized. You just push a button and pages are printed. [So the expense of printing new catalogues is not –] – a big deal, no."

2.4.1 Related Literature

Zbaracki et al. (2004) have used interviews, direct observation, company data, and industrial engineering studies to describe and measure the costs of price change in a large American industrial company. The total costs are substantial and the main costs are the managerial costs associated with deciding on a price, the cost of communicating the logic of price changes to members of the firm, and the cost of negotiating with customers who object to the new prices.

Akerlof and Yellen (1985); Mankiw (1985); and Parkin (1986) argue that even small menu costs can have large effects in macroeconomic models where price-setting firms have market power.

Caplin and Leahy (1997) make an argument for dismissing the macroeconomic impact of costs of price change. They contend that firms with significant costs of this sort would change prices in jumps and would change price only if their current price was outside an interval of no change. A change in a firm's circumstances would induce it to move a price only if the change moved the interval of no change so that it no longer contained the firm's current price. The only firms in an economy likely to change price if economic circumstances changed by a small amount would be firms with a current price near an endpoint of the interval of no price change. A small positive fraction of firms are likely to be in that position at any given time. If circumstance changed by a small amount, most prices would not change, but a small fraction would change with a jump. As a result, the average of all the firms' prices would move nearly continuously. That is, the average price would respond to change in economic circumstances in much the same way that it would if no firm had to deal with costs of price change. Golosov and Lucas (2007) make a related argument.

2.5 Evidence of Constant or Declining Average and Marginal Variable Costs

Respondents discussed the relation of output to average variable cost in 183 of the 290 interviews in manufacturing firms. These interviews were in 175 firms. The topic was irrelevant for twenty of the 175 firms, because the firms' production processes obliged them to run at near full capacity or not at all.[15] Table 2.5.1 summarizes the responses. Some respondents were able to speak with authority about the behavior of marginal as well as average variable costs, but their responses are not tabulated separately.

Judging from the distribution of these responses, it is unusual for firms to experience increases in average variable costs when product demand increases within its normal range of variation. Average variable cost might well increase if output were near the capacity limit. Of the 163 respondents to whom Table 2.5.1 applies, fourteen mentioned that average variable cost does rise when their firms operate at near full capacity. It appears to be unusual, however, for manufacturing firms to produce at such levels. Only four of the 163 mentioned that they were currently producing at near capacity levels, even though the topic of capacity limits came up in many of the interviews with respondents from manufacturing firms.

For many manufacturers, it seemed to be a well-known fact of life that average variable costs do not increase as output increases over its normal range. The Marketing Director for Dimension Lumber for western lumber company B said:

> "[How does the variable (average variable cost) react to volume?] Well, the variable is pretty flat to volume. If you shut a shift off, you send the crew home. That is the major part of your variable cost. If you send the crew home, you are using less electricity, because you are not running that shift. Less steam. Less everything. You can generally get your (average) variable costs down pretty close to where they were when you were running three

Table 2.5.1 The Effect of Increased Output on Average Variable Costs[16]

When Output is Higher, Average Variable Costs Are	Number of Interviews	Number of Firms
Lower	109	104
The Same	41	39
Higher	4	3
Higher or Lower Depending on the Good Produced	1	1
Respondent Did Not Know	8	6
Totals	163	153

shifts ... (Average) fixed costs you can't do that obviously. They go up."

One respondent mentioned that average variable costs decline with output because labor is in part a fixed input. What follows are notes from an unrecorded conversation with an accountant who worked for western lumber company B. I asked him about the relationship between output and unit variable costs. He said:

"... true unit variable costs are flat. They don't depend on output. But semi-variable costs, which include labor, tend to decline as output increases, because labor is to some extent a fixed cost."

Table 2.5.2

Reason Why Average Variable Costs Decline as Output Increases	Number of Interviews	Number of Firms
Lower Average Setup Costs	39	39
More Quantity Discounts in the Purchase of Inputs	23	23
Employees Work Harder When There Is More Work To Do	19	19
Totals	109	104

When respondents said that average variable costs were lower when their firms were busier, I asked for explanations of why this was so. Table 2.5.2 summarizes the 109 responses. Of these, 39 were that greater output brought longer runs of production of one good on a production line with fewer changeovers from one good to another and fewer setups for new production runs. Setups and changeovers were said to be expensive. Of the 109, 23 said that quantity discounts in the purchase of inputs reduced average variable costs when output increased. In addition, nineteen of the 109 said their firm's employees worked harder and more effectively when there was more work to do, because workers tend to try to protect their jobs by slowing down when business slackens. Respondents' explanations relate their views to concrete experience.

Lower Setup and Changeover Costs and Learning by Doing

A district sales manager for very large manufacturer of branded foods 1 said:

"There is efficiencies to scale on a lot of things, because you get to run high speed lines and not be changing the dies on pasta or not stopping line shipment down and switching sizes . . . You know, only produce 18-ounce peanut butter for a week straight. So they never change the jar. They never change the product. That thing never stops for one straight week . . . I don't know what it takes to shut down those lines, clean them out, change the jars that you are putting on there, change the label. You have a different label, different caps, all sorts of different things are happening. [So with more volume you don't have to change so often?] Sure."

The Vice President of Sales and Marketing for stamper A said:

"[That is true, that your variable costs per unit of output increase, because of this overtime premium?] Variable cost would increase, and that you recoup by running sustained production . . . See, there is a lot of setup cost in our business. When you change a job in a machine, the setup cost can wipe you out . . . This is why we strive to get large volumes, then you can just run uninterrupted other than normal maintenance. So there are some different scenarios here, Truman."

The Director of Marketing in North America for manufacturer B of injection molding machines said:

"[Do you have any idea how much unit variable costs of production depend on your output?] . . . I think (with large orders) the guys become more efficient on the floor. From one machine to the next, they know exactly what needs to be done. They know what materials they need. They know where to get those materials. So they are not out searching around talking to engineering, trying to figure out how this thing should mount on a machine or how they are going to have to pipe it or anything special. They have done it on one. The second, the third, the fourth, the fifth become much easier, and we see that in our margin reports as well in terms of labor."

Employees Work Harder When There Is More to Do

The Chairman and CEO of machine tool manufacturer C said:

"[When the volume improves, variable unit costs – ?] Variable costs might go down slightly. I mean, you know, there is an old expression in our industry called the 'empty bench syndrome.' When people know that things aren't busy they tend to slow down a little bit. And so our variable – when things slow down our variable costs probably actually go up a little bit."

The President for North America of a manufacturer of specialized paints said:

"I was the plant manager for a while and one of the things that – it wasn't a secret, it was pretty open – was that as we got more and more busy there was a greater sense of urgency and there was also less, if any, sense of concern over job security and hence a need to feel that the work was getting spread over the day and that everyone looked busy. And so when we took a look at our average outputs on certain pieces of equipment when we were busy versus when we were slower, we found pretty interesting changes and it was pretty clear that when things slowed down work was spread out to fill the day."

The President and COO of folding box manufacturer C said:

"[Are you more efficient as an operation when you are busy?] Absolutely. [So your variable costs per unit of output are lower?] Yes. No question . . . People when they see the work in process at a low level they tend to slow down because they figure they are protecting their jobs, and there is a lot of discomfort when things get slow. They are worried about next week's paycheck; protect the backlog type of thing . . . When we are busy, we are much more efficient. [It doesn't get confused when you are trying to meet orders?] Oh, sure it does . . . [And that doesn't cause inefficiency?] To some degree it does . . . But, it is offset."

A few respondents commented on why average variable costs tend to rise when output approaches capacity. The Vice President of Sales and Marketing for steel service center 1 said:

"There is a fine line there. There is an extreme amount of business when we are not that efficient, because the customer is still looking for from one to two days' delivery and we can't do it on all the orders that they want us to . . . Carelessness, rushing, tired, overtime. Yeah. Things like that. From everybody. From whether inside sales make a mistake on what they put on the piece of paper to be done or people putting up (on a delivery truck) the wrong gauge or the wrong alloy."

Vice President 1 of a huge producer of branded and unbranded foods said:

> "The raw inputs that go into it are, in most of what we buy, not affected by whether we run our plant at 60 percent, 80 percent, or 100 percent. But when you start having people with overtime costs, you have lower yield from a plant, because you have too many things going on at once . . . Some operations we run during peak season three shifts for six days and then one shift on Sunday and that leaves us 16 hours to do any plant repairs. Well, if the margins are so good that you don't run those – if you run the full seven days or run additional, you have only got eight hours for repairs and you start to run into natural problems and hiccups . . . You get breakdowns, where you are less efficient."

2.5.1 Electricity Generators

Respondents who worked for electricity generating companies knew a lot about the marginal variable costs of their plants, because the generating companies where I interviewed sell electricity to semi-public authorities through reverse auctions and need to know marginal costs as a function of output in order to calculate optimal bids. Some generators, such as gas turbine generators produce at essentially a single level of output, but the generators that produce at variable levels have marginal costs which decline with output and then climb steeply as it approaches capacity. The Manager of Governmental and Market Relations for electric generating company A said, speaking of steam turbine generators:

> "[Your marginal cost increases, though, doesn't it with your power output?] No actually in electricity, it often goes the other way around . . . There is a level, which is almost at full capacity that you are operating most efficiently. Your heat rate, in other words, how effectively you are making electricity for the fuel you put in is the best near the top . . . There is a point where you try to crank a little bit more out of the machine than the machine was designed for, that you really start losing efficiencies. So you start up high, because you are running inefficiently at low levels. You drop to a point of optimal efficiency, and then at the end you

get a little steeply upward curve, because you are really running your plant in a way that it is not supposed to be run, which increases the chance of a forced outage considerably. [And that is a marginal cost too?] That is a marginal cost . . . You have got hydro facilities that are dependent on the amount of water that is pouring through . . . You have got nuclear facilities that basically just try to go full out when they are in operation . . . They don't really run well at lower levels particularly . . . Hydro facility. Once you have built the dam, the water is free, so you are going to bid zero."

A Principal Economist for the New York Independent System Operator said, speaking of steam turbines:

"[Why would they ever want to operate in an area where it (marginal cost) is falling? You would think that if there was a given price, they would want to go right up to where their marginal costs is increasing.] They do . . . Typically (at) the last 2 to 10 percent of the capacity, marginal costs are distinctly rising, because it is more difficult to get power out of the last – [There is a danger apparently of failure too?] You have got failure, because they don't often operate there. We just don't take them there. You have to do things to get that power out. You may have to take more pressure in the boilers. You risk tube leaks. That is where your failure part comes . . . The New York system is a funny system. We have got a number of nuclear units, which really do have – they are pretty flat. Actually the marginal cost is probably close to zero . . . and they don't move very much anyway. I am not sure whether the rising piece is even relevant for nuclear. At the other end of the system, we have lots and lots of combustion turbines, and they operate typically at one point . . . So whether they have declining marginal costs is irrelevant . . . They are on or off. [These are those turbines that are like a jet engine attached to a generator.] That is right."

2.5.2 Related Literature

A few researchers have gathered evidence relevant to the assertion that for many manufacturing firms, average variable or marginal variable costs are constant, or decline as output increases, until just before reaching a capacity limit. Andrews (1949, p. 110), in a book based on fieldwork, reports that average variable cost is constant over a wide range. Fog (1960), in his interview study of Danish manufacturing, encountered arguments for both increasing and decreasing average variable costs. Some of his respondents argued that the overtime premium makes average costs increase with output. Arguments for decreasing average costs were that workers work harder when there is more to do and that a portion of labor is fixed. Constant average variable costs seemed to be common, but the increasing and decreasing cases could not be excluded. Blinder et al. (1998, pp. 102, 216–218), have gathered convincing evidence that in a large segment of American manufacturing average variable costs either remain constant or decline as output increases. From data on the production schedules and inventories of several large industrial firms, Valery Ramey (1991) inferred that their marginal costs might be declining functions of output. In a questionnaire survey of French businesses, 36 percent of the respondents said that their unit variable costs were constant as a function of output: see Loupias and Ricart (2006).

2.6 The Treatment of Fixed Costs and the Use of Fully Absorbing Cost Systems

A fully absorbing cost system is a way of computing a product's unit cost of production by adding to average variable cost an assignment to the product of the firm's average fixed and overhead costs. Firms that use these cost systems typically set the price of a product equal to a markup over its fully absorbing cost. It is hard to reconcile this practice with standard microeconomic theory, but it is understandable that a firm would act in this way, if its average or marginal variable costs remained constant or declined as output increased. For this reason, the widespread use of fully absorbing costs is indirect evidence that for many firms average or marginal variable costs do remain constant, or fall as output increases.

The complaints I heard about the use of fully absorbing costs suggest that those using fully absorbing cost systems to choose prices may often fail to maximize profits. Without detailed information, however, we cannot know whether a firm chooses price and output levels so as to maximize the difference between sales revenue and total variable cost. Whether or not this maximum is achieved, the firm needs to verify that a product is worth producing. That is, the firm needs to calculate whether the difference between a product's sales revenue and its total variable costs exceeds the increase in fixed costs created by manufacture of the product. Fully absorbing costs seem to be designed for use as simplifying approximations in this calculation. If the firm's marginal variable costs rise steeply as a function of output, the difference between price and marginal variable cost on inframarginal units of output can create a cushion of net revenue that diminishes the importance of the calculation of whether it is profitable to produce a product. Therefore, the popularity of fully absorbing costs may be evidence that the cushion often is small or not there and hence that marginal and average variable costs are often non-increasing or close to it.

Overhead costs are costs other than operating expenses, which are those directly related to the production of goods or services. In firms that produce multiple products, some overhead costs may be viewed as the costs of joint inputs that contribute to the production of more than one good or service. Examples of overhead costs are payment of accounting personnel and payment for utilities and for the maintenance of facilities. Many overhead expenses are fixed, in that they do not depend in the short-run on the level of productive activity within a firm. The distinction between overhead and operating expenses can be ambiguous, and overhead expenses can be many times greater than total operating expenses.

The distinction between fixed and variable costs is also ambiguous, because what is classified as variable depends on the amount of time allowed for cost adjustment. Examples of costs typically labeled as fixed are debt service, depreciation, and maintenance of plant and equipment, insurance premiums, the salaries of top management personnel, and the cost of developing new products.

The systems for assigning fixed and overhead costs to products vary among firms. It is inevitable that such cost assignment systems often seem arbitrary, since they tend to assign the cost of joint inputs to the individual items produced. The Controller of manufacturer A of architectural hardware said:

> "Overhead and all those fixed costs that you were talking about . . . the way we have assigned those costs is we have created departments. It is really a department based on a product that is being made as opposed to a manufacturing process. So we will take an area of the factory . . . Most of our machinery is dedicated to these product groups. So we have a product group, for example, called mortise locks, and we have all the machinery that is in that physical area . . . We will take that physical area as far as overhead goes, which would be the lights and the property taxes, and the building and depreciation, and things like that, and that would be allocated to that product group . . . We apportion

based on square footage or sometimes it is square footage and the asset value of the equipment . . . We have some support areas, like the receiving department, purchasing on the front end, and on the back end it would be like the shipping department . . . Our maintenance department actually bills those individual product groups . . . for their services. Things like receiving and shipping are pretty much an allocation based on the amount of material that they buy. Something like human resources would be based on head counts."

There are extreme forms of cost systems, called Activity Based Cost or ABC systems, which attempt to treat most overhead and fixed costs as variable. In such systems, marketing executives might keep track of how much time they devote to each product and their salaries might be charged to the products accordingly. I was told that such systems had dropped out of fashion, because administering them took too much time, though two of the companies where I interviewed used them.

Systems for assigning fixed and overhead costs to products are so common that business people have a special terminology for discussing them. People speak of the overhead and fixed expenses assigned to a product as burdening it and they say that the product absorbs fixed and overhead expenses. They say that a cost system is fully absorbing, full absorption, fully loaded, or full cost if it assigns all fixed and overhead expenses to some products.

Even if average variable costs do not decline as output increases, average fully absorbing costs could do so, because fixed costs would be spread over larger outputs. Many businesses offset this tendency by using fully absorbing costs at normal rather than current levels of output. They do so, because they realize that if they used current output levels, then the average fully absorbing costs would increase as output decreased, so that if selling prices were tied to these costs, prices would vary in the wrong way; they would rise when demand fell. Fully absorbing costs at a normal level of output are called standard costs.

Respondents explained that the main purpose of fully absorbing cost systems is to provide a way to check that sales revenue covers fixed and overhead expenses. Use of the systems seems to be especially common among contract manufacturers, probably because they bid for business against many competitors and hence have so little market power that they must be careful to ensure that they earn enough to cover fixed and overhead expenses. All of the 35 contract manufacturing companies where I interviewed included some specific allowance for fixed and overhead costs in their bids.

The Pricing of Manufactured Goods 63

Although many manufacturing firms use fully absorbing cost systems, their use is not universal. Their use seems to be less common among manufacturers of commodities, probably because these manufacturers have little control over their selling prices.

I list tendencies in the ways manufacturing firms handle fixed and overhead costs.

(1) A defect in the use of many full absorption cost and pricing systems is that they do not allow for the possibility that sales growth resulting from a price reduction may be so large that the decrease in average fixed costs increases the difference between the product's total revenue and total cost. Firms that do not take account of this effect may hurt themselves financially by insisting that the price of a product be high enough to cover the assigned average fixed and overhead expenses at current or average output levels.

(2) Some firms that have excess capacity and set price equal to a markup over fully loaded costs, arrange additional sales of a product at a discounted price that is higher than the product's average variable cost of production but lower than the fully loaded cost. Because the price exceeds average variable cost, the extra sales contribute to the surplus that pays for fixed costs and profit, though that contribution is less than it would have been if the extra sales had been made at an undiscounted price. Of course, if the firm charged such a price, those sales might not occur. Reducing price in this manner on additional business is often called contribution margin pricing.

(3) Customer firms sometimes argue that the price they pay should decline with increased purchases of a product, because the supplier's fixed costs are then spread over greater output.

(4) Firms sometimes lower a price during an accounting period once they are sure that they have paid for the fixed and overhead cost assigned to the product for the period. This practice does not appear to be consistent with profit maximization.

(5) Companies that develop products sold on an open market do not let the price of a product depend on its development cost.

(6) Firms that develop a custom product for one customer normally charge the customer for its development cost.

2.6.1 The Uses of Full Absorption Cost Systems

The main effect of full absorption cost systems seems to be to make prices depend on fixed costs. The impact of this effect becomes clearest when respondents describe what they thought were the harmful effects of the systems. The Director of Operations for a zinc-aluminum die casting manufacturer said:

> "The problem was, we had a standard cost system in the company, and the standard cost system was what was killing us, because standard costs said your costs per unit today are this. So when you quote a job on today's costs, you have got to cover all those costs and make a 30 percent profit . . . I would quote the work and I would give it to the sales department and they would review it with the accounting department to make sure that that margin was there. If it wasn't there, they went back and raised the price, and we were losing everything . . . Economically to compete in the industry, you have got to . . . base your quotes on the variable costs, because my variable costs compared to my competitors' may be very much alike . . . If I am quoting a job that exceeds my variable costs, I want to win it . . . Well, lo and behold, all the jobs exceed my variable costs . . . [Do you know what the jobs went for that you lost?] Yes . . . From a standard cost basis, it looked bad. It looks like, 'Oh, you only got a 10 percent margin on it.' 'Yeah, but I got two and half times my variable costs.' . . . We had to do some reeducation, because this entire company lived and breathed standard cost . . . The accounting department wasn't happy with it . . . I was very happy, and the consultant was very happy, because now we could see how we could win jobs. Everybody else in the company was like, 'Oh, my God! You can't do that. You are going to give the company away.' . . . Our variable costs are actually very competitive . . . Everybody charges the same price for metal . . . The variable proportion is . . . (natural) gas, electricity, labor, benefits associated with that labor . . . and it is only the labor that you would add to run that job . . . What we are finding, is that there is just tons of work out there at two and half, three times our variable costs, and we want it all. [And you are sure you will be profitable if you get enough of it?] Yes . . . The variance – let's just say the number (for the cost of running the factory) is $100 an hour (man-hour). If we run the factory at $90 an hour, we have a positive variance. If we run it at 110 we have a negative variance . . . When I had low volumes, I had high (negative) variances (because fixed costs per man-hour were high) . . . One month, I run 4,000 hours, I have no variances. Three months later, I run 3,000 hours and I have high variances. Now the reason I had high variances . . . [High negative variances?] High negative variances. And the reason I

ran 3,000 hours was mainly because it was summertime and a lot of guys were on vacation ... This happened two years in a row. In summertime, they would see I had negative variances. Well, their solution is to lay people off ... Guys in the shop ... It was like this big circle of stupidity."

Many respondents saw advantages in full absorption cost accounting systems, the main one being that they made it easier to ensure that companies paid for fixed and overhead expenses. The CEO and President of a manufacturing and industrial distribution company said:

"[What is the point of allocating your fixed costs at all?] ... We really want to be sure that we are covering the fixed cost. I mean, we want to be sure that we understand what our fixed costs are and what can we do ... If that cost is unreasonable, then you have to do things to change that fixed cost."

The Vice President of Operations for pressed powder metal manufacturer E said:

"[Why have a fixed markup for SG&A[17] and stuff like that?] That is just the way we have been doing it. [These are fixed costs, right, this SG&A? It doesn't depend on how much business you have?] Right. [So why should that enter the pricing at all?] Because somehow we need to cover it, and the simplest way was to figure out what it was."

Some respondents advised against thinking about marginal costs, which is consistent with the emphasis on covering fixed and overhead costs. The next quotation uses the word "incremental," which in business jargon refers to additional business that does not require an increase in fixed costs. The Director of Price Improvement of a large manufacturer of electrical equipment said:

"[Why did you say you don't like looking at marginal costs? Because you are not considering fixed costs?] ... I am underneath a lot of pressure for bookings and orders and I say ... 'I am going to get an increment above variable costs.' ... A couple of things happen. One that happens is that pretty soon your people and your salespeople start to look at all of your business as incremental, and at the end of the year you found out you didn't make any money. You didn't cover your fixed costs . . . That is one danger. The other danger leads more towards what I would call pricing integrity . . . If there is a chance of that customer in the future expecting similar pricing or if . . . it is an industry where people discuss pricing . . . that specific decision there to gain that incremental margin might put price pressure on me from another point."

Another use of full absorption cost systems is to motivate salespeople to sell at a good margin. The President of pressed powder metal manufacturer D said:

"I wouldn't give them (his sales force) the variable cost model, because I think that they would go too low in the marketplace. [Just to get the work?] Just to get the work . . . I don't want them to say, 'Look, just sell above variable,' because, for one, that is too easy. Anyone could do that. You got to try to get a good margin . . . So occasionally, I will go into the computer and increase the burden rates, just to do it, just to make them try and get a higher price."

Price is, of course, influenced by market conditions as well as cost. The President and CEO of a manufacturer of metal storage containers said:

"[How do you come up with a price in the first place?] . . . You go through that (full absorption costing) and you come up with a number of what this thing is going to cost to produce and you adjust that . . . [You don't look at what the competition is charging?] We do. Yeah. So then, that is how we come up with a price and we go to market, and if they say no this is where your competition is, then we have to negotiate and adjust accordingly."

Some companies sell products that are nearly commodities under cost plus contracts that set the price equal to the full absorption cost plus a margin. The firms I know of that used such pricing were the low cost producers in their industries. The Vice President of Sales for steel manufacturer F said:

"We have also cost plus arrangements, where we have a negotiated margin, and we build it on a quarterly basis relative to the prior quarter's actual cost . . . [What kind of costs are they? Are they full costs?] Yeah. They are fully loaded costs. [So with all the overhead and everything?] Correct."

2.6.2 Attitudes toward Fully Absorbing Cost Systems

Not all respondents thought that absorbing cost systems should be used in pricing. Some thought them silly. Perhaps they felt this way because they had so much market power or such low costs that they did not need to use a special accounting scheme to assure adequate profit margins. The President of a company that manufactures energy conserving lighting controls said:

"[The decision for setting your price depends also on your costs?] It hasn't had to, *per se*. [Why is that?] Because the market prices are such that our costs are substantially lower. So I haven't really bumped into any kind of constraint . . . [When you are talking about costs, you are talking about –] Direct costs. [Direct costs of materials and labor? And then, what fraction of your total costs is overhead?] A lot . . . Probably 300 percent (of labor costs) . . . [So you don't go around and assign this overhead to each product?] No. [You don't think that way?] No, I don't think that way at all. [Some companies do.] I know. I hate that . . . [Why do you hate that, by the way?] Because I think it is ridiculous. [How do you make sure you cover your fixed cost?] Well, you have got to cover your fixed cost by covering your fixed cost. Making a pricing decision on this widget because I assign some bogus percentage overhead to it I think is the most ridiculous accounting practice ever invented. So it is just dumb."

In some companies, issues other than covering fixed costs dominate pricing, issues such as keeping factories running and maintaining the loyalty of customers. The Vice President of Sales and Marketing of manufacturer B of major household appliances said:

"In the month of January, we made one million dollars of gross margin on that refrigerator. [That is the difference between price and variable cost?] That is correct. That does not include base cost. [Base cost would be including all the fixed costs?] Right. And we don't actually look at it that way. We basically measure it to variable cost . . . [So you are not really allocating fixed costs?]

No. We don't mess around with it. That happens below the line. We do that mainly on a business group level . . . I know off the top of my head, it (fixed cost) is about 15 percent . . . If I am not at 15 percent here, I am pretty much below cost, total cost. [Is that a concern to you in any way?] Sure. It is a big concern. Like here. Here is a washer I sold 9,000 of last month. We made no margin on the piece. Zero. Now you say, 'Why do you do it?' Well, I have got a factory here that needs volume. If they don't get the volume, we start laying off people. The unions go crazy . . . We probably sell about 10 or 15 percent of our volume below variable cost, and it is basically to keep plants running. It is to meet low-end deals . . . [Why would you want to meet a low-end deal?] . . . Because here is what a customer (a retailer) will say. A lot of times, a customer will say, 'Well, if you don't give me the low-end product, I am not going to support you on the high-end product.'"

For some companies, selling prices are so high relative to costs that there is no need to keep track of fixed and overhead cost absorption. The Director of Marketing, Research, and Pricing Administration for manufacturer of specialty materials B said:

"Pricing to value doesn't – we don't even think in terms of cost . . . We are trying to get the most value out of the product and still make sure the customer is getting a better value than what he is from what he (could get from the next best alternative) . . . Raw chemicals and things like this may fluctuate a little bit. But . . . the actual cost is a small percentage of the value that we bring . . . [So fluctuations in raw materials prices don't really affect your prices?] No, we wouldn't change our price because of that]."

Internal company discussion of absorbing cost systems seemed to be debates between the accounting and sales departments. The Vice President of Commercial Sales for stamper B said:

"That is the fight that I make as the sales guy to the financial community all the time. I got a press sitting, to use a term from show business, in the dark . . . It is not running. Give me the blue light special for that press. I will discount it. I will fill it up. 'You can't go there.' 'Why not?' 'Because if we sell everything like that, we won't cover our burdens.'"

2.6.3 Contribution Margin Pricing

Recall that contribution margin prices are between fully absorbing costs and average variable costs and are typically used by firms with excess capacity. The use of such pricing seems to be fairly common, though some respondents were strongly opposed to it. In 29 of the 90 companies where respondents discussed fully absorbing cost systems in detail, the respondents said their companies had in the past or were currently using contribution margin pricing. The President of corrugated box manufacturer A said:

> "Anything that gives us a reasonable contribution over that variable cost, we will take when we are not at capacity... We will still take stuff below full cost... We will never go below our out of pocket (i.e. average variable cost)."

The owner of small prepared food manufacturer 1 said:

> "[Do you ever... do what they call contribution pricing?] I think you do that subconsciously sometimes... I have actually taken ... low pricing knowing that not only did I keep it away from my competitor, but this is going to cover some of my overheads down the line somewhere. [Even though it is not going to give you profit by your standard calculation?] Right. Right. And I have done that many times."

The President of steel service center D said:

> "[When you are operating below capacity as in a recession... would you take orders at a lower margin just to cover some of your fixed costs, even though you wouldn't by your standard measure make a profit on it?]... Any businessperson would tell you that you have to do that, because you have got to cover your payments, and then the thing starts to spiral. [What do you mean spiral?] Death spirals... It depends on how long and how far you have to go and how much access to cash do you have to weather that."

One argument against contribution margin pricing is that though reducing margins in slow times might gain business, it would be difficult to restore margins on that business or to get rid of the low margin business when good times returned. A Marketing Consultant working for large chemical company A said:

> "[Did you ever take on products, where you are actually by this calculation not making a profit, thinking it is contributing something to fixed cost?] ... Most of the businesses that I have been in don't like to go there. [Why is that?] Well, you know you are not going to want the business when your asset utilization gets better and often we are in the types of industries where our customers can't get in and out easily and it is just customer relations reasons. You are either stuck with it or you are creating so much ill will in the industry for a short-term gain."

Another argument was that any use of contribution margin pricing, by breaking the rules of full absorption costing, could be an invitation to salespeople to fill the factory with low margin work. The President, CEO, and owner of folding carton manufacturer E said:

> "[So you really have two kinds of business, direct cost business and fully burdened business?] Right, but I would tell you 95 percent plus of our business is fully – we have 100 percent of the burden on 95 percent of the business, let's say it that way. [What would be the danger if you had 25 percent of your business be this direct cost?] The danger is this ... A marketing guy could go out and fill up your plant overnight with low or no profit business and put you out of business. You are busy as hell, but you are not making any money ... They (salespeople) usually are highly motivated by closing a deal, making a sale, bringing in the work. Then they think it is somebody else's problem to drive the costs out of the products."

Another argument was that any use of contribution margin pricing could spoil a company's reputation for doing quality work, and the loss of reputation could drive away the most desirable customers. The connection with quality is that potential customers might assume that a company earning low margins could not afford to maintain good quality. A Senior Industrial Engineer with injection molding company D said:

> "[If you are in a recession and this place isn't being used, would you reduce price?] No. The bean counter (accountant) would normally want me to kick it up (raise prices) ... I look at them and I say, 'What you are trying to tell me is you don't want to be in that business.' You can't raise the price like that. [So when you have bad times, like the beginning of the '90s, do you reduce price

to try to fill the place up?] No. You can't. [Why not?] Because you are already at your best economic run . . . Perception is a tremendous amount of it. You can't undercut your margin . . . [What do you think would happen to your reputation if you did that? What would be the effect, the consequences?] What would be the consequences is that the word would go around very quickly that this is willing to happen and therefore what are you looking at for the quality? Are you putting the engineering into the tool when you are setting it up, when you are taking it down. Are you maintaining the tools . . . It is the quality perception."

2.6.4 Other Evidence that Fixed Expenses Can Affect Prices

I came upon two types of additional evidence that fixed expenses can affect prices, usually in the context of pricing based on fully absorbing costs. One type of evidence was the use of fixed costs as an argument in price negotiations between a company and another that manufactures parts for it. The company in the next quotation sells parts to manufacturers of big equipment, an example being door seals for dishwashers. The President and CEO of a manufacturer of synthetic rubber seals and gaskets said:

"We are successful to get small, incremental (price) increases, but they (customers) pressure us just as much to go down in cost or price . . . They say, 'Jee (the rubber company's name), you have had this thing now for four years. You must have absorbed all your fixed costs on this and you certainly have grown by the volume we have given you. How about giving some of that fixed cost absorption back to us?' They don't use those words, but that is what they mean."

The second bit of evidence that fixed costs affect prices is that respondents from eleven firms mentioned that their companies lower prices of a product once the companies have covered the product's fixed and overhead costs.[18] The Vice President of Engineering for a producer of metal doors and vents for buildings said:

"If we have overhead covered already, and now we have got what we call incremental work, so we can prepare our cost and not burden this particular project, because all the other – [Not burden it at all?] No, we burden it, but not to the extent we normally would. That obviously makes us more competitive, and then the only other consideration is the strain on capacity, which I do not want to do. But anyway, that technique has worked very well and has secured us some very large projects."

The President and COO of folding box manufacturer C said:

"[So you are more likely to take these low margin jobs towards the end of the year, when you know you have covered your fixed costs?] I will take them at various points during the year, but I will price them differently . . . [In what sense?] In the sense that once I know that I am fully absorbed, even if I take it at less than my cost, I have a higher potential of ending up on the plus side, because I have already . . . covered my fixed costs."

2.6.5 The Need for Absorping Cost Systems

Although absorption cost systems may seem arbitrary, I heard stories that made it clear that they sometimes serve a valuable policing function. The former CEO of a cleaning products manufacturer said

"One of the issues was many of the people that went into the trucking business during deregulation were gypsies. You know, we call them gypsies. People would show up at our shipping bay with a woman in the truck and a shotgun in the cab. One of the issues was most of those guys that went into the trucking business weren't very sophisticated and didn't realize that in the trucking business depreciation is real. It is not an accounting fiction. Your tires do wear out. Your engine does need an overhaul. Transmissions do fail, and for the first couple of years it was wonderful, but then I can remember very distinctly getting a call . . . a fellow saying, 'I have got a 40,000 pound load here. You guys have got to send me more money. I need tires. If you don't send me more money, this load is going over the side of the road.'"

2.6.6 Development Costs of Products Sold to a Market

Respondents in nine companies described the impact on pricing of product development costs when the products were sold to broad markets. Four of the companies were large manufacturers of pharmaceutical products. In all nine cases, respondents said the costs were sunk and did not affect prices. The four pharmaceutical companies budgeted a substantial percentage of sales revenue every year for

The Pricing of Manufactured Goods

new product research. No one said or implied that this budgeting affected pricing. Since development costs are fixed, one wonders why they do not affect pricing through some fully absorbing cost system. I suspect that the explanation is that the nine companies considered are so wealthy and have so much market power that they need not take special measures to be sure to recoup fixed costs. A Vice President of Marketing for pharmaceutical manufacturer B said:

> "[The cost of developing that particular drug, does that ever enter the pricing?] . . . Most pharmaceutical companies have a very difficult time saying, 'I spent this amount of money on this particular compound . . . I want to get it back.' What happens, it is more or less an investment on a yearly basis against total sales. Most pharmaceutical companies will invest about 14 to 15 percent of total sales into an R&D capacity. It is very difficult to say of that 14 and 15 percent of sales, 'So far that has been the one that seems to be placing a return on the table.' . . . You may have started with a field of molecules in order to reach a new product for a, you know, anti-hypertensive . . . It is very hard to go back and singularly pick out that one particular product until you get to phase 3 (of testing a new drug), and in phase 3 you will spend between 50 and 150 million dollars just to study it. But this does not include the other 100 million dollars that is allocated to all the other compounds that have failed. I believe that is somewhere between one in a thousand that actually come to market. So one doesn't go to recoup those types of costs, but the industry actually focuses on a level of investment that they feel is sufficient to then produce compounds that will yield a satisfactory return to investors."

The Chairman of a manufacturer of telecommunications equipment said:

> "[Now when they compute the cost, do you know how they take account of fixed cost? . . . Development costs?] Development costs they don't take. . . . That is something of the past . . . I mean, when we decide on developing the products, we will take that into account. We will say, 'Well, this is the product. We think we can sell so many of that and we think the price will be that high, so we could have a nice margin and so let's invest in development.' So the decision that was taken two years ago. Now you have the product. The costs may be different. The price may be different.

Everything has changed by that time, and the development cost is gone ... At that point of determining the price, we don't take the development cost anymore into account. That is simple."

The CEO of a geological imaging company said:

"Software is completely value pricing, because there is no cost of manufacturing. I mean, the only thing you have in software is the R&D cost, but the R&D cost isn't amortized, so it is basically a sunk cost by the time you get to the pricing step. So the cost of software is zero effectively."

2.6.7 Development Costs of Custom Products

Companies do let development costs affect prices, when they design and make products for just one customer. Three of the companies where I interviewed produced such custom products. These were robotic machines for forming and assembling complicated objects, such as automobile car doors. All three companies charged the entire development cost to the customer. The development cost was viewed as part of the direct cost of producing the product. The Vice President of Finance of machine tool manufacturer D said:

"The main products are large custom made machine tools that sell for – the average price may be around two million dollars ... There are three basic intervals in building the machine, the engineering, the manufacturing and buying the components, and then the assembly of the machine and the debugging of the machine and testing it and trying it out. And each one might be a third of the total time. And so on the engineering hours, we would have standard charts that we would use to kind of describe different types of machines and how long it would take us to engineer different parts of machines. [This is your guess in advance?] Correct. Well, we price a fixed price quote. [So you do make a quote? It is not like a law firm, where you get paid for your hours afterwards?] No. It is a fixed price quote. [So you are committed to your price? You may lose money or make money on the machine?] Correct."

A respondent from one firm mentioned that the price of a new product could be reduced once the cost of developing the product had been amortized. The President of machine tool manufacturer B said:

"If we are going to build one press and never going to build another one and we have to amortize all of the costs for development, let's say it is a new press, on one unit, that is one situation. Now we may not get the business if we put the full price on based on that cost. What we are looking for is the opportunity over time to credibly supply multiple units, and then once we see that we have that, then some price consideration could be available to the customer because we now have amortized our cost. Now once we get our costs flat, and we know what they are, then we might be able to reduce the price on future units and still enjoy the same margin, because we no longer have the development cost to amortize. So the general statement is, until and unless we get to that point, there is no point in reducing price."

2.6.8 Related Literature

The findings of observers of business are mixed but, judging from the literature, the use of fully absorbing costs is fairly common and has been for a long time. Fog (1960, pp. 76, 118–119), finds that the majority of the companies he studied undertook a full allocation of fixed costs. He asserts that the companies did so because they believed that fully absorbing costs were their true costs. He also asserts that the use of fully absorbing costs amounts to a tacit price agreement among competitors that keeps prices higher than they would be otherwise. Kaplan, Dirlam, and Lanzillotti (1958) found that pricing using fully absorbing costs was fairly common. For instance, in their description of steel pricing (pp. 13–24), they say that US Steel as the price leader aimed to have a stable margin over standard costs. Haynes (1973, pp. 25–26) finds that most of the companies he studied did not adhere strictly to fully absorbing cost pricing, but that the use of some form of it was quite common. The modifications to fully absorbing cost pricing had to do with looking at demand and competitors' prices (pp. 27–29). He also asserts (p. 71) that fully absorbing cost pricing seemed to be used for tacit collusion in the printing industry. Lanzillotti (1964, p. 15), on the other hand, found that the companies he studied did not make much use of standard costs. Accounts of fully absorbing cost pricing systems used by manufacturing firms may be found in Balkin (1956); Pearce (1956); and Pearce and Amey (1956–1957). Balkin concludes that although all kinds of considerations go into pricing, they do little to change the equality between the products' selling price and the price calculated from fully absorbing costs plus a fixed markup. Pearce and Pearce and Amey present a more flexible picture of pricing.

The use of fully absorbing cost accounting for pricing can be interpreted as evidence that businesses do not use marginal analysis and do not set marginal revenue equal to marginal variable cost in order to calculate profit maximizing prices. Some authors have reacted strongly against this train of thought. For instance, Edwards (1952) argues that actual prices are not mechanical markups over standard cost estimates but result from extensive consideration of what the market will bear and of the effect of price on the quantity sold and hence on unit costs. Earley (1956) makes a similar argument, based on a questionnaire survey of modern American companies. The replies led him to doubt whether the companies make serious use of standard costs, especially when pricing.

2.7 Formula-based Pricing

Many companies use formulas to specify a commodity's price in a long-term contract. There are diverse types of formulas. Some make the price a function of the costs of inputs used in producing the commodity. For example, the price of a chemical resin may be a margin plus a weighted sum of the published market prices of the chemicals used to produce the resin. Other formulas have the price depend directly on an estimate of a product's cost of production. A common type of formula makes a commodity's price a function of published survey information on spot prices of the commodity priced. A goal in designing such a formula is to keep the price close to current spot prices so as to minimize the temptation of the buyer or seller to trade on the spot market rather than at the contract price.

Typically, such a formula-based price is a published assessment of the spot price for the commodity, plus or minus some fixed amount that reflects circumstances specific to the contracting parties. The circumstances may relate to the costs of transporting the commodity or to the average quality of the seller's product. Some formula-based prices are indexed to futures prices. Prices indexed to futures prices are said to float, though this term is sometimes applied to formula-based prices in general.

A recurring problem with contract prices indexed to assessments of spot prices is that the contracts are so convenient that they can attract much of the trade volume away from a good's spot market and so undermine its reputation as an appropriate basis for formula pricing.

Commodities priced by formulas include many agricultural products, fish, lumber, logs, petroleum products, natural gas, bulk chemicals, steel, scrap metals, and aluminum beverage cans. In the chemical, natural gas, and petroleum industries, and especially in the steel

The Pricing of Manufactured Goods 77

industry, I had the good fortune to talk to people who had participated in the transition from the use of fixed price to formula-based contract prices and could explain why they thought the change had occurred.

2.7.1 Market Risk

Traders apply the term "market risk" to the possibility that spot market prices drift far from a fixed long-term contract price. This risk can be costly if it leads to contract default, because the parties to the contract may have invested in plant and equipment to produce, deliver, or use the commodity. An advantage of formula-based pricing is that it diminishes market risk by allowing long-term contract prices to fluctuate with market conditions. In so doing, the formulas create price risk, which is uncertainty about future levels of the contract price. A potential advantage of replacing market risk with price risk is that it may be possible to use futures markets to hedge against price risk. There seems to be no easy way to hedge against market risk.

2.7.2 Price Indices

Various organizations produce assessments of market prices, where, in the context of commodity trading, the words "market prices" usually refer to freely negotiated spot prices. The assessments may be single numbers or include highs, lows, and ranges of high incidence. The process of going from surveys to assessments is often neither mathematical nor formal and may involve a lot of judgment. The creation of assessments is called price discovery, though this term also refers to the processes that create market prices. Survey respondents may have an incentive to influence a survey's results, because their companies buy or sell commodities priced using assessments derived from the survey. The market reporters who make the surveys of spot market prices try to avoid bias by talking to many respondents, both buyers and sellers. Reporters are careful never to use in their surveys prices generated by formula-based contracts, for using them would involve circularity and could arouse suspicion that the survey was a mechanism for collusive market manipulation. The President and Publisher for a lumber market-reporting company said:

> "How we gather prices is mostly call around and phone interview. We use fax and email now as well . . . We talk with primarily wholesale distribution type companies. Some mills go direct to retailers, and we have had some contact with buying coops . . .

> When it all comes down to reporting a price, it is our judgment. [You take volume-weighted averages?] There is no mathematical process that goes on here at all. It is an educated judgment . . . Most of the time when people say contract, guess where the price is coming from. [You.] Us. [So you can't use it.] We can't use it, correct . . . We don't want to get involved in that kind of circuitous process, because then we start to move toward a price fixing mechanism, not a price reporting service. [It is dangerous?] Sure it is . . . [How do you deal with the fact that buyers will try to influence what they report to you and sellers too . . . because part of their purchases or sales are contract based on you?] The basic answer there is that is why we would talk to both buyers and sellers and get a read from them . . . We talk to enough people, Truman, so that if a source is consistently kind of out there, does not fall into the range, we may continue to talk to them because of their size and because they want to be contacted, but we are well aware that they are not exactly forthright in providing us information . . . [What do you do if they make a spot sale and they say it is (the reporting company's index) plus five? That still counts for you?] If the transaction was negotiated and they used (the reporting company's index) as some sort of a marker and the buyer says, 'Well, I will take at $5 over what (the reporting company) reported last week,' I guess that is a negotiated price. It is not a long-term deal. One aspect of what we do is provide people with a cliché benchmark to start from in any kind of negotiation. 'Where was it last Friday according to (the reporting company's index)?' 'Well, it was at $200, but we know the market is stronger, so it is $200 plus what?' . . . This is a little over 200 key commodities coverage, and then Friday we come out with this full report . . . That is (called) print."

A beef reporter for and the CEO of price consulting company C said:

> "(Our company) quotes something that is termed as the bulk of sale . . . The bulk of sale is basically where did the majority of product trade on a given day . . . [But you are only doing negotiated settlements, not formula price type?] Exactly."

Because market indices are often generated from spot prices, heavy use of pricing formulas based on such indices can create markets in which spot trading directly or indirectly gives rise to prices for almost all transactions. This is so, even though spot transactions often result from unexpected circumstances. The Marketing and Sales Manager for olefins in large petroleum corporation B said:

> "[What is the spot market for?] So if you have a little more or you need a little more than you thought or you just want to get the normal flexibility in the contract, which is kind of plus or minus 10 percent. For some reason, if you are a buyer, if you need more flexibility than that, then you might leave some to buy spot, risking that you can't get the last increment at some time if you have to, but it also gives you the flexibility to move your production around more than normal contract terms. On the seller's sale, sometimes you have more than you expected, either because your contract customers took at the bottom end of their range instead of at the average or because your plant ran a little better than you thought it was going to or for whatever reason."

Some respondents were unabashed about their attempts to hide information from surveyors, though no one admitted lying. The Director of Raw Materials for a large German chemical corporation said:

> "Spot prices usually get to the publishing companies. They are, of course, phoning traders . . . 'Have you done some spot deals this week or this month?' and some traders say, 'Yes, we have,' and they give numbers . . . Then it is the quality of the person . . . who contacts both sides, if you want, to figure out what is true . . . Me as a buyer, I am interested to have low market prices. [So you could lie about it?] Well, maybe not lie. I never lie to somebody, but I try to put some fog on my information."

There have been scandals caused by false reporting to price discovery agencies, offenders have gone to jail, and the process of data collection for some markets has been reformed to make it harder to cheat. The three quotations that follow are part of a continuous conversation between myself, ED who was Editorial Director for Gas and Power and SE, who was Senior Markets Editor for North American Power. They both worked for market-reporting company B. The conversation took place in July 2010. ED said:

> "In the way back ten years or so ago, reporters used to call traders. That all ended years ago when Enron collapsed and there was a bunch of court cases about traders lying to publishers about prices."

SE then said:

"After the different price reporting issues broke out, we insisted to companies that they report their transactions from their back office instead of their front office. Instead of traders reporting their deals to us, we wanted somebody from their back office that is watching the traders (to) report their transactions to us."

ED then said

"So we got the reporting away from the traders, who have a direct interest in where the index comes out, and all the reporting now is very formalized . . . Every company has to track every trade that they are doing. So what they do is they query their system and say, 'Give us all the Bid Week trades that match what (the market-reporting company) wants and pull them out and put them in a sheet and email them to (the reporting company).'"

Some traders are reluctant to use the available indices because of suspicions about how they are created. There are few good alternatives, however. A partner in turkey meat broker and trading company A said:

"We don't use the index (an index for poultry prices) . . . Only a fraction of all transactions that happen in a given day or year are reported to the agency. And that is part of the downfall of that pricing mechanism. The benchmark is that people only report the things they want to report. If you are trying to take the market up, you will report strong sales. If you are trying to bring the market down in a particular area, you will report those sales . . . The majority of them, there is an agenda behind what is reported. [So the index is manipulated?] Could be . . . We have no other benchmark to use, so we can either use that or we can go to things that are cost plus."

2.7.3 Why the Shift to Formula-based Prices?

I tried to learn why the use of formula-based contracts was so widespread and why the steel, chemical, natural gas, and petroleum industries were switching from fixed price to formula-based contract pricing. This change was especially noticeable in the steel industry, where because of the change much of what I had learned no longer applied a few years later. Respondents claimed that the increase in use of formula-based contracts was a reaction to dramatic increases in the volatility of commodity prices, which some respondents blamed on globalization. Another factor seems to be increased consolidation of business enterprises. Associated with consolidation is a need for stable relations between large supplier and customer firms, so that they can count on earning profits from investments made to enable one firm to supply the other. The need for stable relations creates a need for long-term contracts governing trade. When commodity prices are volatile, the most stable contractual pricing mechanism is formula-based rather than fixed price, provided suitable indices exist. The respondents with whom I discussed these issues all gave similar explanations, though some emphasized the drawbacks of formula-based pricing and preferred to avoid it. There was no disagreement about the need for contractual relations between suppliers and customers. The Director of Raw Materials for a large German chemical corporation said:

"The advantage for the customer is the safety of supply, and for you as producer, of course, also the safety to have a certain base load of your production. That is the main reason why companies agree to (long-term) contracts, and if you agree to contracts and your raw materials are fluctuating, because these are oil based or, yeah, the whole oil chain, olefins based, then it is usually indexed pricing."

The Executive Vice President of steel manufacturer G said:

"Some customers want a guaranteed amount of tonnage and they want to pay a market price for it. [So that would be the (a steel price index)?] So that would be a (the same index) type . . . [But why have (the same index) rather than just negotiate every time they call up with an order?] A couple of reasons. One in a tight market, if they don't have a contract, they may or may not get the steel. The contract guarantees them a certain amount of steel. [They can't say, 'The price to be negotiated,' with a guarantee.] We won't do it that way. That is a one-sided contract. What if all of a sudden, they say, 'Oh, we don't like the price. So we are not going to give you the order.'"

The Sales Manager for a company that upgrades and prepares iron ore for blast furnaces said:

"[There is a fixed formula (for the price of iron ore)?] A fixed formula . . . [There is no negotiation in years two, three, or four?] No. Not for price . . . We have resisted it, and the steel companies have resisted it a bit too, because it (formula-based pricing) is allowing us to budget and plan."

According to respondents, there is a real danger that spot price negotiations end in an impasse, disrupting a supply relationship. The Marketing Director for Dimension Lumber for western lumber company B said:

"What we find is if you have a program where you are determining price at time of shipment, like if you would call the customer today and say, 'Let's establish a price for next week.' It is never an ongoing program. At some point you get where you can't establish a price in our business. They think it is too high, or we think it is too low, and you don't establish a price or come to agreement. So pretty soon your program is gone. That is kind of what I have seen over the years."

Some respondents attributed part of the preference for formula-based contracts to a desire to eliminate the strain of repeated negotiation. The Vice President of Container Board Sales for paper manufacturer E said:

"A lot of people don't want to haggle and fight and discuss about the price every month again. So they try to center the discussion about, 'Okay, what do we use as a mechanism to define our prices going forward?' And that is when you start talking about indices, publications, and so on and so forth."

Some respondents asserted that formula-based contracts protect profit margins, and that the reduction in negotiation costs was not a significant issue. The Marketing and Sales Manager for olefins in large petroleum corporation B said:

"[So it was really increased risk that brought this on?] It is the increased risk. [Brought this use of formula-based pricing?] Yeah. Increased risk of change in hydrocarbon prices. [That is a way of handling that? You just appeal to an index? Does it save negotiation costs?] A lot of it saves negotiation. The cost of negotiation is time, which viewed against the cost of these products is nothing. [It is not a consideration?] No, because people like to have certainty around their margins, especially if you are dealing in a lower margin period."

A common concern among respondents was that contract prices stay close to the market, which formula-based prices are designed to do. The Vice President of Sales of northeastern lumber producer C said:

"Some of our relationships are dealt off Friday's (a lumber price index) prior, which you hear a lot of in our business . . . [So the price fluctuates during the course of the contract?] Some, yeah, because some customers want to commit to your wood and will pay more money for it, but they want to be tied to a market. [Why is that?] Because they have competition right next to them buying lumber that they have got to compete against."

Formula-based pricing is advantageous for large firms that have integrated their operations with those of other firms. A senior vice president of huge meat packer A said:

"We are a large supplier to (a huge retailer). We supply a large portion of their – they are all case ready to sell. If you go into (the retailer's) meat section, it is all prepackaged, prepriced. We are a very large supplier to them, and you can't have the risk of not coming together on a price, because we have specific large plants that are dedicated to them and it is not like we can go some place else and sell that, and they can't go any place else and buy it. So there is so much interdependence on each other. You are going to find a way to come together on price, because you have to, and it does not matter if it is (one of three large food products firms), you have to find a way to come to terms."

The owner of northeastern lumber producer C said:

"[Why have a formula-based price like that rather than just continually bid it, continually back and forth over it?] . . . I think the answer is that regular buyers want fewer more meaningful relationships with suppliers. They would rather buy from a single mill, because quality and communication and all those things can be simplified."

Some said that an increase in the volatility of commodity prices precipitated the switch to formula-based contracts. The General Manager of Sales of steel manufacturer C said in 2013:

> "So you saw this enormous price change from end of 07 within six or seven months, up to $1,000 a ton, and it became obvious that the arrangement of having some sort of fixed pricing even if it was for just six months was not working for people. So you got a lot of – there was a lot of discussion about okay, how are we going to approach contracts moving forward in 2009 after we went through this period in 2008, and that is where really I think the indexed concept kind of started to make its way in force into the discussion. [Prices started to fall in 2009?] Prices had already started to fall, so there was no confidence – you know, the recession hit late in 08, so if we are negotiating all these contracts, people were seeing the price of hot rolled go down just as quickly as it had gone up, so the steel mills said, 'I can't get locked into a low price.' The buyer said, 'I can't get locked into a high price, so we need to do something to fix this.' And I think there was a feeling that as long as you were being able to sell product at a rate that generated a return, if it was a variable price mechanism, that would work. So you saw the evolution of index based contracts. Now some contracts are based on, as you said earlier, an outside index, like a publication like (a steel price index). Some contracts are indexed based upon raw material costs, like scrap. There are others that are indexed based upon a basket of raw materials, like scrap and coal and coke and iron ore and natural gas. So there are a lot of different ways that people evolved their contracts."

The General Manager for a producer of chemical resins said in 2011:

> "About 85 percent of our costs are from our raw materials, and those are commodities, methanol and urea and phenol and melamine are all commodities and they fluctuate quite a bit. So we – typically we will tie our price to what the raw material costs are doing . . . [So it is really formula-based pricing?] . . . Yes. Typically that is the way it goes. Now it was not always that way. In the last ten years, it has moved in that direction as our – we have gotten such big swings on our raw material costs that we have had to do that to justify some of the big swings that we have had on our pricing, because we have had to like double our pricing and we have had to justify that to the customers. So we have had to

make them aware of what our raw materials are doing, and then once they are aware of that then they want to have some proof of what is happening here, so we go to these indexes of what is published prices for urea or methanol, and we show that to them, and so kind of that transparency has grown . . . [What did you do before ten years ago?] We adjusted prices based on movements in our raw materials and based on what demand is. So it was more of a no contracts really in place or not as many contracts in place, not as specified a system for adjusting prices. So if we had our costs changing, we would go to the customer and say, 'Look. We had our costs going up. We have got to go up on the price.' . . . It is not hard to come down on your price, but going up is difficult. So that is where the discussions always happened . . . Then the customer would see if somebody else was going to support that price or if they were going to hold back. If a competitor was not going to go up also, then he may switch some of his volume to the competitor. So it was more of a negotiation going on with the individual customer . . . [Ten years ago or fifteen years ago, before you had these indexed contracts, was price increase more difficult?] Yes . . . [Because it wasn't an automatic thing?] There was more skill involved, making sure that you didn't lose the business."

2.7.4 Disadvantages of Formula-based Pricing

There are drawbacks to the use of formula-based contracts. The most serious problem seems to be that because formula-based contracts tend to replace spot trading, there can be few spot transactions on which to base the indices. This problem can lead to downward bias in the indices. The General Manager of Sales of steel manufacturer C said:

"There are a very small number of spot transactions that are going into these indices, like (a steel price index), because so many people have all their contract business that used to be spot. Now contract is driven off (the same steel price index), so you don't report those transactions, because it is a circular report. So you have got this enormously small population now of spot transactions every week driving an enormously large piece of our business, and it is not healthy . . . [So you are not going to do any more of these indexed contracts?] Or do them the way they are structured now. I mean, a discount off of an index. There is no way. It is a perpetual downward spiral in price. If you have a customer who bought 10,000 tons of steel a month two years ago under spot market conditions that he negotiated every month, and now he has taken that and he has 10,000 tons of (a steel price index) contracts . . . So now he is no longer buying spot prices, his spot volume, so there is no volume, first of all, to report, but secondly if it is – I am just going to pick a number – if it is (the same steel price index) minus 5 percent. That is his contract that he has with multiple suppliers, and the price of hot rolled is $600 a ton, let's say. Well, you now have the ability of that buyer to know that you can buy all of the business you need to at $600 minus 5 percent. So let's call it $570 a ton. So all that does is it serves to put a cap on his spot price that he is ever willing to pay. So now you have these spot sale people trying to sell this same guy some of the extra volume they have on their mill, and he says, 'Well, I am not going to buy from you unless it is 550 ton.' [Unless you run out. If all the mills he is buying from run out, he has to.] Yeah, but the capacity utilization rates in this country are 75, 77 percent, so there is plenty of supply. So he will say, 'Okay, I will buy from you Mr. Spotseller, but I am not going to pay more than 550 a ton,' and maybe they come to a deal where it is 560 a ton. Well that $560 a ton steel that he just purchased goes into the number, which then lowers his number in the contract, so next month, which then makes his new spot price that much lower. It is a do loop. [And there are no contracts out there where it is (the same steel price index) plus something?] If you were a purchasing agent and you agreed to (the same steel price index) plus, you would be fired."

3
Retail Pricing[1]

This chapter covers pricing by non-restaurant stores and does not cover pricing by Internet outlets. The main topic is the contrast between the retail pricing of commodities and of highly differentiated goods. I present evidence on a related matter, which is the similarity of the roles played by fixed and formula-based prices in long-term contracts between large retailers and their suppliers. Both forms of pricing are designed to avoid a breakdown of price negotiations that could interrupt a flow of sales. Other topics are the impacts of the administrative cost of price change and of recession on retail pricing. The reaction of retailers to sales downturns during recessions is usually to increase the frequency and depth of temporary promotional discounting. Manufacturers bear most of the expense of such discounting. This is so, probably because retailers' margins are so slim relative to their overhead expenses that they cannot afford to reduce prices much on their own. An interesting observation is that the total sales of grocery stores are little affected by recessions.

There is an important aspect of retailing that I heard about and regret not having investigated systematically. This is that a large part of retailers' costs, other than the cost of the goods retailers buy to sell, are almost fixed. A retailer's variable costs are mostly what it pays for the merchandise it sells. Hence a retailer's markup of the selling price over the acquisition cost of a good nearly equals the markup of price over marginal variable cost.

3.1 The Role of the Wholesaler

The basic functions of wholesalers or distributors are to store goods needed by retailers and to reduce their procurement costs by enabling them to receive diverse items from one source. Wholesalers have other functions as well. They advise client retailers on what kinds of goods are available. Some manufacturers persuade several distributors in the same geographic area to carry their goods in the hopes that the distributors compete with each other in marketing the goods to retailers. Wholesalers inform their retailers of opportunities for temporary promotional discounts that manufacturers make available to retailers. Wholesalers may advise retailers on how to price their goods. Usually only small retailers accept all these services. Large retailers tend to act as their own wholesalers and have warehouses and trucks for handling the bulk of what they purchase. However, even large supermarket chains may make arrangements with specialized wholesalers or even manufacturers to have them go into stores and place on the shelves products such as soft drinks, bread, or imported foods. Retailers always retain responsibility for the choice of retail prices.

Retailers pay wholesalers for their services in a variety of ways. Usually retailers pay a wholesaler its purchase cost for the goods it delivers plus an upcharge or markup. The wholesaler's markup as a percent of its selling price is typically 30 to 35 percent. Wholesalers may vary their percent markup among goods and do so in a way that supports the retailer's pricing policy. For instance, if a grocer wants to place a lower percent markup on rice than pasta because of the ethnic composition of its customers, its wholesaler may agree to do the same.

3.2 Retail Price Setting

Most manufacturers recognize that it is illegal for them to dictate retail pricing and has been since the repeal of the last fair trade acts in 1975. Retailers know that their right to set their own prices is legally protected. A regional manager of a large supermarket chain said:

> "[So they (manufacturers) have no say in what your margin is on what you retail?] No. They will come in with suggested retails, based on where your competitors are or where that class of trade is in a region. [But you don't have to pay attention to that?] . . . You can establish whatever retail you want on it."

There are exceptions to this statement. Some manufacturers of high quality and expensive products withdraw their merchandise from retailers who charge so little for it that they threaten its quality image.

The basic pricing strategy of most retailers is to lure customers into stores with low prices that customers are likely to notice, because the prices are of items customers tend to buy often. Market studies have convinced store managers that shoppers favor stores they perceive as low-priced and that shoppers' price perceptions are dominated by the prices of items they buy frequently. The retailer may make little or no money on these items, but knows that while in the store customers often buy other less popular items on which the store earns more margin. A General Manager of a large wholesale drug company said:

> "Most of the margin that we receive, that a chain pharmacy receives and that a chain drug store receives, would be in consumer products for health and beauty aids. That is why when you walk into (a particular pharmacy) and you walk back to get your prescription, you walk down a power aisle where you see impulse items and other items that you might need and want to buy that are going to return 50 percent to the pharmacy. You go get your prescription. If you are on a prescription plan, you would be paying a small co-pay payment possibly and maybe not even that. The pharmacy would make very little margin and have to wait 60 days for their money probably."

A retailer's markups of the prices it pays for goods are likely to be especially high on items that most consumers seldom buy and would buy on impulse, such as wooden spoons hanging in a supermarket aisle. Store managers term goods with negative markups loss leaders and call goods that a large fraction of customers buy frequently price sensitive, or market basket, or a number of other terms. Retailers label as peripheral the goods that are not price sensitive. The price sensitivity of a good has nothing to do with its elasticity of demand, because what is sensitive to the good's price is consumers' patronage of the store, not sales of the good. The identification of goods as price sensitive can depend on the ethnic and economic composition of the neighborhood of the store, so that the prices of goods can vary sharply among stores belonging to the same chain. A counterintuitive consequence of this pricing method is that a store's percent markups are often lowest for the items that are most in demand. An advantage of large stores relative to small ones is that because large stores carry a greater variety of goods, a bigger fraction of their goods are peripheral and so have high percent markups.

Temporary promotional discounts are another way retailers entice customers into stores. Retailers offer low prices on selected goods for a short period of time, and the temporary discount is often heavily advertised. Retailers try to create a sense of urgency, so that consumers feel compelled to take advantage of the deal during the brief time it is available. Store managers hope that the customers they attract with promotions buy, while in the store, high margin peripheral items that are not on sale. In order to make promotions attractive, stores normally promote goods in high demand because of the season or holidays, and stores often promote groups of goods that consumers use together. Examples are steaks and charcoal just before Memorial Day, school supplies just before schools reopen at the end of summer, and turkeys, roasting pans, and stuffing just before Thanksgiving. Consequently the prices of promoted goods are priced lowest when they are most in demand. Promotions can have a tremendous impact on the sales of the promoted items. Although manufacturers pay a large share of the promotional discounts and advertising, retailers and even wholesalers sometimes contribute by reducing their margins on promoted items. The prices of promoted manufactured goods normally return after a promotion to their levels before the promotion. The price before and after a promotion is called the regular price. Retailers return prices to their regular levels in order to convince consumers that promotional discounts are truly temporary discounts that consumers should take advantage of. Part of the psychology of promotional discounting is to give consumers the thrill of finding a bargain. Prices of promoted fresh foods often do not return to their pre-promotion levels, because such promotions are normally timed to take advantage of periods of seasonal abundance.

Promotional discounts should not be confused with markdowns, which are reduced prices for merchandise that is not selling well and that the retailer hopes to get some money for. Markdowns are usually permanent in the sense that the price is continually reduced until the inventory is sold out to make room for new merchandise.

While promotional discounts are a normal part of merchandising for many retailers, there are retail chains that disdain them. By generating demand surges, promotions increase retailers' distribution costs. By avoiding these costs and running efficient operations, some chains are able to offer stable regular prices that are low enough to counter for many consumers the allure of promotional deals offered by competing retailers. Chains that offer stable low prices are said to be everyday low pricers or EDLP, and chains that have many promotions are said to be high-low, because they have high regular and low promotional prices. Retail pricing policies usually fall somewhere in the spectrum between extreme EDLP and extreme high-low. Despite the strength of EDLP retail chains, promotions are of great importance to many manufacturers. Food broker[2] 1 said:

"[What is the purpose of promotions?] To drive sales. To increase trial . . . You can increase an item's sales by . . . featuring in a display ten, fifteen times. That is called lift. Your regular business is called base line, and then when promoted it is called the promotional lift . . . [And that has permanent effects?] Yes, because the whole idea is, once you get that trial, to increase the base line."

A Marketing Director for very large manufacturer of branded foods 3 said:

"Promotion . . . in the supermarket business is critical. You have over 20,000 items in the supermarket. There is a lot of stuff to look at, and you are just not going to get noticed unless you get on an end aisle or if you get in the feature ad or something that the retailer will support to buy more of it and put it on the floor . . . There is a very significant portion of that segment that will not buy anything unless it is on promotion . . . A lot of times the argument is if you don't promote, you don't get the shelf space or you don't get the distribution and you give that to a competitor who will promote, who will get the shelf space and get the distribution."

A common retail pricing technique is line pricing, where the retailer displays a range of quality and of features for goods of the same type with price increasing in modest intervals with quality and additional features. A salesperson can use this progression to convince a customer to buy a more expensive item than they would otherwise. The salesperson starts by showing the customer an inexpensive version and then brings them up through the line, pointing out at each step that for only a small additional amount of money they can enjoy valuable advantages. Line pricing is appropriate for goods expensive enough to make their sale worth a salesperson's time. A Marketing Manager for manufacturer A of major household appliances said:

"What people (retailers) have found is that in selling appliances, you can't just buy everybody's best deal. What you have to buy is you have to buy a lineup of appliances that can be merchandised and make sense, so that when you come in as a consumer off of an ad, and this ad says that you can buy a supercapacity washer for $299. We have a well-thought out and planned strategy to sell you up. It is not bait and switch, but we will sell you this for $299 and we will sell it to you if you want it, but we will be able to show you how for $349 what we can give you in capacity, what we can give you in energy efficiency, what we can give you in features . . . But it takes a logical, legitimate step of features and benefits to the consumer, so that when you come in prepared to spend $299 and you walk out spending $500, you are still happy about it, and what we gave you for the $200 more you spent is more than you expected. See that does not happen by accident in appliances. That is planned and prepared."

Retailers devote considerable resources to keeping track of competitors' pricing, and the pricing of each retailer is a compromise between the desire to match or undercut competitors' prices and the achievement of other pricing objectives. Some large EDLP retailers promise to match the prices of any nearby competitor, even promotional prices.

Many retailers put a considerable amount of thought into choosing prices. Despite concern about competitors' prices, they believe that competition does not tightly constrain their prices. The owner of a bicycle store said:

"With retail, we set our pricing realistically on what you would consider, I guess, a keystone, keystone plus, depending on the product. Keystone is a 50 percent margin (as a percent of the retail price) . . . Keystone plus means that there is an extra amount of percentage built into that . . . [What does this image come from?] Image I can show you. Take a product like – this item is a computer that tells speed, distance, time and the like . . . It is pretty interesting looking. It has an LCD display, a multiple display . . . So this item . . . costs us $14.40. A keystone or 50 percent on that would be $29.99.[3] But we look at it and say, 'Okay, a regular (a brand) watch is a $30 item and it doesn't do anything compared to this. So we will get $32.99 for this.'"

3.2.1 Related Literature

There is a literature on promotional sales, and many of the papers are theoretical. Early papers were on markdowns: Lazear (1986); Pashigian (1988); and Pashigian and Bowen (1991). Most of the theories of promotional sales are based on customer heterogeneity. For instance, promotions can be viewed as a substitute for price discrimination between bargain hunters and customers loyal to certain brands. Papers that explain promotional sales include: Guimaraes and Sheedy

(2011); Nakamura and Steinsson (2011); Narasimhan (1988); Simester (1997); Sobel (1984); and Varian (1980). Some of these papers do not explain why prices return to their regular level after a promotion. Nakamura and Steinsson have a novel explanation, which is that the return to the regular price is a device designed to commit retailers and manufacturers not to raise their products' prices after consumers have become habituated to them. The explanation I heard repeatedly was more mundane – that prices return to their regular level in order to convince consumers that promotional discounts really are discounts that should be enjoyed while they last.

Chevalier, Kashyap, and Rossi (2003) present detailed evidence from a large supermarket chain that the retail margins on many items are lowest during times of the year when demand for the products is greatest, presumably because those are the times when the items are likely to be promoted at discounted prices.

3.3 Commodities and Highly Differentiated Goods in Retail Trade

The distinction between commodities and highly differentiated goods is central to the thinking of many retailers and, in particular, to that of grocers and to those who run big box home improvement stores. Fresh foods, and some building materials, such as lumber, plywood, gypsum wallboard, and PVC pipe are examples of commodities sold by retailers. Most manufactured items other than the building materials just mentioned are highly differentiated goods, because they are branded. Retailers view the wholesale prices of commodities as volatile and those of highly differentiated goods as stable. Retailers help to reinforce the price stability of highly differentiated goods by resisting manufacturers' price increases. Although retailers may try to resist increases in the wholesale prices of commodities as well, they normally have much less success in doing so. A produce manager for a chain of four supermarkets said:

> "There is manufactured items in a supermarket, whether it be the (canned) peas, or whatever. They may start as commodities, but they still end up as manufactured items. Then there is true commodities. Typical items to talk about are butter, milk, produce, fresh fish. They are commodity driven markets. They are fresh markets. Sometimes they have got to be sold (before they rot). So those are like one group for us. Then this other group is like – it is very funny, like the price of (canned) peas

stays the same for 18 months very very easily. Believe it or not, the manufactures stay the same."

A Senior Vice President of a huge supermarket chain said:

"[So you don't make any attempt to resist price increases for perishables from vendors?] No. That wouldn't be true, but I am just saying that it is true that the perishables and in particular produce will fluctuate significantly with wholesale prices. That is true. More than the others."

The Merchandise Manager for chain A of home improvement stores said:

"In the categories of lumber and plywood – that is one of the last true supply and demand markets in this country, as I am sure you are finding out. I mean, it is not like signing a contract with (a brand of) faucets and you are going to buy this product for $5 for the calendar year ... There is no price. It changes every day."

The Director of Customer Development (A) and a marketing manager (B) for consumer products manufacturer 1 said of aluminum foil:

"(B) We have had in the last ten years one price increase. (A) No, two. (B) Okay, you are right. Two. [Were they big or small?] ... (A) An average of 4.25 percent, the last one, and I think the one before that was probably around 5 percent. (B) If you want to know why we don't go down (in price) anywhere, anytime, it is because it is almost impossible to get it back up ... Roughly aluminum is about half the cost (of aluminum foil). [Oh, so the fluctuations of aluminum prices do affect your cost?] (B) They substantially affect it, but we do a pretty good job on the division level of hedging against those fluctuations."

Aluminum foil is a good example of how pressure from retailers can oblige manufacturers to stabilize prices, because the market price of aluminum ingots can double or halve in a few months.

Retailers who specialize in supplying building materials to contractors buy lumber and plywood at spot prices that can change from hour to hour. Big home improvement retail chains buy lumber and plywood spot and under long-term contracts with formula prices based on indices produced by a market-reporting company. Both systems yield volatile prices. The Marketing Director for Dimension Lumber for western lumber company B said:

> "[So how does the pricing happen? Do you do program (formula-based) pricing?] We do both. Most of our (big) box store type business is program . . . Generally it is priced based on what (a lumber and plywood market-reporting company) prints on Friday plus something or minus something, depending on what the product is. [This would be (two large home improvement retail chains)?] Yeah and a few other programs, but mostly (those two chains), and that is 20 percent of it (sales), and then the other 80 percent is just traded open market, day to day, hour to hour, moment to moment almost, and we determine pricing by how much we have to sell, how quick we need to sell it, and, of course, what the demand is at the time drives where the pricing goes, whether it goes up or down."

The Merchandise Manager for chain A of home improvement stores said;

> "I need to buy a truckload of lumber to go into this store, and then you call around and see what you can buy it for . . . That price is up and down all the time . . . We can buy lumber from 50 different people."

3.4 The Retail Price Behavior of Lettuce

Figure 3.4.1[4] shows a time series for average retail prices in the U.S. of fresh iceberg lettuce. The extreme seasonal volatility gives an idea of what grocers have to contend with in pricing fresh food.

3.5 The Difficulty Grocers Have Controlling Commodity Prices

The grocery industry makes some use of techniques adopted by the restaurant industry to control fluctuations in the prices of fresh foods. That is, some large grocery chains make fairly long-term fixed price contracts with fresh food producers. The motives for the contracts differ in the two industries. Restaurant chains try to procure fresh foods at fixed prices, because they want to avoid being obliged to increase menu prices. Some grocers believe that their customers prefer stable prices, but the main motive for procuring fresh food at stable prices

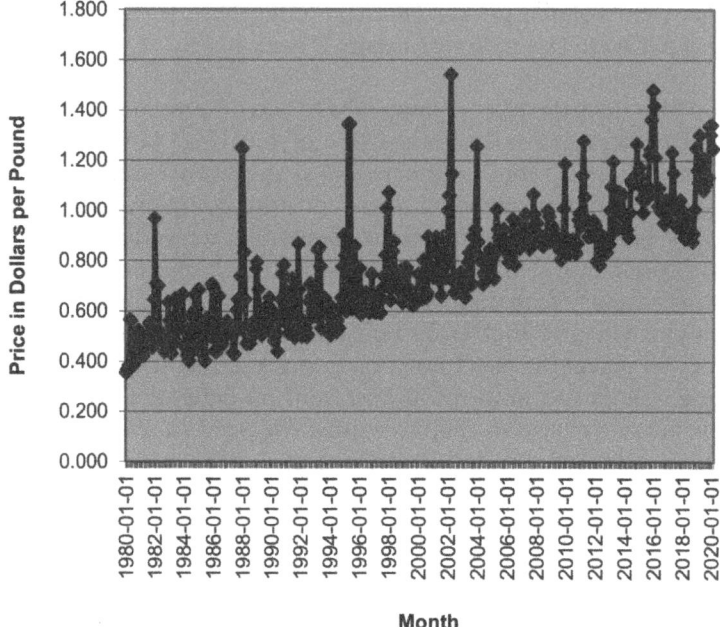

Figure 3.4.1 Retail Prices of Iceberg Lettuce in Dollars per Pound, Monthly Data, Not Seasonally Adjusted, January 1980–February 2020

is to encourage large-scale production by guaranteeing producers a predictable return on their investment. Fixed price contracts for fresh foods are not as common in the grocery industry as in the restaurant industry, perhaps because of the difference in motivation. Many of the contracts between grocery chains and food producers use fluctuating formula-based prices rather than fixed prices.

Some food producers prefer a procurement system that uses contracts with stable prices. The President of a pisciculture firm said:

> "I think the business model of selling everything spot is wrong. The business model we have, it is very predictable . . . It is a very predictable cost side of the business model. It is heavy capital investment and it is cages, boats, inventory, feed . . . We plan out our fish, because it is a two-year growing cycle . . . The problem with the business is if you go spot it is not a predictable revenue side . . . So to me, some of the value of this business of getting into long-term contracts . . . is to put some certainty into the

revenue stream ... [So you are subject to some price fluctuation?] Yes. [It just minimizes it by having a contract?] Yeah."

The use by large grocery retailers and their suppliers of fixed price contracts explains how bagged salad and spinach can be treated as branded manufactured goods with stable prices that do not follow the gyrations of lettuce and spinach prices. In the following quotation, the respondent explains why a company he had worked for adopted a fixed price contracting system for purchasing most of its fresh food. The company made the switch in order to encourage production, but later abandoned the contracting system. A former Senior Vice President and General Merchandise Manager of a huge EDLP chain said, after explaining that the chain had been growing at a rapid rate:

"The problem with that became that how were we going to be able to secure the volume and the quality of produce that we needed as we continued to grow at that rate, because the produce industry is highly fragmented ... The things you want to accomplish is first of all you want to get the product that you need, and secondarily you want your suppliers to be profitable, because they have got to reinvest in their business to grow with you ... Historically in supermarkets, your meat is bought in larger quantities, as much as a whole side of beef, and it is further broke down at store level. They had butchers in the back of the store. We were evolving into what is called a case ready program to where there is a central processing plant that does all the various cuts of meat and shipped to the store, who just puts the product out on the counter ... In the retail, particularly to the scale that we were doing it in, it was unheard of to do it at that scale. So we had to really work closely with people (at major meat processors) to contract quantities and pricing, so that they could make the capital investment necessary to be able to keep up with the need from a production standpoint. [Was the price fixed in these contracts?] Yeah ... [There are good indices for meat prices, especially chicken and pork. Why not index the wholesale price of these items?] Well, that was taken into consideration, but when you have to think about it from a longer term perspective, our most important goal is to ensure that we were to get the quantities that we needed. It wasn't necessarily to pay the cheapest price or the market price at a given particular period of time ... [Are bagged salads treated as manufactured goods because the supply is contracted or because of pressure from merchandisers or both?] ... In industry at large you see that further processed produce, not just salads but things like cut melons and fruit and things, tend to be more contracted for the same reasons that I just described in case ready (meats)."

Respondents had divided views about whether consumers prefer stable or fluctuating fresh food prices. A former Senior Vice President and General Merchandise Manager of a huge EDLP chain said:

"[Do you think your stable price strengthened your image as an EDLP seller?] Certainly, because I didn't just stabilize the price. I stabilized the expectation the consumer would see when they went in the stores ... What gets customers upset is ... if you did your shopping one day and you paid $2 a pound for grapes and then the weekend you had to go get a gallon of milk and you walk in and you see those same grapes at 99 cents. You are not a very happy camper. That is the beauty of EDLP."

A retired executive of a high-low supermarket chain said:

"[So there is no feeling that consumers prefer a steady price?] No. I would say they don't prefer a steady price. [They do not?] Right ... I think it has been proven over time that a customer will travel past a store for a better price or a significantly better price on highly perishable items and go to a store that will offer those products in probably more abundance and in often cases a better quality at a lower price. [So you think that this EDLP idea of having a steady price is not necessarily a good one?] Not in perishables, and certainly not in produce, and that is my opinion, of course, but it is an experienced opinion."

The CEO of a wholesale club chain said:

"[Do you think the consumer reacts better to a stable price?] Does the consumer react better to a stable price? I don't think the consumer knows whether there is a stable price. The consumer only knows whether it seems like a good price. I mean, I don't think that they say, 'This is 6.99, and I like it better, because it is always 6.99.' They say, 'It is 6.99, and I like it because it seems like a good deal.'"

In the fixed price wholesale contracts described to me, there were provisions for adjusting the transaction price when the spot market price deviated too far from the contract price. The contracts nevertheless seem to have been difficult to live with. (I had asked in writing as a follow-up question why some supermarket chains buy perishables, such as salmon, bananas, and apples from wholesalers under long-term contracts with constant or nearly constant prices?) A retired manager of merchandising for a large supermarket chain said:

> "The few times we tried to hold the price on a perishable item it was a rather harrowing experience . . . In my experience it just did not pay . . . The fluctuations in perishable products can be dramatic and unpredictable."

One reason fixed price contracts were difficult for grocers to live with is that the grocer had to resist the temptation to profit from declines in the wholesale prices of what they were buying. I have described efforts by a large EDLP retail chain to use fixed price contracts for fresh food to encourage production. This chain eventually gave up its fixed price contracting system in favor of having producers bid competitively for the company's fresh food business. This bidding system created fluctuating prices that allowed the chain to take advantage of declines in market prices to run promotions.

3.6 Holding Wholesale Commodity Prices Temporarily Fixed for Retail Promotions

Grocers who run reduced price promotions usually need to arrange the advertising for the promotions a month to a few months in advance, and to do so grocers must choose the prices they will advertise. If the wholesale prices of the promoted items are volatile, fixing their retail prices beforehand creates a price risk for the retailer. One way to deal with this risk is to make a fixed price contract with a large producer or wholesaler of a promoted item, so that the producer or wholesaler bears the risk or hedges it by using a futures market. If the promoted items are beef or pork, hedgers can use the futures markets for live beef cattle and for lean hogs. Hedgers take advantage of the correlation between the prices of cattle or hogs and the prices of individual cuts of meat from the animals. This kind of hedging is called cross hedging or ratio selling or buying. The difficulty with it is that its effectiveness relies on correlations that are not very close, so that meat packers and wholesalers using it charge a premium to compensate for the risk they take. Another method for reducing the price risk associated with a promotion is for the producer or wholesaler to buy and store the item, if that is possible. It is very common to freeze hams and whole body turkeys and store them for promotional sales. Most turkeys sold for Thanksgiving are frozen and sold on promotion. A Senior Vice President for Perishable Sales in a large supermarket chain[5] said:

> "Meat buyers have to commit for as long as four weeks or they may not get the product they need. The producer needs to plan production. He needs three or four weeks notice of a (promotional) sale. Promotions work to drive a lot of product through the system. When advance orders are made, buyers and sellers settle on a range of pricing. We own what we order, but the price is settled on two weeks in advance of delivery . . . A typical price range might be $1.25 to $1.29. There is no danger that the supplier will gouge by insisting on the maximum price, because the buyers know the market and there is a give and take relationship between buyers and suppliers. Credibility is important."

A retired senior vice president of manufacturing for a huge supermarket chain said:

> "We are sitting here today the 15th of March and let's suppose that I (the buyer) want to get ready for the Fourth of July (steak promotion). We are both going to be looking at the July futures and agree upon pricing . . . The price is fixed . . . The processor . . . is going to turn that very day and he is going to buy (live cattle) futures, so that he is guaranteed that he will be able to sell at no profit or loss what he just agreed to from a commodity market standpoint."

A vice president of a large pork packer said:

> "[Hedge in that sense. Have a fixed price?] Yeah, a fixed price. I will go in with the lean hog futures or I have my own hog production, because I am raising the hogs ourselves. All I have to do is buy the grain. So I know the cost of grain. That cost of grain converted into hogs, they can convert it into meat prices. [Also you can buy your grain forward on the futures market?] That is right. That is what we do. So we either go with the lean hog futures or with the grain . . . One of the things I am looking at is the freezer stock. The government publishes how much hams in the freezer . . . Back right after Easter the ham market was depressed. The market was 60¢, and I will do the calculation. I

think the (Christmas) holiday hams are going to be 85¢. It is 60 now. If I put the hams away (in the freezer), it is going to cost me a penny a pound every month. One pound costs interest and storage, and 5¢ for freezing. So my cost of the ham coming in that door will be 72."

3.7 The Use of Fixed and Formula-based Contracts in Retail Trade to Secure Supplies of Branded Products

The stability of the retail prices of highly differentiated goods is in part a natural outcome of the need for stable business relations between manufacturers and retailers, particularly when retailers are large organizations. General reasons for having long-term sales contracts between large businesses have to do with assurance of markets and supply. Advantages of a fixed price are that it enables the retailer to plan its merchandising and the supplier to plan its production. The next quotation articulates these considerations, but does not clearly express an important one, which is the danger that if price were renegotiated frequently, negotiations might reach an impasse and supply would cease. The phrase "continuity of supply," I believe, refers to this danger. The Merchandise Manager for chain A of home improvement stores said:

"(In products other than commodities) you have manufacturing contracts and you have a static price for whatever the period of time you agreed to . . . [For one or two years?] Generally no longer than a year. [Why have a contract? Do you dislike having costs fluctuate?] No. The prices on a lot of products, a lot of draperies and rugs and faucets and a whole mess of products that people in our business have, the contract protects us, number one, and we are probably more interested in the continuity of supply. [Just getting the stuff.] Getting it . . . We can significantly impact a single manufacturer. I keep saying faucets. There is a brand awareness for faucets, and it is when we advertise it, when we display it, when we offer it to our customer, we want that brand recognition. So you do it on a contractual basis with the manufacturer, number one, so we can keep some consistency of our offering, and number two it helps the manufacturer, 'Okay, I know I am going to have this business for a year, and maybe I can generate some economies purchasing my raw materials, because I have got a pretty steady quantity I can count on.' [So this contract does not specify the quantity though. It is just you give him an estimate of what it will be?] It is an estimate. [Why have the price constant over that period?] We want the price constant so that it does not fluctuate. That is how you want to back into it. [What is the matter with fluctuation? Is it costly to you? Suppose it went down. You would like that wouldn't you?] Oh, yes and no. Number one, in the product assortments that this is the normal way of doing business, manufacturers won't bill on a spot market, because you cannot have a contract on it. So if it was a fluctuating market for us, we couldn't count on (the faucet brand) this week or next week. Number two, there is only one place you can buy (the faucet brand), and that is (from the manufacturer), as opposed to lumber ... And number three, there is some consistency that now we can advertise. Since our advertising gets locked in three months in advance of publication date, it is almost suicide but obviously borders on folly trying to put a price to the consumer when you don't have a clue what your costs are going to be three months from now. [But your advertising does name a price?] Yes."

Retailing firms and their vendors sometimes make long-term supply contracts with fluctuating formula-based prices, and they do so for the same reasons that manufacturing firms make such contracts.[6] In all the contracts I learned about between manufacturing firms that used formula-based pricing, the pricing was for commodities. Contact with retailers brought to light contracts that use formula-based prices for branded goods for which a large portion of the production cost is the cost of a commodity with a volatile price. These are the only exceptions I know of to the generalization that highly differentiated products have inflexible prices. The main examples came up in a discussion with the respondent just quoted above. The discussion started with the pricing of PVC pipe, which is a commodity. The Merchandise Manager for chain A of home improvement stores said:

"PVC pipe is plastic resins, and plastic resins are traded on commodity markets and they go up and down with the price of oil, and no PVC pipe manufacturer will enter into a guaranteed pricing arrangement for longer than two weeks because of that. And the other side of that coin is, there is no brand identification with PVC pipe, so we may have a purchasing agreement with a PVC pipe manufacturer and prices go up and down and when we see cheaper prices from other manufacturers, then we have got the ability to go to that manufacturer ... We can get back to him and say, 'We have a competitive situation at 29¢,' and, 'Can't do it.' 'Okay. I will call you in a few weeks.'"

The same person explained that if there were brands of PVC pipe and if his company were intent on buying a particular brand of it, he would enter into a contract with formula-based pricing for purchasing that brand of pipe, probably to be sure of receiving an adequate supply. Moreover, his company buys some branded products, such as windows and subflooring, using such contracts. The Merchandise Manager for chain A of home improvement stores said:

> "[Suppose someone succeeded in making PVC a brand. Would you then fix the price or you would still have a fluctuating price, you think?] That would depend on a lot of stuff. [Like what?] Number one, do we feel it was important ... If we decided that was the brand we wanted and assuming the manufacturer had the capacity, we would enter into a purchasing agreement with a floating scale (i.e. a formula-based price) for a cost standpoint, whether it is based off an industry market report or tied to the cost of plastic resins or tied it to the tide table. I don't know. But you tie it to something. [So that kind of thing exists?] It does exist. [What kind of commodity is like that?] In some wood products, it is that way. Windows ... [So there are some wood products that have some sort of brand identification and you do enter this kind of agreement?] A case in point (a company), has an OSB (oriented strand board) underlayment, which they market under the brand named (a brand). Basically 3/4 tongue in groove OSB, and that is what you use for subfloors in 80 percent of the houses. [They have gotten used to that brand?] The builder has gotten used to the brand. The homeowner does not know and does not care, and the product is a little better ... So builders say, 'I want (the brand).' We are under contract with (the company) for (the brand), and it is on a floating scale."

Hence brands of subflooring and windows are examples of highly differentiated products for which contract prices are formula-based.

3.8 Does Brand Alone Stabilize Price?

Since most branded products have more stable prices than do commodities, one wonders whether there is something magical about brand that stabilizes prices. Some foods offer test cases. For instance, there are brands of pork, chicken, and steak, and I inquired about their price stability. I learned that producers can charge a little more for branded pork and chicken than for the unbranded meats, but the brands do not stabilize prices, because the branded and unbranded meats are close substitutes. The brands do not differentiate the products enough to impart price stability. The opposite is true of a brand of steak. That brand seems to be so strong that the producer can ignore fluctuations in the prices of unbranded steaks. An egg reporter for price consulting company C said:

> "[One question I had was whether (a brand name) chicken prices – that is sort of a branded item – are they less volatile or more volatile than (unbranded chicken)?] . . . Generally they work in a different price structure than your average chicken, but they still go to some sort of basis around what we are quoting here (as a market average). (That is, the difference between the average wholesale market prices for the branded and unbranded chicken is nearly constant.) . . . Traditionally speaking, the (branded) market will garner maybe a penny, two, three cents (per pound) above what the traditional markets will."

The President of a hog producing subsidiary of medium-size pork packer A said:

> "[So does that stabilize the prices at all that you can get for your products – having a brand?] Well, what it does, Truman, it helps you to enhance the profitability of the company by branding the product. [You can have a little higher margin?] Yes. [But it doesn't stabilize the price?] Oh, no. It is a dog eat dog world out there. [It moves up and down with the regular pork?] It still moves up and down. It sure does."

Meat pricing consultant 1 said:

> "[Why is stability associated with a premium? You are saying that (a branded steak company) can charge a lot. But why should it (the price) be stable? Why not just let it fluctuate? Do you think there is some disadvantage to them of having the price fluctuate?] What is the incentive for him (the company owner) to bring the price down? [Well, he could bring it up.] I guarantee you that he is getting as much as he thinks he can get. [As much as he can get is not going to change much over time?] Sure, it will change

over time. [But slowly?] Yeah. More or less . . . He doesn't really want to be foot balling (changing dramatically) the price . . . He wants to position himself at the high end. The guy is selling a Rolls Royce . . . For the guy that is in that neighborhood, it just doesn't matter."

So the branded steak seems to be highly differentiated and to enjoy the price stability typical of such goods.

3.9 Retailer Resistance to Manufacturers' Increases in the Prices of Highly Differentiated Goods

I now discuss the resistance of powerful retail companies to manufacturers' attempts to raise the prices of highly differentiated products. They do so by demanding explanations for increases and even by refusing to pay them. The main reason for resisting increases is to protect the reputation of the retail organization as a source of low-priced goods. The resistance was pronounced in the grocery industry. Most of the respondents in the industry mentioned it. Food broker 1 said:

"A lot of these power retailers, they fight price increases. They say, 'Why are you going up? I am not going to accept your price increase. Justify it. I mean, let's have a discussion. What is going up? Freight? I am in the freight business. I own 2,000 supermarkets and I am dealing with freight all the time, and my freight manager is right here. Freight has gone up 1 percent. Why are you giving me a 10 percent increase? I am not going to accept it.' . . . [Not to accept it means they just won't pay?] I won't pay it. [I will do without your goods?] Right."

The CEO of large dairy cooperative 2 and a large cheese manufacturing company said:

"So it is kind of as we are raising prices, it is kind of a dance. Who is going to go first amongst the suppliers? . . . As I said, this is a pretty messy process getting the prices up here. [The retailers have a fit?] Yeah . . . and some of them have policies that you can only increase your price one percent a month, sometimes some really weird policies."

A marketing manager for consumer products manufacturer 1 said:

"(A huge retailer), if you raise prices, has significant penalties and such, in a sense, that they will not allow you to do certain things after a price increase, like promote. They figure if you have to have a price increase, then you don't have money to promote or otherwise you shouldn't be able to increase price. [So they really punish you.] They pretty much punish you for a price increase. It is very difficult to get a price increase at (this retailer)."

Retailers object to price increases, not price change. They like price decreases. A Marketing Director for very large manufacturer of branded foods 3 said:

"There is an unbelievable pressure on us not to change pricing. [Upwards, you are talking about?] Upwards, yeah, certainly downwards they love. [Oh, everybody does?] Everybody does, except for us, but upwards is very, very difficult to do."

Supermarket managers are more likely to resist manufacturers' price increases and less likely to pass them on to consumers, if the goods are price sensitive than if they are peripheral. The Director of Merchandising at a wholesaler and supermarket chain said:

"A lot of times, price increases can hurt us . . . (a popular sandwich spread) is a great example. We have never ever made money on (it). Don't ask me why. I don't understand it. [It is a price sensitive item?] Yeah . . . We have to pay $2.90 a jar for it and sell it at $2.29 every day, but for some reason, that is one of those items that is extremely price sensitive. And, if (the manufacturer) comes out with a price increase tomorrow, chances are nobody is going to raise their prices, and we will end up losing a dollar a jar instead of 80¢ a jar . . . If you came in and told me today that you are going to raise the price on (i.e. cost of) (a minor brand of) corn oil, I am not going to care that much. If you come and raise my price on (a major soft drink), I am going to sit here and argue and fight with you, because I know that that is going to cause me to lose money, because . . . I can't raise the price. Nine times out of ten, if I am able to raise the price, I can only raise it as much as the cost increase, which hurts my margin. If I can only go up a dime on a ten-cent increase, my margin, from a percentage perspective, I am in trouble, because now, you know, I was making 20 percent, now I am making 15. Even though I have recaptured the penny profit, from a percentage perspective I am in trouble."

Retailers resist manufacturers' price increases, because they do not want to be obliged to raise their retail prices and they hope they will be more successful than their competitors in holding down manufacturers' price increases. A retired district sales manager for very large manufacturer of branded foods 2 said:

"[Why do supermarkets resist price increases on a branded item?] Because they are competing against other supermarkets. They resist despite the fact that they will all face the same price increase. They hope that others won't be able to resist. Another concern is the loss of sales. They are concerned about consumer response."

Food Broker 3 said:

"If a manufacturer takes frequent price increases . . . why they (retailers) are annoyed is it hurts their margin. Say the manufacturer goes up three dimes in a row. Thirty cents they have gone up on the price. Depending on competition and what is going on, they (retailers) may be able only to take 25 cents of the 30 cents. [Because competing brands don't go up?] Right. So that is the classical answer to why they don't like it."

Large retailers of building supplies and office supplies showed the same resistance to manufacturers' price increases as did large grocery chains. The Merchandise Manager for chain A of home improvement stores said:

"[You say, for most of your manufacturers you contract for a year for the price. Do you dislike it when . . . at the end of the year . . . they increase the price?] We certainly dislike it, and that is part of the negotiating process. [Just because you don't like paying more, even if your competition is going to have to pay more?] We are as greedy as the next guy . . . We are in business to make money, and we want to lower our costs. Now whether that is the cost of goods or whether that is the transportation costs or the distribution costs or the merchandising costs, all those things that go into cost of goods we want to keep reducing that . . . The manufacturer comes in and says, 'You paid $2 this year. I have got to go to $2.25

next year,' and we will posture and 'No, you can't do that . . . And why?' 'Well, because I am using plastic and petroleum is up and it is not projected to go down and I did not secure next year's raw material cost on the petroleum futures market.' . . . At some point in time, the manufacturer says, 'That's it. Take it or leave it.' . . . So then you make a business decision."

Despite all the references to price rigidities and resistance to price increase, both wholesale and retail prices of branded goods do rise and fall. The resistance slows adjustment.

3.10 The Effect of Sellers' Administrative Costs of Price Change

For supermarkets and stores selling general merchandise, there is no doubt that the costs to the stores of changing prices are real, though not big enough to discourage anything but small price changes. The use of computers and electronic shelf tags has reduced the costs of changing prices, and retailers consider price change to be part of the necessary routine of doing business. A general manager and part owner of a two-store supermarket company said:

"When we were with (a wholesaler used previously), they had price changes every day, which was annoying, because it took up a lot of my time and a lot of work. [You mean to change – ?] To change prices. I mean, you may get 25, 50 prices, you have got to go figure out the individual cost for that product and profit that you want to make and see what your retail is already set and standing. You have to go up and down (stairs), and then you have got to come up here and change it in the computer, issue it a sign. So it is a hassle . . . Does this cost of marking things, does that inhibit you from changing prices?] No . . . I don't worry about it. If I get them to change prices, and they cry because there are a lot of price changes, that is too bad. The guy that doesn't change prices is the guy that won't be there in a few years. I have heard other people say that they don't want to do price changes. It is too much work. That is how you make money . . . If you have got an opportunity to make more money on something based on what your competition is doing, you are going to raise the price. They (the store staff) are going to do the price changes. That is all there is to it. [It sounds like it is not that expensive then.] It is labor. That is all."

Retail Pricing 109

A produce manager for a chain of four supermarkets said:

"[Do you take into account the actual cost of the process of changing a price? Going around stamping on the things.] It doesn't cost anything with bar code and the computer. You go into your computer. It sends out a signal in the store. It is a matter of seconds. How do I relate to doing 1,000 price changes? I don't know. It is nothing. We don't physically mark anything. It is done automatically at 1:00 on Saturday morning. Years ago you had this huge inventory and you had 1,000 items to reprice. [You don't think about it now?] We don't."

Food Broker 3 said:

"[Does that cost of changing prices, you think, inhibit them (supermarkets) from changing price?] No . . . They have been doing it for a hundred years, every week, the weekly specials. All supermarkets across the United States have weekly specials and they change their prices every week . . . That is the way they do business."

Respondents said that the administrative costs of price change were less important for perishable foods than for non-perishable goods, so that the volatility of the retail prices of perishables does not contradict assertions that costs of price change do discourage small price adjustments. A Senior Vice President of Perishable Sales in a large supermarket chain[7] said:

"The costs of changing prices are always a consideration, though more so in groceries than in perishables . . . Changing the prices of perishables does not involve a lot of labor, because the product is sold by the pound and sits in bulk on the counter. You just have to change the sign and change the price in the register and on the scales."

Some respondents made it clear that the costs of price adjustment discouraged small price adjustments. The Director of Pricing for a large consumer electronics and appliance retail chain said:

"To get back to addressing your question on the cost of price changes. They aren't that great on larger items, but when it comes to music and movies, we try to be very careful of that, because we would have to obviously, when there is some thousands of titles and when you want to change prices on all of those ... The labor can get pretty expensive taking care of that ... [So then you really do pause when thinking about a price change.] When it comes to music and movies, yeah."[8]

Related Literature

A team of four researchers has collected evidence on price adjustment costs at supermarket and drug store chains: Dutta et al. (1999) and Levy et al. (1997, 1998). They found that the costs were large, about 0.7 percent of annual revenues. They also found the costs inhibited price change to some extent.

3.11 The Effect of Retail Buyers' Administrative Costs of Price Change

A great many retail stores specialize in a single class of goods, such as clothes, sporting equipment, or lawn and garden supplies. Many of these specialty stores have a selling season. It is considered to be bad form for manufacturers selling to specialty distributors and stores to change prices in the middle of the season. This prohibition exists in part because of the distributor's and retailer's administrative costs of price change. These costs can be the expense of printing catalogues or the cost of rethinking the store's pricing. A former officer of a company manufacturing sporting goods said:

> "[How often do those prices change on this price list?] Usually the goal was to only change them once a year. [Why was that?] Just for stability . . . They (retailers) are dealing with a competitive environment and they are trying to come up with a program that is going to be successful with them. They don't want it to keep changing. This is upsetting, because they would have to come in everyday and figure out how to start again. That takes a lot of energy and most people don't have that much energy."

The former owner of a small manufacturer of children's clothing said:

> "[During the season you didn't change prices, because that is bad form?] You really can't get away with it . . . I once tried it with (a woman's name), when we were first starting. She ordered something, and then when I sent her the confirmation, I raised

the price just a little bit and she was right on the phone with me. 'You are starting. I can understand these things, but don't do it again. I am not going to buy from you.'"

The Executive Vice President of a chain of stores selling products for patios and swimming pools said:

> "We have for the most part spent the winter planning out our whole marketing strategy for the full year . . . I don't have time really to renegotiate a higher price. Now I have to rethink my whole marketing strategy for not just that item, but all the items surrounding it. So no matter what it is, it is very difficult to accept a price increase in season. [It is not just relabeling?] No, it is your whole marketing strategy . . . The packaging is price sensitive, being that the price tags are either printed on the package or price tags are put on the package at the manufacturer. So most of my items are priced for the season. If I get a big enough price increase that forces me to raise the retail, the expense is astronomical."

A situation similar to that in specialized retailing exists in the retailing of expensive durable consumer goods. For most of the goods, there is a selling season and manufacturers tend to avoid changing list prices during that season. They do so in part in order to avoid distracting retailers during the season. The CEO of a recreational power boat building company said:

> "[He (another respondent)] has dealers or distributors and they don't like the price to change during the season. I guess that is true of your dealers too?] Of course. [Why is that?] Well, kind of by definition if you think about it. What does in season mean? It means it is the time to sell. So the less disruption to that process the better . . . Twice a year we look at prices, every June just before a model change and every December just before January. [And neither of those disrupts things?] No, because it is all part of the process that has gone on for a bizillion years."

Manufacturers and retailers of expensive durable consumer goods are likely to adjust special incentives during the buying season in response to sales levels and competitors' moves. The incentives could be temporary discounts or rebates. These do add administrative costs, but are an expected part of merchandising. A high official of automobile manufacturer A said:

"[Is there any administrative reason not to change these things too often? Is there a big expense to announce a new – ?] . . . The dealers would tell you it is awful complicated. They like to know what it is for at least three months, so they can get all their advertising and get everything lined up, their promotions, based on this is what the deal is going to be. But if it is not working, we do change it. I mean, it might be out there for a month and they say, 'Hey, it is not working. It is not enough,' and we will change it."

3.12 The Impact of Recessions

Respondents from retail companies explained that the items whose sales fall the most during recessions are the more expensive and luxurious ones and the ones whose purchase can be easily deferred, such as automobiles and pleasure boats. Respondents from supermarkets claimed that their sales are recession resistant, because consumers tend to substitute home cooked for restaurant meals when hard-pressed financially and they buy the ingredients for home cooked meals at grocery stores. The main impact of recession on grocery stores is substitution of staple for luxury foods. In retail businesses that suffer sales declines during recessions, the main effect on the pricing of highly differentiated goods is an increase in temporary promotional discounting. There is little reduction of regular or list prices of highly differentiated manufactured items. The reaction of regular and promotional prices seems to be shaped more by manufacturers than by retailers. The prices of commodities such as fresh food, lumber, and plywood sometimes plunge.

All respondents in the retail grocery business said that their companies do not suffer in recessions. A General Manager of a large supermarket chain and with 45 years in the business said:

"[Were you hurt by the recession in 91, 92?] No. A lot of times when there is a recession, our business is better . . . A recession sometimes slows things down overall, but it keeps a person at home, where they can feed their families, and it favors guys like us, that have stayed in the meat and potato business, because that is where we make our money, and it keeps them out of other places and it keeps them home. They don't take off for a month (on vacation)."

The impressions of respondents in the grocery industry are borne out to some extent by the statistical evidence illustrated in the two graphs that follow. The first shows a time series for total sales of U.S. grocery stores.[9] The graph climbs steadily, except for an upward jump and abrupt decline in 2020 brought on by the temporary shunning of restaurants during the pandemic. The claim of some respondents that recessions increase the sales of grocery stores is not visible in the graph. Although some respondents in the grocery business said that during recessions consumers switched some of their purchases from restaurants to grocery stores, this tendency is not visible in the data for grocery and restaurant sales displayed in Figures 3.12.1[10] and 3.12.2,[11] except when it becomes prominent with the onset of the pandemic in 2020.

The insensitivity of total grocery sales to the business cycle casts doubt on the appropriateness of using supermarket scanner data to estimate the sensitivity of consumer goods prices to the business cycle. However, recessions do shift the assortment of groceries consumers buy. A retired manager of merchandising for a large supermarket chain said:

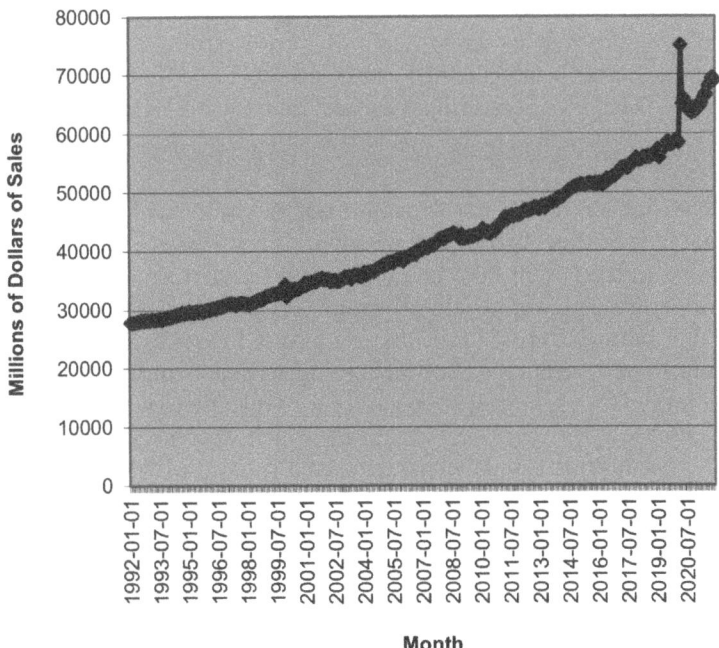

Figure 3.12.1 Total Grocery Store Sales, Monthly Data, Seasonally Adjusted, January 1992–December 2021

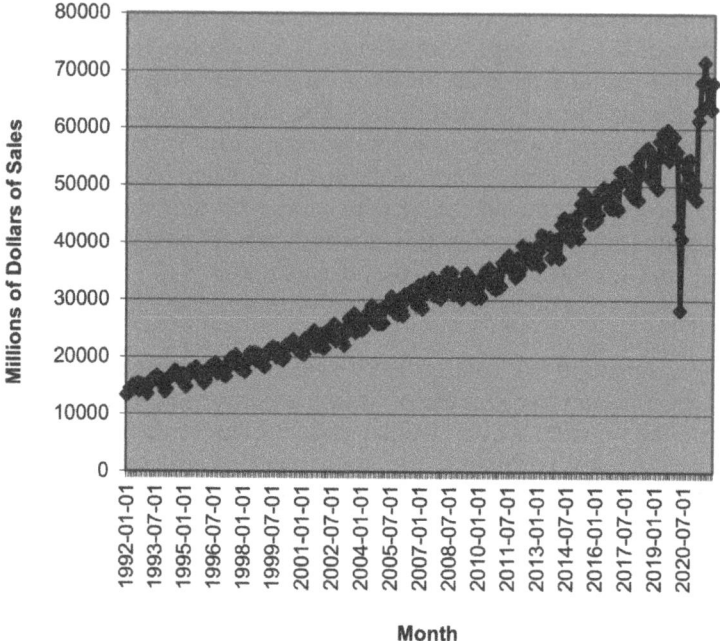

Figure 3.12.2 Total Sales of Restaurants and Other Eating Places, Monthly Data, Not Seasonally Adjusted, January 1992–December 2021

"Recession doesn't affect your unit volume much as I remember. What it does affect is your mix of goods. It takes you to the cheaper cuts of meat. It will take you to the less luxurious produce type item. You sell fewer whole pineapples, fewer raspberries, things of that nature. But you are still going to sell lettuce. You are still going to sell tomatoes. You are going to sell bananas. It takes you away from gourmet foods and more into generic type foods. It increases your private label sales, which decreases your total sales, because private label sales are at a discount from brand."[12]

Similar shifts in demand occurred in other types of retailing. The Executive Vice President of a chain of stores selling products for patios and swimming pools said:

"A recession is going to slow business down . . . In a recession, people that would have bought an in ground pool will look at the very expensive above ground, because an in ground pool is $20,000. A good above ground is $8,000. Those people that would have bought a good above ground will work their way down. So we are, I don't want to say 'recession proof,' but the above ground swimming pool industry is not affected by recessions as much as it is by weather."

All types of retail business followed the pattern of increased temporary promotional discounting during recessions and sometimes reduced regular prices. A Senior Vice President for Perishable Sales in a large supermarket chain[13] said:

"There is always a tendency for trading down in recessions. People use more than one store for shopping. We know this because the average order size shrinks. People buy less when they are going from store to store. If that process continues, we have to do something. We increase our promotional activities. We put stronger items in the promotions, give better prices in them. Price sensitivity increases, because people are doing more comparative shopping. We may even reduce regular prices."

The founder and former president of a large chain of electronic and appliance stores said:

"I think retailers promote harder to generate – to drive traffic in slow times. [And so they actually have more sales?] We are on sale more often and the drops are more dramatic . . . [This is to move inventory?] It is to maintain, I mean, it is both. If you have a big slug of inventory that is not price protected and you have a six-months supply and you only want a three-months supply, you are going to focus on that and drop more. But it is also to maintain the momentum. I mean, the theory of this business is that you cover the – it is the turnover that keeps your cost of doing business at that lower and lower percentages" (because the costs of a retail company other than the costs of the goods sold are largely fixed.)

The Vice President of Strategy and Business Development for a fashionable clothing store chain said:

"[How has the recession affected you? Has that impacted pricing?] Well, yes. As I mentioned, the entire Q3 and Q4 of last year (2008), the entire competitive landscape turned extremely promotional, because basically most retailers were stuck with inventory levels that they had to clear. People weren't spending money, so they had to go pretty deep on discounting to make that happen. But we have seen competitors lower initial ticket prices. Not universally but there has been movement amongst some people on initial tickets."

4
Restaurant Pricing[1]

A central phenomenon in restaurant pricing is the reluctance of restaurateurs to increase prices on their main menu. The reluctance is in response to customer resistance to increases. Customers tend to notice price increases and react by buying less or patronizing the restaurant less. The reluctance to raise prices leads large restaurant chains to try to avoid increases in the prices they pay for ingredients by buying them under long-term fixed price contracts. The desire never to raise menu prices gives rise to a tendency not to reduce them during recessions. This is so even though sales at some types of restaurants tend to fall during slumps. The administrative cost of changing menu prices discourages small and frequent price changes. I also present evidence that changes in fixed costs can affect restaurant pricing, just as they can affect manufacturers' pricing.

4.1 Industry Competition

According to respondents, the restaurant industry is extremely competitive. The Chief Marketing Officer for a fast casual restaurant chain said in 2008:

> "The industry is over built. There has been a forty year trend of eating away from home, but there is very low barriers to entry in the restaurant industry. So everybody, every celebrity, every entrepreneur thinks they can open a restaurant chain . . . As a result of that, you have hyper-competition, and if you talk to people who built the industry in the '60s and '70s, literally it was open a restaurant and make a ton of money, because at that time the trend of eating out of home was growing faster than the supply of restaurants. The key year, I guess, was 1999,

when the number of women working outside the home peaked. It has been flat. The number of restaurants continued to increase monthly. So it is really a share game, and in a share game pricing is extremely difficult."

Customers' awareness of prices depends on location. The CEO and Chairman of a retail pricing consulting company said:

"If you went to (a Southern city) in a very competitive environment with high Hispanics and people over 70, they will know the price points brand to brand to brand. If you go to an airport at five o'clock in the afternoon that is 90 percent business travelers on a Wednesday and you were to perturbate (change prices), they would not even look."

Because restaurant offerings vary, competition does not tightly constrain pricing. The Vice President of Purchasing for a large restaurant chain said:

"[Do you pay a lot of attention to your competitors' prices?] Yeah . . . Our competitors could . . . be almost anybody. If there is a restaurant next to you, they are a competitor. Yes, we look at their pricing, but the quality of the items are not always equal, the accompaniments are different. There might be more accompaniments here than there. Portion sizes are not exactly matched up. So it is used as a guideline and we will look at it, because we don't want to be too far away from the competition . . . [It sounds like it doesn't tightly constrain you. You have some latitude in your pricing.] We always have a latitude."

The more unusual a dish is, the less its price is confined by competition. The Director of Marketing Analysis for a large restaurant chain said:

"What we use competitive data more for would be like soda, things like that, where you are going to get a direct comparison. But when it comes to some of the plates on our menu, they are pretty unique."

The Vice President of Product Development for a fast food restaurant chain said:

"The restaurant business tries to stay out of directly comparative packaging sizes, presentations, all those kinds of things, if they can, because then it becomes a commodity."

4.2 Franchisees' Pricing Freedom

Restaurant chains do not necessarily control prices at all their restaurants. Chains control pricing in the restaurants they own but not in restaurants owned by franchisees, and these may be a large majority in a chain. Most franchise agreements specify that the franchisor determines the items appearing on the menu and is allowed to recommend prices, but legally franchisees are supposed to compete with each other and with the franchisor and so should not coordinate pricing. An exception occurs when a chain organizes a promotion with advertised prices. Franchisees are free not to participate in such campaigns, but if they do participate they have to charge the announced prices.

Franchisees usually want to charge more than what their franchisor recommends, because the franchisee pays the franchisor a royalty that is a percent of sales. Microeconomic theory implies that the royalty should increase the franchisee's profit-maximizing prices, if the franchisee has any market power. To see why this is so, suppose that the royalty is the fraction α of sales. Then the marginal revenue of the franchisee for a product is $1 - \alpha$ times what it would be if there were no royalty. If we set this marginal revenue equal to marginal variable cost, then we see that the effect of the royalty is the same as setting the marginal revenue with no royalty equal to marginal variable cost divided by $1 - \alpha$. Since $1 - \alpha$ is positive and less than 1, the royalty has the same effect as an increase in marginal variable cost. Such an increase normally increases profit maximizing prices. A Senior Vice President and the Chief Marketing Officer for a fast food restaurant chain said:

> "We do not dictate pricing to any restaurant . . . We have established what I would describe as some pricing principles . . . [Does (your company) control the menu in the franchise? Do you decide what they are going to have on their menu board?] Yes. Not the price, but the products."

The Chief Marketing Officer for a fast casual restaurant chain said:

> "The menu is set by us in corporate . . . When you talk to different restaurant companies, you will find that usually the menu is a matter of the basic contract as well as practices that have been

built up over time ... [Your contract allows you to impose a menu?] Yeah, and the distribution company. Basically in order to receive a rebate, you have to buy everything from us ... [What is the rebate?] The rebate is when you buy all your distribution (i.e. food and supplies) from us, we actually rebate money every quarter for doing so. That is our way of coercing, our way of enforcing."

Franchisors achieve some compliance with their price recommendations by advertising price points, which it is awkward for franchisees not to respect. The former Vice President of Marketing of a fast food restaurant chain said:

"As part of pricing you will have promotional offers. That tends to be set by the franchisor, and the franchisee, while perhaps not required contractually to abide by the price, is forced to abide by the price because it is generally something that is advertised. So if you have a 99 cent hamburger advertised in the market, it is difficult for the franchisees to sell that hamburger for something else, because the customers walk in and say, 'Where is the 99 cent hamburger?'"

There is a divergence of objectives in price setting between franchisor and franchisee. The CEO and Chairman of a retail pricing consulting company said:

"The franchisee system in the United States is economically dysfunctional, because the corporate makes its money on a percentage of total sales, so their total impetus is to drive sales. The franchisee makes his money on the margin difference."

4.3 Pricing Tiers within Restaurant Chains

In many restaurant chains, an important fraction of the individual restaurants are company owned, and the pricing in these varies according to local circumstances. Some chains organize this variation by classifying company owned restaurants into tiers, with all the stores[2] in one tier charging the same prices. The Director of Marketing Analysis for a large restaurant chain said:

"We have basically eight price tiers across the country as well as one price tier for Hawaii and one for Times Square, because of

Restaurant Pricing

the much higher costs . . . [So it is like zones or regional zones or does it just depend on the neighborhood?] Generally states kind of define, because one of the biggest costs are defined by the minimum wage, and since normally states have different minimum wages, that is a big driver."

Pricing is especially high in some restaurants where rents are high. The Chief Marketing Officer for a fast casual restaurant chain said:

"The only place you see . . . in the restaurant industry, that sort of captive customer mentality, is what are traditionally called non-traditional locations. The best example would be airports. Our pricing is significantly higher in airports. Our cost structure is higher. Airports just nail us on the leases."

4.4 Labor Costs and Variable Costs

Restaurant managers think of labor costs as fixed. The size of the kitchen staff hardly changes with the demand for meals. The waiting staff may fluctuate with demand, but its compensation is not a big expense, especially if much of it comes from tips. There are few variable costs other than food and paper costs, where food costs are the cost of the meal ingredients and paper costs are the cost of any plastic or paper items customers need to carry and consume the food. Paper costs are important only for fast food restaurants. The former Vice President of Marketing of a fast food restaurant chain said:

"[Labor costs aren't variable?] Not that much. I mean, if you have huge spikes in business, you do see some increases in labor, but not typically. The only other variable cost (besides food and paper) really is royalty, advertising fees, and then some of the stores have a sales based rent structure, so they are paying their rent based upon sales. Other than that, there is very few variable costs. So the total variable cost picture on a franchised restaurant could be . . . 35 to 40 percent. So you can give up a little bit and still make a bunch of money, if you can drive traffic . . . That is why it is such a profoundly lucrative business, if you are growing traffic."

Labor costs are seldom assigned to individual menu items. The Chief Marketing Officer for a fast casual restaurant chain said (he reads from my list of questions):

"Are fixed costs assigned to products? No. Labor, I have never met a chain that actually assigns the labor costs by product. It is true that it varies, but generally labor is looked at more as a fixed cost."

4.5 Food Costs and Pricing

Discussions of pricing in the restaurant industry focus on the food cost percentage, which is the percent of an item's price that is the cost of the materials used to produce it. In sit-down restaurants, the materials are the food ingredients. In fast food restaurants, the materials are the ingredients plus the paper. As food and paper costs are almost the only variable costs, they nearly equal marginal variable costs. Hence marginal variable costs are nearly constant as a function of sales or output, though not declining as they seem often to be in manufacturing. Respondents spoke of prices as markups over food or food and paper costs, where the markups are the residual that pays for fixed costs and profit. More frequently, restaurateurs speak of percent food costs or percent food and paper costs. So the higher is the percent food or the higher is the percent food and paper cost, the lower is the percent markup. The markups are almost always positive, so that price usually exceeds marginal variable cost, as one would expect of a monopolistically competitive industry.

Restaurant selection of food cost percents or margins for individual items is the one area of pricing I learned about, where price setters seemed truly to take account of each item's elasticity of demand in a way consistent with microeconomic theory. Restaurateurs say that they earn higher margins on items with prices that customers are not likely to notice, such as beverages, desserts, and sometimes low cost main dishes. Because consumers notice these prices less, the elasticities of demand for the items are low.

Restaurateurs' pricing decisions are influenced by other considerations than demand elasticities. For instance, restaurants try to avoid having any exaggeratedly high prices that might offend customers and restaurants try to have a smooth progression from low to high priced meals to encourage customers to buy the more expensive items. This last consideration resembles line pricing for expensive consumer goods.

Managers usually have a target for the restaurant of average food costs or food and paper costs as a percent of sales. The Director of Purchasing for a large restaurant chain said:

Restaurant Pricing

"I don't know how much you know about restaurants. Restaurants try to operate (at) about the 30 percent (food) cost factor theoretically."

The food cost factor can vary from item to item. The Vice President of Purchasing for a large restaurant chain said:

"[Roughly what fraction of costs are ingredients versus . . . ?] You mean of the whole price? [Yeah.] . . . The overall is somewhere . . . in the 40 percent range . . . Within that, you could have a range of probably the mid 20s all the way up to mid 50s. Desserts[3] tend to have much higher food costs, and pastas (as main dishes) would have much lower food costs."

Since food costs for main dishes vary widely, their prices would also vary widely if food cost percentages were kept constant, and the resulting high prices for some dishes would stand out and might discourage customers. The Assistant General Manager of an upscale casual dining restaurant said:

"[So you even them (the prices of different main dishes) up so the customer is not shocked?] Shocked by pricing and offended by pricing, right. So also, it is a more affordable price range and they will be willing to say, 'Great, my wife could have the filet,' and he could turn around and say, 'Great, I am in the mood for pasta,' and it works out for both parties."

A restaurant owner said:

"You hope to justify they buy coffee, dessert, because that is where the profit is. But as far as profit on the food, there is not that much profit at all. [Why is there more profit in things like coffee and dessert?] . . . People they don't complain about the coffee and dessert what they pay . . . The main dish they complain."

The Director of Marketing Analysis for a large restaurant chain said:

"Everybody has been taking beverages up, because there seems to be less elasticity in beverage pricing."

Some restaurants charge very low prices on a few items in the hopes of attracting customers who will buy other more profitable items as well. This is close to the pricing strategy of many non-restaurant retail stores. The Chief Marketing Officer for a fast casual restaurant chain said:

> "The classic in this industry is kid meals. The line is, nobody under seventeen drives to the restaurant themselves. So people will take in much lower margin on kid meals in order to attract mom and dad."

Some items, such as filet mignon, appear on the menus of many restaurants. Since the resulting competition holds down the prices of such items, it is natural to wonder why restaurants do not try to populate their menus with unusual items. One answer is that consumers tend to prefer the familiar. The Assistant General Manager of an upscale casual dining restaurant said:

> "[So why not have unusual items on your menu that people can't comparative shop?] It is a market driven business as well. Our friend down in New Haven having that (African) restaurant, as you notice, there is only one in New Haven, because the drive is just not there for such a variety of those things."

It should not be believed that low food cost percentages or high profit margins imply high profit. The contrary is often the case. The high food cost percentage dishes are often the most profitable, because they are so expensive that the low percent markup on a high cost exceeds a high percent markup on a low cost. The Director of Marketing Analysis for a large restaurant chain said:

> "[So you really try to keep the same 30 percent or whatever of food costs per price?] . . . We definitely don't do that. In fact, we use the cost of the product kind of as a proxy for value to the guest, so the lowest cost item we expect to get the least amount of margin from. The highest cost items we expect the most. So we might actually have a 20 (percent) cost of sales on our cheapest seafood and the plate might deliver $10 in margin. We will let that cost of sales creep up as you get to higher cost items like lobster and you will get up to close to maybe 40 percent, but we will be getting $15 in margin on that entree. [So your dollar margin would be bigger, but your percentage margin would be smaller on the expensive items?] Right. That is generally the basis for our overall strategy."

An important part of pricing strategy is to have the prices of low cost dishes be high enough relative to the prices of high cost dishes to encourage consumers to buy the more expensive rather than the cheaper ones and at the same time have the absolute margin be higher on the more expensive ones. The former Vice President of Marketing of a fast food restaurant chain said:

> "How you might change demand on the strip steak is to raise the price of the flat iron steak to a certain point where they are all transferring over ... from the flat iron ... It wouldn't do you much good to be real low price on that, except maybe in a tough economy and then advertise it, because you don't really want to sell it. I mean, it cannibalizes."

Some pricing tactics take advantage of the complexity of consumer demand in ways more sophisticated than simply encouraging consumers to trade up to more expensive items. The CEO and Chairman of a retail pricing consulting company said:

> "In our system what we do is suppose there was an increase in gross cost of a product, say, the coffee, and we need to make that up. Well, we might not raise the price of coffee. We might raise the price of the (a popular soft drink), because the (soft drink) might be very inelastic. So you look at the item, and you say, 'Gee, coffee looks like it is sensitive. We need another dime. We will make it up here in (the soft drink).'"

An important aspect of designing menus and menu pricing is to have different parts of the menu appeal to customers of different levels of affluence. The Chief Marketing Officer for a fast casual restaurant chain said:

> "I remember when I was working at (a restaurant chain), a woman in a focus group in Knoxville, Tennessee said ... 'I have seven kids. I live in a rural town. We are very poor, and the rule of my house is when you are up to ten, you get one item off the dollar menu in (a fast food chain) when we go. When you get to ten, we allow you to have two.' And the franchisees behind the mirror looked at this person. I had been trying to convince them to adopt a dollar menu. None of the data convinced them. When they heard that woman, they got it. They went, 'Oh my gosh. There is this whole group of consumers out there for whom this

is how they consume food.' . . . And in that consumer base, if you took them away from fast food, fast food would collapse . . . What you hope to do simultaneously as a marketer is intelligently segment your menu to appeal to a broad set of people, including value (low budget) customers. But then through advertising and in store communication, push your brand up, so that you can justify a bigger price and a different level of consumer in effect who cares less about value."

4.6 Pricing and Fixed Costs

Fixed costs clearly influence restaurant prices, because prices vary with local rent and wage levels and wages are thought of as fixed costs in the restaurant industry. It is conceivable that this variation exists only because of the impact of restaurant entry and exit decisions on market prices for restaurant meals. However, fixed costs probably influence restaurant pricing directly, because restaurant pricing is consciously adjusted in response to changes in the minimum wage, which is the main determinant of restaurant wage rates. The minimum wage varies locally, because state and local governments as well as the federal government determine it. The Vice President of Product Development for a fast food restaurant chain said:

> "Inner city (restaurants) will not be the cheapest necessarily, because you tend to run into high rent districts there. So while the demography might demand lower costs in Harlem, the reality is you can't afford to sell it for lower cost, because you are paying the same hourly wage and you have got very high overhead costs."

The Director of Marketing Analysis for a large restaurant chain said:

> "In January, a lot of times, when the state minimum wage changes (increases) . . . we take some pricing (raise prices) in those states to offset the minimum wage changes."

It is easy for restaurant managers to adjust prices to the minimum wage, because they can count on competitors doing the same. The Vice President of Purchasing for a large restaurant chain said:

> "In Phoenix, we tend to price down. And part of Phoenix is that the labor market there is so much less, so that is reflected in the market place. Our competitors are priced down."

There is some controversy within the industry about whether fixed costs should affect prices. The Chief Marketing Officer for a fast casual restaurant chain said:

> "[Don't varying minimum wages affect your – ?] Oh, I am glad you brought that up. In fact, that is probably the second biggest variable next to leases, and franchisors are often accused of ignoring that in setting prices. We don't actually factor that in. Our argument as a franchisor is the consumer doesn't care whether there is an eight-dollar minimum wage in California and it is still 5.60 in Mississippi. They are still looking for value and assessing you relative to the competition. The franchisees will often push back and say, 'That is not really true. I can prove that the (fast food chain) down the street is significantly higher than the one in Mississippi.' We actually do a once annual survey to try and get at that."

4.7 Specials

A special in the restaurant business is a food offered for sale that does not appear on the regular menu. Specials can be unusual items that are meant to be especially good but are not necessarily sold at a discounted price. They can be items offered experimentally to see if they should eventually be placed on the regular menu. They can be dishes made from ingredients that fluctuate so much in price that the dishes are offered for sale only when their cost is low. Specials can be promotions of items normally on the regular menu. As in most types of business, advertised temporary price discounts are an effective way to attract customers. Specials are intended to attract new customers, please and retain existing ones, increase visits and sales, and encourage trial. Grocers discount and promote a few items in the hopes that when consumers buy them, they will also buy other items that are not discounted. This motivation exists in the restaurant business, but is less important than in the grocery business, probably because restaurant customers buy only one meal. Grocery stores often lose money on sales of discounted items. Loss leaders hardly exist in the restaurant industry. As do grocery stores, restaurants try to promote discounted items at times most likely to attract consumers.

Items such as fresh fish that have extreme cost fluctuations tend to be offered only on a menu of specials that is inserted into the main menu and changed frequently. The Director of Marketing Analysis (A) for a large restaurant chain and a marketing analyst (B) for the same large restaurant chain said:

> "(A) Like the fresh fish sheet, that actually changes monthly, because the cost fluctuates so much on fish compared to shellfish, that we have to change prices more often to offset how the cost changes. [Do you do that on your regular menu?] (A) The sheet . . . It is printed daily in the restaurant. [It is like an insert?] (A) Yes. [So that is like a special?] (B) It is, for the lack of a better word, a daily special, a daily fresh fish menu. (A) And the (restaurant) managers choose the fish that they were able to get in, but we are setting what the price is going to be."

Demand usually responds vigorously to discounted promotions that are advertised, but the effect is temporary. The former Vice President of Marketing of a fast food restaurant chain said:

> "[So demand is very responsive to price?] Yes. [You usually get a big boom out of these promotions?] . . . You will see big traffic booms on a very temporary basis based on price . . . The problem with food is, there is a high satiation factor for a lot of food types . . . We do seek variety in our . . . diet."

Restaurateurs run discounted promotions in the same way grocers do. They either advertise a temporary price reduction or they offer coupons. An advantage of coupons is that they do not require that prices be reduced. In the restaurant business, it is hoped that increased sales of discounted items alone will increase profits, something I seldom heard from grocers. The Vice President of Purchasing for a large restaurant chain said:

> "The purpose of the discounted (promotion) is to drive the (customer) counts and get as many counts as possible into that restaurant in the hopes of retaining them."

The former Vice President of Marketing of a fast food restaurant chain said:

> "You are trying to drive traffic, because if you discount – it is that highly leveraged business, which is the good news . . . You have given up some of your margin, but if you can drive more

traffic . . . you do get to leverage fixed costs very effectively in the restaurant business."

Although promotions with discounted prices are not uncommon in the restaurant industry, I heard complaints that they are not effective. I did not hear such complaints from grocers. The main complaints were that associated sales were small and that customers were likely to buy a discounted item in place of an undiscounted item. Other complaints were that discounted prices give an impression of low quality and that reduced price promotions seldom create loyal customers. Some customers wait for the return of the discounted price before visiting the restaurant again. The former Vice President of Marketing of a fast food restaurant chain said:

> "There are very few loss leaders in the restaurant business. There are some. It is rare. The food and paper cost is generally in the high 20s. So you really have to discount something to be in that true loss leader category . . . What happens if you . . . cut your margins so greatly on a popular item is it creates trade-over from the other items and it ends up dominating your menu to the point where you are not making any money. The loss leader strategy has never really found a home in restaurants. [. . . Because they are not picking up other things, the way they do in the supermarket?] Exactly. You only have one stomach . . . So typically there is not a lot of deep discounting. Discounting as a strategy has its applications, but it is not a terrifically strong strategy."

The President of a buying cooperative for a fast food restaurant chain said:

> "You can discount your flagship product and drive a lot of traffic. Your gross profit percents go down, but your gross profit dollars go up for a while. The question is how long before it is not sustainable. And then you get yourself into a trap where you get all your customer base that is accustomed to paying a dollar for (the flagship product), then all at once you take the promotion off and you price it where it needs to be priced. You could potentially lose all those customers and they won't come back."

Except for introductory discounts, suppliers do not seem to discount items promoted by restaurants. The COO of a large bakery serving restaurant chains said:

"[If (two restaurant chains) or whatever have sales at a promotional discount price, does that come back to you? Do you have to offer a discounted price?] Generally not, because they are expecting us to have everyday low prices to begin with. A promotional price is really up to them."

4.8 Importance of Repeat Customers

Restaurateurs assert that an important fraction of their profits comes from sales to repeat customers, who are often so governed by habit that they order nearly the same thing every time they come in. The Chief Marketing Officer for a fast casual restaurant chain said:

"For anybody in the restaurant business, it is . . . like 20 percent of your people drive 80 percent of your profits. In our case, we probably, in an average year, of adults 18 to 54 . . . maybe 120 million (eat at our restaurant chain) at least once a year. But of the percent who come four times or more a month, there are like 5 and half million people."

The Director of Marketing Analysis for a large restaurant chain said:

"About 90 percent of our customers we would say come four times or more a year . . . There are a lot of people who come in here and order the same item every time they come. It goes back to a majority of the business being a core group of guests that come fairly often."

4.9 Price Change

Restaurateurs expressed a great deal of reluctance to change regular menu prices as opposed to the prices of specials. This reluctance stems partly from the costs of changing the menu, but a more central issue is the anticipated reaction of consumers. Most changes in menu prices are upward, and repeat customers are likely to react negatively to them, either by shunning the restaurant or by shifting orders to cheaper items. Competition and anticipated reactions to price increases tend to hold restaurant margins to such a low level that restaurateurs are reluctant to reduce prices when costs fall. Restaurateurs believe that sales don't respond much to reductions in regular prices, though they may to temporary promotional reductions. A deterrent to any price reduction is that any later attempt to undo the reduction would

Restaurant Pricing

probably antagonize customers. Regular menu prices seldom change and almost never fall, and restaurants may temporarily cut portion sizes in response to transient food cost increases rather than raise prices. Restaurateurs believe that customers are more likely to notice price increases than portion size reductions. The former Vice President of Marketing of a fast food restaurant chain said:

> "There is not a lot of talk about price reductions. There is not a lot of talk about price increases either . . . Price movement of any significance is soberly contemplated."

Restaurants tend not to pass food cost declines on to consumers. The Vice President of Purchasing for a large restaurant chain said:

> "[You say you almost never decrease prices. Do you think customers would dislike decreases?] Well I think part of it is more we are always trying to catch up to the pricing. If we get some decreases (in costs) on some things, we take it as a catch up point . . . We are probably always a little bit behind in raising prices to where we probably should, and the result when we see a decrease (in food costs) we will just leave it there."

The Vice President of Product Development for a fast food restaurant chain said:

> "[So when they get a reduction in food costs, they don't pass it through?] Exactly. No, they very rarely do that. They figure they are putting up – they call it putting hay in the barn."

A restaurant owner said:

> "When last year . . . veal went sky high . . . I went up $2 a piece for a dish. Oh, they mostly would kill me . . . I learned one thing now that how to raise price. Cut the portion like everybody else is doing . . . They don't notice so much."

Menu price changes are usually made in reaction to cost changes, which are usually increases. The Vice President of Purchasing for a large restaurant chain said:

> "[Why do you change them (menu prices)?] Costs . . . Food costs are generally going up. Not too many food prices go down.

Although we do get downturns at certain times on certain commodities."

Regular customers notice price increases. The former Vice President of Marketing of a fast food restaurant chain said:

"Price increases are recognizable by customers pretty easily, especially your best ones. 'You were ten dollars last week, and now you are eleven. What is going on?' So it is something that is highly visible."

The Manager of a chain of truck stops, hotels, and restaurants said:

"We have a lot of repeat business in all of our sites . . . This restaurant over here is, I think, the most popular restaurant in Utah. We do a couple of million covers a year. If we increase the price 25 cents on halibut, we will get a couple of hundred letters of protest. So people watch that very closely."

The Assistant General Manager of an upscale casual dining restaurant said:

"Usually customers come in and they end up purchasing some similar items time and time again, and they would actually notice the price changing and question it themselves at that point."

Restaurateurs are very concerned about possible negative reactions to price increases. The Chief Marketing Officer for a fast casual restaurant chain said:

"I can send out tomorrow stickers to take everything up ten cents. My daily conversation with franchisees is, you can do that all day long. You are not going to get that dime for dime from the consumer. They are going to manage their check down or they are going to go somewhere else . . . They (a fast food chain) have had to keep the price, because of that twenty to thirty percent of the population who – if you take out the dollar menu, they are gone."

The Director of Purchasing for a large restaurant chain said:

"[Why don't you like changing (prices)?] Because it is not an easy thing to do in a restaurant, and sometimes it is perceived from a customer negatively, where maybe you have raised something up and all of a sudden he says, 'I can't afford to bring my family here anymore' or 'I can't afford to have lunch here anymore.' [So he will switch to another restaurant?] Yeah."

An additional concern about customer complaints is that they can disrupt customer service. The Vice President of Product Development for a fast food restaurant chain said:

> "What the fast food guys, in particular, try to avoid is any discussion at the counter, because let's face it, the person that is doing the transaction on the other side probably isn't really armed to have a very good conversation with you about why the price is fifty cents more today. It is all about speed of service. So that one minute conversation you and I are going to have about why I am paying a dollar more today because of my orange juice means three more guys are going to pull out of the line behind me, and it is a transactions speed of service game."

Another argument against price increases is that customers like to know what they will eat and what they will pay before they enter a restaurant. The Vice President of Product Development for a fast food restaurant chain said:

> "The customer – they like the consistency. One of the reasons they seek out fast food and they seek out chains is they want to know what to expect and that includes pricing."

One reason restaurateurs are reluctant to reduce regular menu prices is that price reductions have little impact on the quantity sold. The Director of Marketing Analysis for a large restaurant chain said:

> "Very seldom do you take prices down . . . probably the best example is snow crab. Crab is very cyclical, and costs will go up and down . . . year to year, and so you would say, why don't you lower the price down when the costs fall. Very seldom do you get much benefit from lowering prices, we find . . . They don't seem to buy more."

Another argument against price reduction is that margins are too small to permit it. The Manager of a chain of truck stops, hotels, and restaurants said:

> "We are definitely reluctant to lower them (prices). [Even if the price of halibut goes down?] Oh, we would never lower it. I can't imagine that we would, no, because the margins are so thin in the restaurant business."

An argument that applies to major chains is that price reduction can lead consumers to focus on price comparisons among competitors rather on product comparisons. The Vice President of Product Development for a fast food restaurant chain said:

> "We . . . live on differentiation . . . That is part of the reason you try to avoid pricing wars is again you want people to perceive (the company's main product) to be a better product than a (competitor's main product) . . . If you standardize pricing (by matching competitors' prices) you are basically saying, each of them is worth a dollar (and) you start to take away from that value of differentiation, of customization, of all the things that you do that makes yourself stand out. It undermines a brand something awful, and these are very brand driven, consumer driven businesses."

This person also argued that price reduction could degrade the brand's reputation by giving customers the impression that it had been too greedy before the reduction.

> "[It is perceived that maybe there is something the matter with the quality that they have to reduce their price? Does that ever come up?] What comes up more often than not is the fear that they will be perceived as having ripped off (customers) prior. It is not so much that they will have degraded quality as there would be a fear that it would have been perceived to have been egregious before."

4.10 Menu Costs and Price Change

I tried to gauge the impact on price change of the administrative cost of changing menu prices relative to a restaurant's concern that increases in regular menu prices might antagonize customers. The comparison is difficult to make, because respondents' views varied and were ambivalent. I conclude that the administrative costs can discourage short-term price change, especially when menus are expensive to print, but that these costs are not the main reason for avoiding price changes. The Director of Marketing Analysis for a large restaurant chain said:

"[And why not change it (price) every week?] We could. It is just the cost benefit with the administrative effort made . . . [So this (having only one) annual price change, that is not coming from the administrative cost of making price change?] No, not really, because we are printing menus anyway, pretty frequently, because they wear out . . . You get such a significant impact from a price increase that that more than offsets any administrative effort. So it is more from the guests seeing increases too frequently."

The CEO and Chairman of a retail price consulting company said:

"[Do the administrative costs of price change, such as menu printing costs, inhibit price change?] Slightly. The opportunities for cash based on the new margins are so huge that the print is a small cost in a cost benefit analysis discussion. If it would cost you $100,000 to print it, you should have a ten fold return easily on the new margins that should yield."

All respondents agreed that the administrative costs exist, and some felt they were an important impediment to price change. The Vice President of Purchasing for a large restaurant chain said:

"We have got 87 restaurants . . . and the cost is over $100,000 to print a menu . . . So we put a menu in and if the prices start going up on us, we just struggle with it all the time, because it is such a process to go through . . . It is not just the cost. It takes time to reset these prices and go through the printers and do all of that and then the shipping and everything else. If you reacted to it every week and the damn thing will change on you. I mean, it doesn't make a lot of sense to do it on a frequent basis. [What about your decision costs? Having to meet as a committee, does that count too?] I don't think we have ever looked at it that way, but if we were looking at it every week, yeah, we couldn't do it. We couldn't give up six or eight hours every week to do that. That is an interesting point. Maybe we just intuitively feel that we just wouldn't bother with it."

The administrative costs of price change do seem to reduce price volatility. The Vice President of Product Development for a fast food restaurant chain said:

"[So it is an expense to change pricing on a menu?] Yeah, absolutely . . . They have got to physically go through the process of changing out their menu boards and any attendant thing, make sure their programming and their cashiers are up to speed . . . [These costs of changing the menu, that really affects the decision not to change price?] It does. It certainly keeps the volatility down, because it is just a hassle."

4.11 Purchasing

Restaurants have such a strong interest in avoiding price increases that the industry goes to great lengths to stabilize ingredient costs. It uses futures markets to hedge price risk and may require that suppliers use their financial resources to manage risk. Restaurant food suppliers can be manufacturers or farmers or wholesalers. Particularly important are large wholesalers, who supply many restaurants. These are of two types; broad line distributors that service independently owned restaurants and systems distributors that service large restaurant chains. Large chains usually make their own supply and price agreements with farmers and manufacturers, and system distributors execute the agreements and make the deliveries. Independent restaurants buy from manufacturers directly, buy at wholesale markets, and buy from broad line distributors. Broad line distributors negotiate the prices they pay their suppliers.

It is much easier to enforce price-stabilizing agreements between large restaurant chains and farmers or food manufacturers than it is to enforce such agreements between independent restaurants and broad line distributors. Independent restaurants buy from so many sources that they are likely not to buy from a distributor if they can buy more cheaply elsewhere. Large restaurant chains, on the other hand, are not likely to engage in disloyal behavior in dealing with manufacturers or farmers, because few are big enough to supply a large chain. The enforcement issue may be one reason broad line distributors do little to stabilize prices and tend to let the prices that independent restaurants pay for ingredients fluctuate with spot market prices. The President and Chief Operating Officer of a large broad line food service[4] distributor said:

> "[When you are buying like pork and hot dogs and things like that or ham, is that on a fixed price long-term contract or is it some sort of formula-based?] It is formula-based, because you can't – you know, it is a commodity. Our product is for the most part commodities and for the most part – and I am looking for the word. [Volatile?] It is volatile and it is consumable and it

perishes . . . [What happens if you buy – suppose you bought on a fixed price contract hams and the price of hams went down . . . What would happen?] Here is the part you are missing is then that our – everybody isn't contracted to you for ham, so you would be off the market and then you would be hung out to dry on hams . . . There is kind of two groups of customers. Ones that is the chain business that does that and a whole bunch of people that don't do it. [Don't do what?] Contract. For instance, all your friends on Cape Cod are most likely not contracting. Yale is. [So Yale is obliged to take it from you, but some seafood restaurant . . .] You would be out the door, and that is the business that we worry about. You know, you have it, don't have it. They can just wait for the next guy with the ham to come in. [You really have to be market competitive.] Absolutely and if you are not, again it is a commodity and you are out."

Another reason that broad line distributors do little to stabilize the prices paid by small restaurants may be that the restaurants do not have enough buying power to be able to insist that distributors bear risk for them. A Vice President of a huge meat packer A said:

"[Who would buy market based (i.e. formula-based)? (A big broad line distributor), you say?] Sure, (they) would . . . you have got a lot of the ethnic restaurants, Hispanic and Chinese or Asian restaurants . . . [They don't mind the price fluctuations from (formula-based pricing)?] They don't like it, but they are willing to live with it . . . [So the ones who really resist these price changes are the big chains?] Yes . . . [So the small restaurants aren't so keen on that?] They just don't have the leverage to do it . . . These big guys may be buying three or four million pounds a week of a product versus somebody who wants to buy 50 cases . . . They just don't have the leverage to try to negotiate pricing that way."

It is common for systems distributors to service agreements between restaurant chains and manufacturers or farmers that fix prices for periods from a quarter to a year. These agreements work for some goods but not for others. French fries are a good example of a good for which fixed price contracting works. French fry manufacturers buy potatoes from farmers at prices contractually fixed for the season. The manufacturers make the French fries, flavor and par fry them and sell them to restaurant chains, often under long-term fixed price contracts. Vice President 1 of a huge producer of branded and unbranded foods said:

"We contract for the potatoes. The potatoes are harvested by farmers, who we have contracted for their output. They bring them in. We may contract the acres at a certain price and then we will process them. They will yield so many French fries per a hundred pounds of potatoes and then we will have already sold those by contract . . . And we will size them and spice them and maybe par fry them . . . [You contract for the potatoes ahead of time? Can you explain that?] Yeah. With producers . . . It is irrigated, so the yields are pretty constant. We typically will tell them, 'We will take all the eight (a size) potatoes you have.' . . . At a set price, and then if they are – the potatoes are a funny one, because if they are stressed, they become a little bit deformed and they yield less French fries. So there is a grading system, and if these potatoes grade as – instead of being an A they are a B or a C, . . . we discount the return to them . . . We might pay them 30 cents a pound for all the potatoes they grow on a thousand acres . . . We might do it January and February and then the potatoes are harvested in the fall and then we use those potatoes for the next year. So you are planning out twelve to eighteen months, nine to eighteen months in advance . . . So that is a fairly risky proposition. And then we will try and sell forward to the large buyers of potatoes and French fries in the brand names you know (two fast food restaurant chains), those people have those French fries at such and such a price. [So you sell for a whole year in advance?] Sure. [You say, 'We will fill your needs at this fixed price?'] Yeah."

Chicken is another food for which fixed price contracting has succeeded at least partially. In this case, producers or farmers can protect themselves against increases in feed costs by hedging them on the futures markets for corn and soybeans. A marketing analyst (A) for a large restaurant chain and The Director of Marketing Analysis (B) for the same restaurant chain said:

"[When in the meat, in the steak, do you make long-term contracts?] (A) On beef and chicken, we do – (B) Actually, we do one-year contracts. [With fixed prices?] (B) Yeah."

The founder, owner, and CEO of a large chicken producer said:

"[There is really a custom in this industry to have fixed prices?] On food service chain business, yes, and if you don't do it, somebody does it. [And they are under pressure to hold their prices fixed, because restaurants don't like to raise their prices?] Bingo, right . . . [How do these long-term contracts work? Were they generally fixed price or are they varied?] Most of those are fixed price. [For a year?] Between a year and three years. [Oh, you fix a price for three years?] Yeah, some of them are three years. That just kind of started in the last year. It stinks, because we can't hedge corn for three years. 66 to 70 percent of our costs are corn and soybean meal to raise a chicken . . . So right now to go out three years at these cheap levels that these people want to pay is very tough, because our conclusion or our understanding is that corn is going to go up."

Recall[5] that meat producers fix prices for future grocery store promotions by freezing and storing large quantities or by using the futures markets for live cattle or lean hogs to cross hedge individual cuts of meat. Meat producers use these techniques and the futures markets for feed grains to provide restaurant chains with long-term fixed price contracts for meat with the exception of hamburger. Hamburger is made from beef trimmings, and the price of trimmings is so poorly correlated with that of cattle that it cannot be reliably cross hedged. Hamburger is usually sold to restaurant chains using formula-based contract pricing. The President of a buying cooperative for a fast food restaurant chain said:

"All of our beef is formula priced . . . It is tied to the commodities, raw materials . . . [So who makes up the index?] USDA (United States Department of Agriculture) reports market prices . . . If we are looking at a one-year, two-year, three-year contract, the month-to-month fluctuations will tend to work out. [And you are not taking special positions in inventory.] No. The cost of holding the inventory on our products is too high . . . We move about 30 trailer loads of hamburger each day. So if we wanted to take an inventory position for more than two or three days, that is a lot of meat that would take up a lot of storage, a lot of costs associated with in-and-out charges, cost of carry . . . [Yet the stuff isn't frozen anyway. It is perishable.] It is frozen . . . Hamburger has about a four month shelf life."

Although growers and restaurant chains do arrange fixed price contracts for produce, doing so is difficult because of the risk of crop failure, the impossibility of long-term storage, and the absence of futures markets. The Director of Marketing Analysis for a large restaurant chain said:

> "We even have long-term contracts with lettuce growers, tomato growers ... A lot of these contracts will have act of God clauses. So when a hail storm goes through California and wipes out half the crop and obviously we (would) put them out of business by demanding – you know, that is not going to be in our long-term interest either. So we work with vendors like that, but if just something like that happens we will give them a temporary one or two month price change."

The Vice President of Purchasing for a large restaurant chain said:

> "[With those produce suppliers, do you fix the price in advance or have contracts?] ... Produce, lettuce could be $8 a case and two years ago it was $60 a case ... A lot of people do contract lettuce and some of those things, but the contracts there, unlike the beef, we could never get lettuce contracts down low enough where we were comfortable with it."

4.12 Market Research

Restaurants devote resources to surveying competitors' prices, and large chains estimate the impact of price changes on demand through focus group studies, test marketing, and statistical estimation done by consulting companies. Restaurants survey other restaurants similar to themselves. Focus groups are made up of a few consumers who are questioned about their buying habits or their reactions to hypothetical new products and prices. Test marketing involves changing dishes or prices at a few restaurants within a chain for a trial period. Statistical estimation uses econometric methods familiar in economics. Focus group studies tend to be straightforward. The Vice President of Product Development for a fast food restaurant chain said:

> "So I would have a photograph of a new sandwich and I would say, 'Given what we have described, what price would you expect to pay?' ... And that is where you really start to establish what their perceived value is."

Test marketing is quite common in large chains. The Chief Marketing Officer for a fast casual restaurant chain said:

"An optimal methodology . . . is this. Six months before you want to take a price increase, go into a DMA (Designated Marketing Area). Take ten stores. Take them up. And take ten stores and keep them down. Then you can truly read the elasticity . . . [And that would be for a month or two?] Generally you want it to be through at least two purchase cycles (of a consumer). So for us that would actually be four or five months. Because you think about what happens. If I am mad, I generally don't leave then. It is just the next time out, I may not buy my family (the typical food of his chain)."

4.13 Impact of Recession

Respondents in the restaurant business, like those in the grocery business, said that recessions bring a shift from restaurant to home cooked meals, so that grocery stores gain at the expense of the restaurant industry. Within the restaurant sector, the impact is complex and varies from recession to recession. In the recession that began in 2008, expensive restaurants and fast food restaurants suffered little, and middle level restaurants suffered a great deal. A senior vice president of huge meat packer 2, speaking in September 2010, said:

"[What has been the impact of the recession on your production decisions? None at all?] Not substantially, because what ends up happening – about half of our business is food service based and about half of it is retail based. So during economic recessions, food service demand usually goes down, which is exactly what has happened, and retail demand goes up . . . They offset each other."

The President of a buying cooperative for a fast food restaurant chain, speaking in February 2008, said:

"Consumers are buying down, buying down to fast food. So in a perverse sort of way, a poor economy may actually help the fast food sector and damage the middle ground, which is the casual dining. And then you have the high end, like (three restaurant chains) and places like that that may be more insulated from both commodities and the economy. [Because their clients are so rich.] Yeah exactly. At the high end, they are not all that income or price sensitive. So the casual dining sector has really taken a big hit in the last year, and fast foods has been strong."

Restaurateurs agreed that it is not a good idea to react to declining demand by reducing regular menu prices. Doing so can diminish the consumer's image of the value of the product and consumers may get used to the lower prices and resent their being brought back up later. A better way to respond to demand declines may be through temporary promotional price cuts, though some respondents found fault with this approach as well. The Assistant General Manager of an upscale casual dining restaurant, speaking in October 2002, said:

> "We do suffer from what is occurring out there in the economic market as well. [And does that affect your pricing?] No, it has not yet. We hope to avoid that actually. [Why?] I think . . . if you start to put yourself in a lower priced market your customers are going to continue to expect that. Even if the economy starts to return, they are going to expect you to stay down at that price range then. Whereas if you deliver consistency of product and the quality and the service, the dollars, everything is consistent right now and it stays and holds through all this trouble, they will continue to come back."

The Vice President of Product Development for a fast food restaurant chain, speaking in June 2005, said:

> "You use pricing as a promotional tool in those times, but you don't change your menu pricing, because of the fear that you are going to cheapen the perception of your product. [And it is also hard to get it back up?] It is very hard to get it back up, again because our customers are so habitual."

The Director of Marketing Analysis for a large restaurant chain, speaking in January 2008, said:

> "[You wouldn't try to get higher counts by lowering price?] Historically back in the late 90s, we did that, and that is definitely something that management does not want to do again. [It didn't work?] It didn't work. The long-term effect of that didn't pan out, did not work. It was a short-term fix, and it takes a while then to get out from under that . . . The guests would wait until you got another one of those offers to come back in. Those were low profitability offers, so actually although you had more guests coming in than before, you are making less money. [So these were sort of announced temporary discounts to try to create – ?] Yeah."

4.14 Price Behavior

Figure 4.14.1[6] shows that the U.S. average price level for restaurant meals has almost no cyclical pattern.

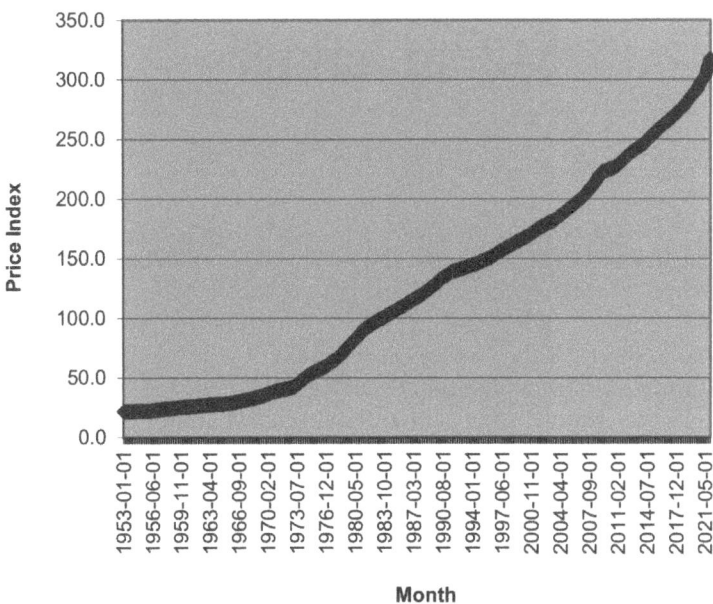

Figure 4.14.1 Consumer Price Index for Urban Consumers' Meals away from Home, Monthly Data, Not Seasonally Adjusted, January 1953–December 2021

5
Pricing by Contract Manufacturers[1,2]

The businesses discussed in this chapter manufacture for other companies products whose design the customer owns. The customer usually requests bids from several companies to manufacture the product and selects the vendor on the basis of price and qualifications.

Although contract manufacturers do not own the designs of the products they produce, they can differentiate what they do as manufacturers through high quality work and service, where service means mainly delivering the product on time. Contract manufacturers seem to be of two types, those that compete primarily on price and those that compete mostly through service and product quality.

When it seemed appropriate, I inquired about whether the prices of contract manufacturers fall during periods of slack demand. Although the question might seem to make sense only when applied to repeat business, respondents interpreted the question as applying to their method of calculating bids. The companies that seemed to compete on service and quality used arguments against price flexibility typical of producers of highly differentiated goods, namely, that price reduction does not attract much additional business and that it would be hard to reverse a price reduction after economic conditions improved. These companies seemed to operate in an environment where customer loyalty to vendors reduced the risk of losing customers to low priced offers from competing contract manufacturers.

All the contract manufacturers where I interviewed used some form of fully absorbing costs when choosing bids. This practice is consistent with the marginal and average variable costs of manufacturers being constant or declining over the normal range of output variation.

5.1 The Mechanics of Contract Manufacturing

The process of awarding contract work begins with the customer company requesting bids. There is a qualification process, which may be complicated. The President and owner of machine shop C said:

> "It might be 5 or 6 other people quoting on the same part. [Do you know who else is quoting?] No, they don't tell you who they send it out to . . . You have to show that you can make the part. You have to show a similar part that you have made . . . If they feel that qualifies you to make the initial part, then you can quote on it . . . You still have to make one part . . . They will choose usually the lowest bidder or the one who is the most qualified."

The prices given in awards are usually good for one purchase order. Because of setup costs and as a result of the assignment of fixed costs to individual products, prices tend to decline as the size of the order increases. The Vice President of Operations for pressed powder metal manufacturer E said:

> "[With your customers, you sign a contract specifying price?] It is a contract on each individual part. So they send in a purchase order with a part and a quantity and a delivery date . . . Some parts, for example, the second-tier automotive and the replacement automotive parts, we will give a price for the whole year . . . [Those long-term contracts, they say that there is a minimum amount that they are going to take?] We quote it on their annual estimate . . . If there is a huge difference between what they said and what they actually ordered, the next year, when they go to order it, obviously, I would change the price, and say, 'We can't accept this price because you didn't order nearly as many as you asked us to quote on.'"

The President of pressed powder metal manufacturer D said:

> "In the market place, to be competitive on the big dollar accounts, you have to be lower . . . [Why is that? . . .] It is just bigger, it absorbs more burden."

Despite the short-term nature of awards of business to contract manufacturers, customers tend to stay with the same vendors for the manufacture of particular parts, especially if the work requires special tooling. Even if the tooling belongs to the customer, it often does not work in the machinery of other vendors. So tooling creates a switching cost. The President of folding box manufacturer B said:

> "There is all these issues, so it takes a long time to get a customer. But on the other hand, once you get them, you really have to screw it up to lose them. Or they find a price that is so much less than yours that they can't say no, and then onward they go. But the tooling costs and things like that become a factor in changing. [So they own the tools?] We own them most of the time."

5.2 Competition

Although contract manufacturers face competition through the bidding process, there is not the continual pressure on price faced by commodity producers. The President of corrugated box manufacturer A said:

> "You can differentiate, somewhat. It is a commodity and it is not a commodity, because everything is custom-made. Every box is custom-made. Somebody can go out and get a price on it from twelve different people, but it is still a custom product. We have tried to differentiate ourselves by providing service and engineering and warehousing, distribution, trying to do just-in-time deliveries through warehouses."

I have mentioned that contract manufacturers seemed to compete either mainly with price or mainly with service and quality. The next quotation is typical of those that compete with price. The President and COO of folding box manufacturer C said:

> "How do we get more business in a one or two percent growth market? We go out and try to steal it from somebody else. And how do you steal it? We steal it through – if you get the opportunity through pricing... Once you get in there, then quality and service are the issues that keep you there."

The next quotation is typical of those who emphasize service and product quality. The Vice President of electronics contract manufacturing company A said:

"I look for customers that I can have a long-term relationship with. As a contract manufacturing company, we are our customer's manufacturing department, so it behooves the customer and ourselves to establish a long-term relationship."

5.3 The Choice of Bid

The first step in the selection of a bid is the calculation of the direct variable cost, which is the cost of the labor and materials needed to manufacture one unit of the product. This step is usually unambiguous, though it can be complicated. The Vice President of Operations for pressed powder metal manufacturer E said:

"[How do you come up with a price?] Okay, basically what we do is we have a program that I wrote . . . We figure out the size of the part, the area of the part, and that determines the size of the press that it goes in . . . Cross-sectional area, it is a start, because you get your tonnage (of pressure) by that. And then you have to look at the overall length of the part, because that will change the fill, what we call the fill ratio. You fill the product about two times the height of the part . . . You know which material you are using . . . You put that into a little equation and come up with a (metal) powder cost. And then we break it down into what operations we need to do. So we need to briquette and we need to sinter it and we need to heat treat it, to tumble it, and then ship it out the door."

Contract manufacturers use a variety of systems to account for fixed and overhead expenses in their calculation of costs and choice of prices. The President, CEO, and owner of an injection molding and metal stamping company said:

"[How do you assign that to a particular product?] You don't. Overhead you don't. You absorb overhead . . . All of your budgetary items that are not direct costs, that cannot be absorbed on a one to one basis – [by that product.] by that single product, get lumped into overhead expenses . . . So you estimate how many direct labor hours you are going to have or how many machine hours you have got and you divide that into the overhead rate. So if you have got two million dollars of overhead and you have a million dollars, let's say $500,000 of direct labor . . . Across the whole factory?] Right. So if there is a dollar of direct labor in this part, there is four dollars of overhead at that ratio . . . Some manufacturing overhead is variable. Some of it is fixed. But usually you assign it as a fixed overhead."

In deciding on a bid, price setters at contract manufacturers typically view their final cost estimate as the basis for a target price. They sometimes adjust the target to account for market conditions and in response to pressure from the customer. The Sales Manager of folding box manufacturer A said:

"A lot of times, they will come back to us and say, 'You know, you were the highest of three quotes, and it surprised us. I would like to give it to you, but we can't give it to you at the price you wanted. I could if you dropped it 5 percent or 7 percent.' . . . That is legal. They are not telling me what the other competition is doing, but they are telling me what they are willing to pay."

The President of a medium-size contract manufacturer said:

"We are paying an employee $10 an hour. We would then add to that the benefits cost, and then we would roll into it our burden cost, the cost of operating the buildings, the utilities, our various insurances, the machine cost. All of that factors in, and we come up with a certain burden number and we say that burden gets added to the wage costs and that becomes what is our factory cost. At the end of that, what we do is we will then multiply for SG&A and profit, another multiplier . . . And that becomes our selling price. [Is that multiple the same for all products? . . .] It is up to me to determine what the multiple is. [For each product?] Yeah, so that if I am aggressively pursuing a product I might adjust accordingly. [Hoping to get higher volume?] Hoping to get higher volume."

The President of injection molding company A said:

"Probably, the next thing we look at is how busy we are or not busy, and based on that, the answer to that question, I will decide which (burden) rate we go in with. If we really need a lot of work, I want to go in with a little bit lower rate. If we are real real busy out there, I will go in at the higher rate."

5.4 Contribution Margin Pricing

Recall[3] that a contribution margin price is one that covers average variable costs and some but not all of the assigned average overhead and fixed costs. It might be thought that such pricing is especially appropriate for contract manufacturers, because they can move in and out of markets quickly. This inference would be incorrect, however. Respondents from eleven contract manufacturing companies discussed contribution margin pricing, and all but two of these eleven showed little interest in it because of concerns about the difficulty of raising prices once they have been reduced or because unexpected problems can lead to losses when profit margins are thin. The President and COO and owner of folding carton manufacturer E said:

> "There are opportunities to pursue business that is less demanding and may be high volume and low margin with excess capacity that you can move in and out of that market, not necessarily at will, but easy, and it helps to absorb overhead and obviously make a contribution. We don't want that to become our business ... The only problem with that kind of business is you can't have any screw ups, because there is no room for absorbing anything."

5.5 Reactions to Reduced Demand

I had unambiguous discussions with respondents from fifteen contract manufacturers on the response of pricing to reduced demand. Ten of these companies had clearly reduced prices and five had maintained prices in current or recent periods of low demand. The ten companies that reduced prices seemed to be of the type that competed mainly on price. The five that had not reduced prices seemed to be of the type that competed mainly on the basis of service and product quality.

The following two quotations are from respondents that claimed that their companies had reduced prices during slow times. The President and owner of machine shop C said:

> "[Has the pressure of less business, has that driven your hourly rate down at all?] Oh definitely, because you are constantly sharpening your pencil, trying to get the work. And not only that, but now you might be lowest bidder today, and the buyer will call you up and tell you that, 'Well, we have a target on this, and you will have to meet the target if you want it.' ... Lowest bidder doesn't mean you are going to get the job. You still might have to come

down lower, or they will go to the next higher one, and if he is willing to come down lower, he gets it. [But in good times, like three years ago, they just wouldn't try that?] Oh, they would try it, and you would just say, 'No, that is my price, and that is it.' And most everybody else would say the same thing, so you would probably get it."

The President of injection molding company A said:

"We have seen a major reduction in manufacturing. [Does this affect what you ask in your prices?] Oh, absolutely . . . We have reduced the bids for the last six months or so . . . Being more aggressive . . . [Does it work?] Yeah, we are busy again . . . [By what percentage do you think would have been the decrease in price?] Probably 20 percent."

The next two quotations are from respondents who worked for companies that had not reduced prices. The Vice President of electronics contract manufacturing company A said:

"[How do you react to these conditions of recession?] One of the only ways we can really weather it is to constantly look for more business . . . [So you don't actually try to solicit business by cutting price or anything like that?] No we don't do that . . . [Do you think that you could get more business by lowering price, quoting lower, especially during a downturn?] I would like to say 'Yes,' to that, but in my experience it is not necessarily – our sales are not necessarily really a function of pricing. Our sales come quite a bit from rapport, come from trust . . . [You said you got one fifth of your new quotes – you wouldn't up it a lot by reducing pricing by 10 percent?] Not really, especially for new customers. I haven't seen any responsiveness when I send out direct mail pieces advertising certain rates that I know are very competitive in the industry . . . [You just don't react to recessions by reducing price.] No. No. We haven't. [If they (customers) are so loyal, why not raise the price? What is the argument against that?] Well, the argument against that is that there are so many competitors out there that it certainly – I wouldn't want to give my customer the opportunity to look at additional – [So they would start looking, if you raised price?] There is no question that would happen. [If you reduced price, you wouldn't have others looking at you?] Not to the extent that I wish they would."

The President of plating company A said:

"[If you are very slow do you charge, say, a smaller fraction for overhead and profit to get more business?] Well, that is hard to really address, because once I price something, I am generally stuck with that price in good times and bad. [Why is that?] Because it is really hard to raise prices. It is easy to lower it . . . The problem is that once I get busy again, then I have got to go back to that customer and say, 'Well, I have got to raise your price,' and then they get mad at me because they have got 10 other things that they send to us . . . I kind of feel like I have got this obligation to him to continue to do it at that low price. [Oh, because he started pricing his product based on what he is getting from you?] Right. Yeah. They really just pass our price through."

6
Pricing in the Construction Industry[1]

It is hard to detect downward rigidity in construction prices, because construction projects vary so much that price decline is difficult to define. Rigidity in the prices of building materials can be detected, however, because the materials are standardized. These prices again show an association of product differentiation with downward rigidity, though I came across few examples of price rigidity, probably because most building materials are commodities or near commodities. It is nevertheless surprising that there could be any downward price rigidity in the construction industry, because its bidding processes apply strong downward pressure on prices. Most of this chapter is an attempt to make this pressure clear by means of a rough description of how the industry prices large projects.

Like contract manufacturers, construction companies normally include in their bids an allowance for overhead and fixed costs. This practice adds to the evidence that manufacturers cannot count on increasing marginal costs to provide an adequate margin between total revenue and total variable cost.

The bidding for large construction projects may be visualized as occurring in three stages, the first at a center and then spreading successively to two concentric rings. The center is a general contractor or construction manager who organizes the work and comes up with a bid for the whole project. The first ring consists of subcontractors from about twenty trades who do most of the work. The center bases its overall price on bids solicited from subcontractors in each of the trades. When calculating its bid, each subcontractor solicits bids from material suppliers, who form the second ring. These suppliers are retailers, distributors, and manufacturers. As a result of this process, dozens of companies may calculate bids for parts of one large project.

6.1 General Contracting

Typically the owner or government organization that pays for a project employs architects and engineers to design it. The designers produce a set of documents describing the structure. If it is to be built for private owners, they usually invite a select list of contractors to bid for it. If the project is public, then a government organization advertises for bids. Large construction projects inevitably involve subcontractors, and each contractor requests bids from potential subcontractors for their part of the work, or subcontractors may submit unsolicited bids. The contractor then submits a bid based on the subcontractors' bids and its own expenses. If the work is public, the contractors' bids are opened publicly, and the low bidder almost always gets the job. If the work is private, the bids are normally opened privately, and the owner may begin negotiations with individual bidders. The owner may lead low bidders to believe that they are high in order to persuade them to lower their bids.

After winning the bid, the first thing a general contractor typically does is to begin negotiations with subcontractors who have submitted bids to her or him, and have them compete with each other in reducing their bids. This stage is called "buying the job" or the "buyout" and is much more prevalent for private than public work. A general contractor is not legally bound to employ the subcontractors who submitted the low bids that the general contractor used in calculating its winning bid. General contractors have a strong incentive to engage in the buyout, because their profits increase by the amount of the reduction in the subcontractors' bids. The President and owner of construction general contracting company B said:

> "On a lump-sum bid, if you went in with a 3 percent markup on the day of the bid, the chances are that you can through the buyout process . . . double that or triple that . . . [By going back to the subcontractors?] Going back to the same subs. In some cases, finding new subs . . . [You are not legally bound to them at all?] No."

When bidding jobs, general contractors anticipate the savings they will make through the buyout and adjust their bids downward accordingly. A Vice President of construction general contracting company C said:

> "Believe it or not, this business is nothing more than a guessing game of trying to figure out what the real number is in each

trade, because each general contractor who is bidding doesn't get the lowest number at bid time in each trade ... At bid time, you have got all these numbers. Now the question is, what adjustment factor do I put on there to arrive at what I think the real number is, and that is the name of the game in this business."

Respondents understood that the buyout would not exist if subcontractor bids were opened publicly and work automatically went to the low bidder, as usually happens with public work. A Vice President of construction general contracting company C said:

"You have got, let's say to make it simple, 5 bidders for each trade, 20 trades. You take the bids. You open them up publicly, because it is a public school. The low guy gets the job. You have got a lowest price in each trade ... [So you don't go back and ask for less?] No. No negotiations on public work."[2]

The general contractor's bid normally exceeds the sum of what the general contractor thinks the subcontractors will cost after the buyout, because the general contractor adds to its bid a percent of the cost of all the work done by the trades in order to cover overhead and profit. This margin can be from two to ten percent and depends on the general state of demand for construction.

Until now, I have described all work organized by general contractors as competitively bid. This is not always so for private work, because the owners may have favorite contractors, and contractors may have favorite subcontractors. In such situations, the prices may be negotiated rather than bid. A part owner of drywall[3] contracting company B said:

"We have a core of eight or ten contractors that we do most of their work. When they get the job, we know we have the job. So you have to take care of those people. [Do those people ask for competitive bids from others?] Sometimes they do. It depends on how they bid the job, whether it is construction management or just a straight negotiated job. A lot of jobs are negotiated, and they just work on a fixed fee and they like to work with the same subs who have worked together a lot."

6.2 Construction Management

A wide variety of arrangements are labeled construction management, but in all of them the construction manager acts as the agent of the owner or public authority in both the design and the building of the structure. When the construction manager is chosen, the plans for the structure may be no more than a sketch or perhaps a 25-page document. The manager advises the architects and engineers designing the structure on how to control costs.

Construction managers typically bear financial risk, because they give or negotiate a guaranteed maximum price. If the actual cost exceeds the guaranteed maximum, the manager pays the difference. Managers are paid a fee of from three to five percent of the total cost. Sometimes the fee also includes charges for overhead costs and some on site expenses.

Part of the function of construction managers is to seek bids from subcontractors and to choose the winning bidders. Like general contractors, construction managers usually have subcontractors compete with each other in reducing their bids, and choose the low bidder in each trade. Construction managers have an incentive to behave in this way in order to keep the total cost of the project below the guaranteed maximum and in order to burnish their reputation as managers.

6.3 Subcontracting

An important issue for subcontractors is how to handle the pressure to renegotiate bids made to the general contractor or construction manager who won the job. Some are able to resist. A Structural Engineer for pre-stressed concrete company B said:

> "There are some contractors that will take the best bid and they will say, 'Well, this guy is $10,000 lower, but I don't want to use him.' So then they will call the other guy and say, 'Hey. Can you come down 10,000, and we will use you?' which is totally unethical, I think, and that is what we steer clear from . . . We make it very clear that no that is not an option, that that number is our number."

Despite resistance, the dominant practice seems to be to renegotiate subcontractor bids and for subcontractors to increase their initial bid by the amount they anticipate they will have to give up in the buyout. The owner and Vice President of a structural steel and steel fabrication company said:

> "There is always the token cut, that you have to throw some money in for. If they get the job, you might be 55. 'Alright, you

can do it for 53.' Sometimes you know already you are going to get that if they get the job. So you throw a few extra dollars in there for the cut. [What is the purpose of the cut, to make them feel good?] . . . You just know that these guys are going to try, that this is where they will make their money on the buy. They are probably going to make most of their profit on the buy. They . . . figure that on a five million dollar job they are going to buy back maybe a quarter of a million, just on the buy."

Subcontractors give lower bids to contractors they have confidence in. The Sales Supervisor for Plant and Heavy Highway Construction for ready mix company A said:

"They are not always the same price. They generally are, but they are not always the same price. We may have customers that we deal with on a more regular basis that we have a good relationship with, good pay, maybe work our concrete trucks in a quick fashion, so it keeps our costs down, and we have that history. We have that experience with them and we may offer them a lower price."

A part owner of drywall contracting company B said:

"[These regular contractors that you deal with all the time, the regular customers, your core customers, do they ever come back to you and try to get a lower price, after they have agreed to take you?] Sometimes, they say, the honest ones say, 'For us to get the job, everybody has to come down a certain percentage.' So usually it is the same team, the same electrician. 'Okay, we will do it,' because we do all the work for them. So we will help the guy out and then sometimes they will say, 'Well, this job is a little heavy. What you paid back last month, maybe we can put it over here.'"

Subcontractors described the calculation of their bids as being routine. They estimate materials, fuel, and labor costs and add on a percentage margin to cover overhead and profit. The margin to cover overhead is calculated as the ratio of estimated overhead expenses for the year to the estimated total costs of materials, fuel, and labor. A similar calculation may be used, if they choose to include overhead costs in a labor rate. The descriptions of the estimating procedures made it clear that overhead costs affect bids, even though overhead costs are largely fixed. The margin added for profit or profit plus overhead costs is adjusted to reflect the likelihood of winning the bid and how near the subcontractor is to full capacity. The President of pre-stressed concrete company A said:

> "So it all comes back to the margin. With that we have to cover our overhead costs obviously and try to make a profit. When times are down, the profit – like in the '90s there was no profit. I mean, we were bidding jobs theoretically at a loss. But you see our business here is volume is the big issue. You are doing 10 million dollars a year or you are doing 50 million a year. There is a huge difference in the amount of contribution you get out of those jobs. [Because so many of your costs are fixed?] Right. So it is basically down to what the market will bear."

The Director of Sales and Administration for a bridge girder company said:

> "I need work for next January or I need work for next December, so how do I get more work? I cut my price, so I can get the job. It is just that simple . . . because I know the other shops, I keep a tab . . . I just record it and I can look at it and find out where everybody is at. Then our competitors, because times are good put on a huge expansion. Well, my gosh, when you spend $15 million for an expansion, you better have some work in it. So now all of a sudden, his prices are depressed again. Why? He wants to fill up that shop."

6.4 Construction Material Dealers and Manufacturers

When subcontractors prepare their initial bids, they turn to distributors for prices of materials to use in their estimates. After the general contractor or construction manager has been selected and subcontractors feel the pressure of the buyout to reduce their bids, they begin a buyout of their own by negotiating with distributors and manufacturers and having them compete to reduce the prices for materials. The subcontractors seek both low prices and assurance that the prices will not increase during work on the project. The Drywall and Acoustic Tile Manager for building supply company B said:

> "Usually what happens is, a commercial contractor, a drywall or acoustical contractor will bid a job and based on their knowledge of the industry they may require assistance from us . . . We will

just give them a run of the mill price ... So they will go and they will bid the job. Now then they land the job and they will start calling around and getting quotes to buy the job and then when they are buying the job, then it is time to be down and dirty and you get more aggressive. [Buying the job means getting actually –]. Finding a distributor that they are going to buy from ... He is pricing, because he has the job and he wants the best numbers he can so he can make the most money he can."

The person just quoted works for what is called a pro-yard, which is a building materials dealer who sells mostly to professional builders. The majority of the business of pro-yards is bid. The President of building supply company A said:

"I would say 60 percent of our business or more is really work that is bid. Maybe 30 to 40 percent is everyday."

In order to meet subcontractors' demands, distributors may appeal to manufacturers for price reduction and guarantees that prices will not increase. These requests are negotiated and typically met when a job requires large volumes. Such requests are usually not met for commodity lumber, plywood, or oriented strand board. Wholesale price margins for these items are too small and the prices too volatile to make guarantees and reduced prices feasible. The normal way to fix the cost of commodity wood products is to buy and store them. The President of building supply company A said:

"We have other subs that will come to us and whether they should or should not just do that and say, 'Listen, I want to buy it from you, but so and so is charging this price.' And therefore we will go back to the manufacturer. So we are constantly negotiating ... [So they (manufacturers) will give you a break in price just for the job? They can do that?] Yes."

The Drywall and Acoustic Tile Manager for building supply company B said:

"The manufacturers are only going to protect jobs with a certain volume, and there are many jobs that we quote that the manufacturer gives us some guidance on, but there is no guarantee."

The owner of northeastern lumber producer company C said:

"On big projects with respect to large quantities of lumber and plywood, if you wanted to fix your cost (with us), you would typically have to buy that product, take delivery of it, pile it up, and hang on to it."

6.5 Downward Price Rigidity of Some Materials

The pricing of building materals shows some evidence of an association between product differentiation and downward price rigidity. Lumber is undifferentiated, and its prices are volatile. Gypsum wallboard is nearly undifferentiated, and its prices fluctuate but do so less than the prices of lumber. At the other extreme, is a company that frequently innovates proprietary products providing access to buildings. Its prices are non-negotiable and stable. The Vice President of Engineering for a producer of metal doors and vents for buildings said:

"We publish a price list . . . Those are our prices. They are not negotiable . . . The construction industry and building materials in general are notorious for engaging in negotiation. We don't do that and we never did that."

I came upon two examples of downward rigidity in subcontractor pricing. Both subcontractors delivered or installed materials that are near commodities. A subcontractor that sold ready mix concrete used a familiar argument to justify the rigidity, namely, that price reduction is hard to reverse. William Brainard said:

"[What is surprising is that somehow you are really able to use those 150 trucks – you don't have periods when you are only using 100 of them?]"

The Vice Chairman of ready mix company C said:

"Yeah in the winter. [Do you reduce price then to get more business?] No. [Why not?] . . . I hate to talk to an economist about this . . . My amateurish feeling about that is, also empirically well-founded, is that it takes ten times longer to get a price back up, or get it to a level and you can undo that ten years' worth of effort in one day by dropping it back."

The other subcontractor, who installed gypsum wallboard, added a new consideration in explaining downward price rigidity, that his customers did not know that the manufacturers' prices of wallboard had fallen. A part owner of drywall contracting company B said in June 2000:

> "Once the prices go down, they are tough to get back up. [Why is that?] Because people are accustomed to paying something for a certain price . . . The past four or five years, it worked out well, because we didn't adjust our prices down because of drywall. (Manufacturers' prices of drywall had fallen because of increased supply.) Drywall went down and we kept it. [Oh, when was this?] Drywall was cheap up until a year ago, and we kept the prices the same . . . [Your clients didn't object to that?] No. They don't really know."

7

The Pricing of Cement[1]

The cement industry provides evidence against the proposition that product differentiation causes downward price rigidity only indirectly, by creating market power that directly causes the rigidity. It is appropriate to think of the cement industry as an oligopoly that sells a nearly undifferentiated good. All cement producers sell almost the same product, and it is clear that cement companies have market power. There are few sellers in each market area, and cement companies tend to reduce output in times of slack demand with the intention of limiting price erosion. Only a small number of cement producers compete in most market areas, because cement is expensive to transport. Furthermore, cement mills are large and expensive to build, so that there are not a great many of them. Cement companies do compete on the basis of price, and prices do fall in times of slack demand, though prices are not as volatile as those of a commodity such as lumber. Price competition is not imposed by customers' requiring cement producers to bid for business.

7.1 Background

Respondents made it clear that different cement companies produce nearly identical products. The Vice President of Sales and Marketing for cement company C said:

> "The two biggest areas that you hear about are color and setting time, and different cements will have variations of both. But typically, for a dollar or a two dollar savings (per ton), there is not even a discussion . . . For the most part, there is enough cement compatibility . . . that you can have competition. There is no leverage."

Transportation costs of cement are high, especially by truck or rail, so that cement markets tend to be local. The Vice President of Sales for cement company A said:

> "It is a local product ... On lakes we can move it a long way ... In a landlocked market, Columbus, Ohio, pretty much you are limited to 100, 150 miles ... It is a transportation limited product. [Even when you ship it by rail?] Even when you ship it by rail ... It is a lot of rehandling with rail ... You have to pump it, which is horsepower ... It is basically a talcum powder and so you have to have the proper environmental bag houses and these kinds of things. So every time you pick it up and do something with it, it is very expensive. And the rail, you have to have environmentally correct loading of the car, horsepower to pump it to the top of the silos, and investment in the silos at a remote site."

In part because of high transportation costs, the degree of competition probably should be characterized as oligopolistic in most areas of the United States. The Vice President of Sales and Marketing for cement company C said:

> "When I last checked there are somewhere about 53, 54 different cement companies. [But in each region, you probably butt up against what?] ... In the Northeast it is more like six to eight different companies from the Mid-Atlantic to New England. In the Southeast, it is probably, it is only about four ... On the Mississippi River ... we are competing with probably a dozen different competitors ... Of those 53 companies, though, the top 10 control 50 plus percent of the market ... The service area around the cement plant is about 100 to 125 miles."

The main cement customers are ready mix companies. The Vice President of Sales for cement company B said:

> "Ready mix concrete buys 70 percent of the cement produced in the United States. So they are the big consumer."

The bagged cement used by masons is only a small part of the market. The Vice President of Sales and Marketing for cement company C said:

> "Only 3 percent of our national market is for masonry products."

The main cement customers tend to buy large quantities. The Vice Chairman of ready mix company C said:

"I guess on a busy day I get 25 or 30 trailer loads of cement."

Cement plants are expensive to build. The Vice President of Sales for cement company A said:

"A modern cement plant of any size is $200 a ton of (annual production) capacity and most of the plants today are million ton plants. So you are talking 200 million dollars."

The plants are run at full speed or not at all. The Vice President of Sales for cement company B said:

"The kiln is either running or it is not running. [You can't adjust the flow through it?] No."

The plants have significant startup and shutdown costs. The Vice President of Sales for cement company A said:

"To heat up a kiln is about five days, because you have got refractory brick in it. When you shut it down, you have to shut it down slowly. When you bring it up, you have to bring it up slowly, so you don't fracture the brick."

For all these reasons, cement companies hesitate before taking downtime. The Executive Vice President of cement company D said:

"You can't really slow down a big kiln . . . [Is it expensive to shut it down?] Sure. You have your fixed overhead. [Oh, you mean, because you still have the interest cost and everything.] Oh sure, the depreciation involved. [But you are not damaging the kilns so much.] No, but most people are going to do anything they can to prevent from shutting those things down. It is very difficult to spend 200 million dollars on a brand new plant and turn around and shut it down."

7.2 Pricing

Cement companies normally have informal understandings with customers about what the price will be until further notice. There are formal price commitments only for sales to customers who sell concrete to contractors for use on large projects where the concrete's cost is stated in the contractor's competitive bid. The Executive Vice President of cement company D said:

> "Usually we don't have a contract. Usually we have just a verbal commitment for preplanning purposes, how much we can expect them to buy in the coming year . . . Price is usually not outlined, unless you have a specific contract for a project, like a highway project or bridge or something in that magnitude. Usually there is a price you start with and as market conditions change and your price increases, you renegotiate the price."

Mills set an FOB[2] price for customers who pick up cement at the mill and a delivered price for cement delivered by the mill to the customer. FOB prices vary among customers because of volume discounts, discounts resulting from past competitive situations,[3] competition from other mills, and because of the need to equalize the delivered prices paid by different ready mix customers who serve the same market. The Executive Vice President of cement company D said:

> "You have to take into consideration if we are going to ship cement 150 miles from there and it is closer to a different mill, that FOB price for that customer is going to be different than for the guy in (a city close to cement company D's mill), because you are going to have to be competitive. So people evaluate their pricing on a delivered basis . . . Our price list is usually based on FOB our plant and then the transportation costs are added on to it . . . At least 80 percent of our business is picked up . . . Our FOB price . . . is published . . . We tell everybody our price . . . [It is the same for all buyers?] No. There is some volume discounts . . . [So that is part of the list?] Yeah. [You don't have special arrangements with some customers, because you had to meet a competitive situation?] . . . Oh, we have to be competitive . . . This is a very competitive business. People will change on you for 50 cents (a ton)."

As was just mentioned, mills announce FOB cement prices. It is not clear what these announcements mean, as they are sporadic and don't apply to all buyers. The Executive Vice President of cement company D said:

"We don't always announce what the exact FOB price of our product is. That is something that, you know, it varies. We may announce it every two years and then adjust a five-dollar increase from that. But we don't come out every time with an FOB price."

An important reason FOB prices may differ among customers is that the cost of transporting cement to different customers can differ, and yet all those who compete selling concrete in the same market should receive the same delivered price. The Vice President of Sales and Marketing for cement company C said:

"Pricing is invariably FOB . . . It is an FOB price our terminal or an FOB price our plant, and then they calculate what their costs are . . . So if you are picking up and you are ten miles away, I know your freight is $3, and I am picking up and I am 35 miles away and I know my freight is $9, then we will have different FOB prices, because we are competing against one another. But your freight plus cement and my freight plus cement are both $75 a ton, even though I have a lower cement price to account for the freight issue."

Equitable treatment of competing customers is important for good customer relations. The Vice President of Sales for cement company A said:

"Most of the time, if we have in a market two very large customers, as an example, and we give a price concession to one of those customers, we will generally go and give it to the other customer unsolicited, because if he ever finds out, he will have your ears and nose and head . . . The ready mix industry is consolidating the same way the cement industry is consolidating. The worst thing to happen is if you sell Joe and Bob at different prices and the high priced guy, Joe, acquires Bob's business and goes through his books . . . and finds out that Bob has been buying cement a dollar cheaper than he has been buying cement. I mean, there is hell to pay then. You have lost two customers then."

The need for equitable treatment can be modified by consideration of differences in the markets served by different customers and by the volume of their purchases. The Vice President of Sales for cement company B said:

"[You have to give the same price to all your customers who are competing with each other in (a city)?] Well, you don't have to. Basically you have got a ready mix industry that has its pricing, and we are a player there, and those folks you try to keep on the same playing field as best you can. They are not all getting the same price in the sense that you have one buyer that is owned by an Irish cement producing company that has 125 mixers and he has got 5 batch plants and he has some power to buy probably a little better than a person that has 13 mixers and has a little different customer base. He does not sell high-rise office buildings. He sells houses. And in those cases, you might have a difference in price, because one is in a different market size and filling a different customer base himself. [It is both because they are filling a different customer base and also because they have more buying power?] More buying power."

One respondent claimed he discouraged ready mix customers from taking advantage of volume discounts to reduce the prices they charged their own customers, because that could lower the market price for concrete and perhaps cement as well. The Vice President of Sales and Marketing for cement company C said:

"It is my understanding that if someone is buying significantly more volume than someone else, then you are allowed to give him a better price, because it allows you to operate your business more efficiently . . . What we have done, is that you go to the big customer, the big dog, the big volume, and you just tell them, 'Look, you have got a $2 a $3 price (advantage) on anyone in the market,' but usually that is all they need to know . . . Basically you are telling that guy, put that money in your pocket, don't build up market share by lowering your price, because then all you are doing, you will take the price per yard (of concrete) from $50 to $45, because you all compete . . . So the idea is to give the big dog a better price, sell that product and let him make more money and not disrupt the market."

Both buyers and sellers treat the prices individual ready mix customers pay for cement as confidential information. The Executive Vice President of cement company D said:

"[Do the customers find out usually what other customers are paying?] No. [They just see that the other customer is able to underbid them for work?] Yeah. That is exactly right . . . Most customers are very protective on their prices. They don't want the competition to know. Everybody thinks that they can attempt to try to get an advantage in the market. That is very difficult to do."

Despite the secrecy about pricing, everyone I spoke to in the cement industry believed that key decision makers were well informed. The Vice President of Sales for cement company A said:

"I assume there is three or four ready mixers here in town, and they pretty much know what is going on. People change jobs, so they know what the pricing is when they go to the new ready mixer . . . Cement salesmen call on all customers, and everybody always asks for a price, even if we are not selling them. So we give them a price and we don't get any business, so we assume they are buying better someplace else . . . Everybody in a market, whether it is Nashville or New Haven or Hartford or Memphis or Chicago pretty much knows what is going on . . . If their competitor gets a lot of work all of a sudden, they understand that there must be an element to the cost, which is allowing him to take all this work below a market price. And they start asking questions either to their friends in town or to the cement salesman or to the aggregate people and they pretty much figure out what everybody is paying for cement."

Cement producers announce price increases to customers in letters. The absolute size of increases is the same for all customers in a region and are added on to whatever price the customer currently pays. The Vice President of Sales for cement company A said:

"We just announced an increase, and the base, to some of the big customers, is probably lower than the base to some of the small customers . . . The base price is lower for the big customer, so he is getting a higher percentage increase . . . [Do you announce these region by region or across the whole country?] No, no. Region by region. [So it is different times.] Well, no. Generally the same time, but different prices for different markets. Basically what the market will bear kind of thing."

The increases are announced six months in advance, so that ready mix customers can make price commitments to their customers when bidding for work. The Vice President of Sales and Marketing for cement company C said:

> "[So this April increase is announced in October already?] Correct. Oh yeah, you give people six months notice. The whole idea is they are bidding jobs, so they know what they are dealing with."

Attempts to increase prices do not always succeed. The Vice President of Sales for cement company B said:

> "We had a price increase for $3 mailed out last September a year ago. We rescinded it. [Why did you do that?] It fell apart. [Nobody was following it?] Nobody was supporting it . . . One company started to go out and make deals, and it lost. I mean, it is a commodity."

High demand encourages price increases for obvious reasons. The Executive Vice President of cement company D said:

> "Right now, you are selling everything you can make. And somebody comes in and says, 'Hey, Joe just walked in and gave $2 a ton (price reduction).' You say, 'Well, do me a favor' (and buy from Joe)."

The cement industry regularly has periods of shortages. According to the four respondents who worked for cement producers, shortages provide an occasion to display loyalty to customers by allocating cement fairly and refraining from increasing prices quickly. The Executive Vice President of cement company D said:

> "We have had periods of spot shortages . . . We have allocated cement, and you allocate cement across the board on some formula that is fair to everybody, and that is when you test the customers, because you better be dealing in good faith, because they will remember you."

The Vice President of Sales for cement company B said:

> "[Does price go up, or is that a no no too, to raise price in a time of shortage?] Generally, you are a partnership with your customer, and if it is going to affect prices, it is usually next

The Pricing of Cement

year's. It doesn't affect them on Monday. [Because you have this commitment for a year?] You really do."

In contrast to price increases, price decreases go unannounced, though they can be part of a price war. The Vice President of Sales for cement company A said:

"[What about price decreases? Are they announced or do they just happen?] They just quietly happen . . . No letters . . . On the downside, there is erosion in the dark kind of thing . . . What generally happens is people see maybe demand decreasing in an area, so they develop a strategy that says we need to get some business and so they will go out and offer a price concession for business . . . to try to get their competitors' business . . . [There is no compunction about fear of price war?] Well, and then that is what happens. It breeds a thunderstorm. Then it breeds a category one hurricane. And then it gradually slips into a category five hurricane before it all settles down. It can be very hurtful."

Price decreases are sometimes brought about by competitive situations, and there are systematic procedures for dealing with these. The Vice President of Sales for cement company A said:

"Our policy is that before we can make a price concession, we need written proof. We need the offer from the other cement company . . . So an invoice."

The four cement producers I talked to were reluctant to admit they initiated competitive situations. The Vice President of Sales and Marketing for cement company C said:

"[So you are not ever initiating a price decrease?] The only time you do it, is when you have too much cement in the silo."

Nevertheless, demand decreases seem to give rise to price reductions and price wars, where one competitor may try to hurt another to teach it not to steal sales through price cutting. The Vice President of Sales for cement company B said:

"One cement company went in to grow his market share, took the price down (in a city) . . . He bought market share . . . He impacted one of our competitors, probably 30 percent of his volume . . . What happens sometimes is he goes to a customer in a disguise and whacks him to get his 30 percent out of their hide some place else, which makes nothing but problems . . . The revenge is not so much to get that tonnage as much as to tell that guy, 'You do this again. I am showing you there is no gain. There is pain. Okay?' That is the only way you can control it . . . [When demand is down . . . there are people who do this and so prices tend to fall?] Yeah, and in some cases I do it."

One of the rewards for having a good relationship with customers is that they give their suppliers the opportunity to respond to competitive situations. The Vice President of Sales and Marketing for cement company C said:

"One of the first things that affects our pricing is what I call 'last look,' and what that is . . . That is where a customer says to you, 'Mike, you have been selling me cement for X number of years, X amount of volume. Truman walked in, and I hate to say it, buddy, but he is $2 lower than you. Now I don't want to give it to him, but I am giving you last look.' . . . What do I do? If I have the product, I match the price . . . So I just took my 500,000 tons that is already sold out . . . I now lost $2 a ton or a million dollars a year and I did absolutely nothing, but because I had last look I accomplished something very important, which is I didn't lose any business . . . A competitor can go to my accounts and if I have a better relationship, I will get last look."

The appropriate response to a competitive situation may require more than matching of a price reduction and so may further decrease the market price. The Vice President of Sales for cement company A said:

"Look at the psychology of it, where you have lost a customer – somebody had cut the price $2 in a recession or in not boom times, and you have lost your customer. So the owner has already made a decision. He is going to change suppliers and he does that, and there are certain costs to him in doing that. He has got to change his mix design, because he has got another product now, because all products are slightly different . . . For you to go in and get the business back, you have got to basically compensate him for the costs he has incurred by going to the other guy plus some kind of sweetener to get him to love you again. So you probably are now cutting the price $3 . . . Then depending on how bad things are, maybe somebody will come back into him again after he has switched back to you."

7.3 Capacity Utilization

Cement producers sometimes react to a decline in cement demand by shutting plants down temporarily, since doing so supports prices. Such a move can have drawbacks. The support given to prices may benefit competitors more than the company taking downtime, and the shutdowns can hurt customers who depend on cement from the mills that have been shut down. A downtime strategy is most appropriate for a company that serves a region from several mills, so that after shutting down one mill it can continue to supply its customers and enjoy the benefit of having slowed price decline. The Vice President of Sales for cement company A said:

> "You could be the one to close down your plant for the good of the market . . . to support the price, and you would hope other people might follow . . . We have shut plants down totally to ride out the recession. Most people don't do that . . . You have a customer base that you have built up through the years and a loyalty, and if you shut a plant down, assuming that it is the only plant of yours that can service that market, then you are basically flushing the customer base away for someone else to prey on . . . We had four plants in (a state) and we shut one down, but we had three others to supply the market, and that worked out fine . . . You have let them (your customers) down, and the only way you are going to get them back when times get good is by price concessions, and that is not healthy either."

7.4 Price Behavior

The cement producers I talked to were impressed by the large swings in cement prices. The Vice President of Sales for cement company A said:

> "The business cycles that I am used to, going back through the years, from peak to trough the average drop in consumption of cement is about 25 percent. [And the drop in price is?] Considerably more than that. Up to 50 percent, say."

Figures 7.4.1[4] and 7.4.2[5] show histories of the U.S. producer price index and of the industrial production index for cement from January

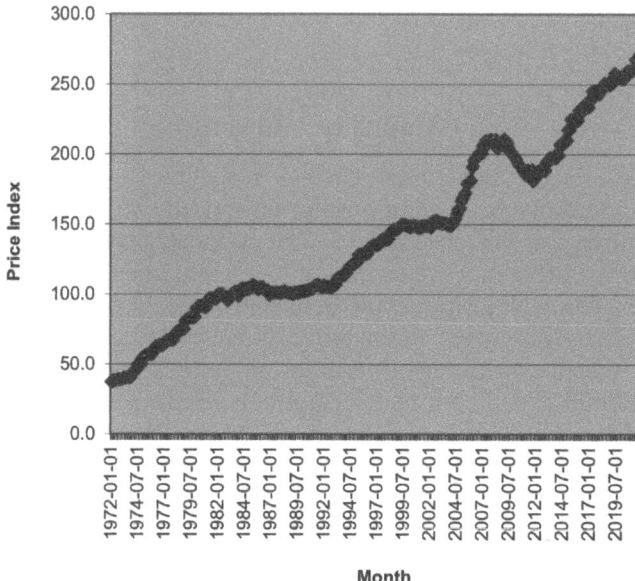

Figure 7.4.1 Producer Price Index for Cement, Monthly Data, Not Seasonally Adjusted, January 1972–December 2021

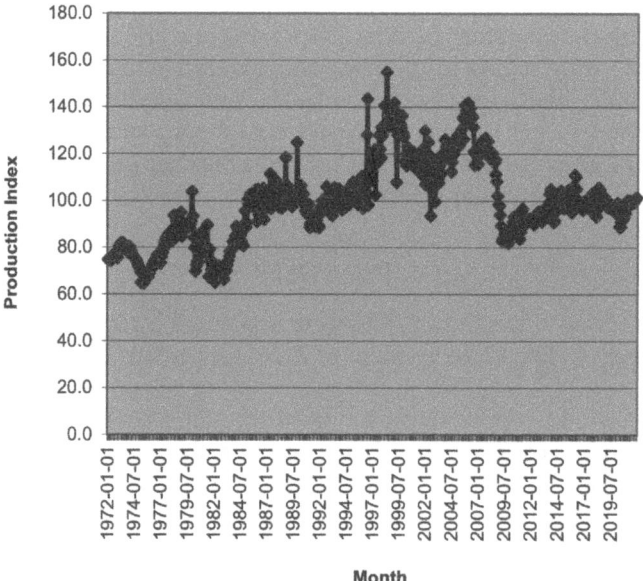

Figure 7.4.2 US Production Index of Cement, Monthly Data, Seasonally Adjusted, January 1972–December 2021

1972 through December 2021. The price index does sometimes fall, but does so slowly and does not seem to be as volatile as respondents said the prices are. Respondents may have described the behavior of local prices that were more volatile than the average national prices shown in Figure 7.4.1. Despite the difficulty individual cement plants have in adjusting output, the industry did reduce production during the recession starting in 2008.

8

The Pricing of Commodity Lumber, Plywood, and Oriented Strand Board[1]

The markets for commodity lumber, plywood, and oriented strand board have a reputation in the business community of being the most competitive of all industrial markets. Negotiated spot prices underlie almost all the industry's prices, and a product's long-term contract prices are normally indexed to a market-reporting firm's assessment of the product's spot prices. Negotiated spot prices are volatile and sometimes destabilized by price-inventory cycles.

Although there is a futures market for 2x4s on the Chicago Mercantile Exchange, prices are mainly created through dickering over spot prices. The Lumber Yard Sales Manager for building supply company B said:

> "People through the years have certainly gotten more in tune with shopping (now) that they have the ability with computers to look at different things, and they never had the ability to price lumber futures, although it is not really a determining factor. But they think it is . . . My sale prices are based on my costs, what we can buy the material for . . . A lot of it is just done by constant contact and feedback from different customers, different vendors . . . We negotiate with our vendors, and our customers negotiate with us. It is a daily thing."

I treat separately the two main steps in going from forests to retailers, namely, the provision of logs to sawmills and the sale through a supply chain of mill products to retailers.

8.1 The Market for Logs

Owners of forested land can be private individuals, lumber companies, state or federal government organizations, or investment groups called TIMOs (Timber Investment Management Organizations). Any of these can harvest trees themselves or sell to loggers the right to harvest selected trees during a specified period of time, a right called stumpage. The sale of stumpage or logs can be done through sealed bid auctions, open outcry auctions, negotiation, or by selling logs to whatever mill posts the highest offer prices for logs. Normally many logging companies compete for stumpage and many lumber companies and exporters compete for logs. Another source of logs is land clearers who prepare sites for construction projects. They are likely to sell logs cheaply to whomever can remove them quickly. Log prices fluctuate, sometimes dramatically and not necessarily in synchrony with lumber prices. Logs are somewhat perishable, which limits the ability of log storage to dampen fluctuations in log prices. Declines in log prices are restrained by the tendency of landowners to ride out price slumps by letting their trees grow while waiting for prices to recover. Logs are seldom sold under long-term contracts with fixed prices. Some buyers and sellers of logs have long-term relationships, however, and regularly negotiate the price of logs. A vice president of resources and manufacturing for western lumber company A said:

> "We are a producer of logs . . . We can contract with you for, say, 10,000 tons of logs. We deliver them to your mill at either a negotiated price or we could put an essentially an auction environment, where we say we have 10,000 tons of logs to be delivered. What would you pay us? And then the different mills would send us or call us with quotes on what they would pay . . . Or you could have it tied to an index. [Oh, they have indices for logs too?] They do, although it is pretty thin . . . Another way to sell logs . . . is to sell the stumpage, and what you do there is you are selling the rights for them to cut the timber off your land, and that could be a negotiated deal or it could be an auction environment as well . . . If we use douglas fir logs in Oregon, for example, they were selling for about $700 per thousand board feet at the peak . . . They dipped down to under $400 per thousand. A tremendous drop . . . which then caused a reduction in the volume of logs going to market, not just from the mills needing less, but from forest landowners just saying, 'At that price, I am not going to sell . . . It is a better investment just to sit on these logs . . . because you are getting growth on that timber, plus you get a price appreciation.'"

8.2 The Markets for Lumber, Plywood, and Oriented Strand Board

Earlier I discussed the pricing of specialized plywood that is highly differentiated and has fairly stable prices.[2] I now describe the pricing of commodity lumber, plywood, and oriented strand board.

A typical first step in the supply chain of commodity lumber, plywood, and oriented strand board is sales from mills to distributors, who buy and store large quantities. A typical second step is distributor sales to lumber retailers. Another route is sales through brokers, who normally arrange direct sales from mills to retailers by calling many mills and retailers to arrange deals. For instance, a mill with excess inventory might call a broker describing what it is eager to sell. The broker then calls retailers until it finds one willing to pay an acceptable price. Or a broker may initiate the process by calling mills until it finds one with an excess inventory that it is impatient to sell. The urgency of the retailer's need and the size of the mill's excess stock influence the price they agree on. Brokers exist, because mills' salespeople and retailers' buyers normally do not have time to do all the telephoning that brokers do. The President and Publisher for a lumber market-reporting company said:

> "You can go around Eugene (Oregon) and find two and three people offices that are lumber wholesalers, and they are kind of brokers ... They have a customer base and they have a supplier base and they are kind of the in between guys that handle the transaction. They are acting as a banker. They are doing the logistics in terms of transportation and so forth."

The President of the Building Products Division (the distributor) for a huge lumber company said:

> "We buy it and we either will sell it as direct shipments from a manufacturer to a customer and, in that case, we provide the connection between manufacturers and customers. [There is no warehousing?] No warehousing, and that is probably 30 percent of our business moves in that channel and 70 percent would go through – we bring it into a warehouse in large quantities, break it into smaller quantities, and ship to our customers ... We would find that generally one of our customers would call three distributors and then understand what their trade-offs are between availability, service, their perception of quality, and price

… When I want to buy lumber or plywood, I will go shop a number of mills, and then understand about availability … The bigger deal on price is availability. If you need it tomorrow, you are willing to pay more than if you need it any time in the next three weeks."

The President of a large lumber and plywood brokerage said:

"Our best customer is the retail lumber dealer where the owner does the buying. We can provide a real value add to him, because he does not have the time to shop all the mills that we cover for product. So when he calls us and asks us for a quote on a carload of plywood, he wouldn't have time to call those 15 mills to get prices and compare them and put blocks together to maximize his purchasing power. So we would do that for him."

8.3 The Use of Market Reports

One market-reporting firm creates the indices used in formula-based contracts for lumber, plywood, and oriented strand board. For lumber and sheathing, the key index number, called print, is that reported on Friday of the previous week. When a buyer and seller arrange the price for a spot sale, they normally quote the price as print plus or minus something. This is equivalent to quoting the spot price as a number, since lumber traders know what print is. A Vice President of Resources and Manufacturing for western lumber company A said:

"What typically happens is that a buyer somewhere will call us up and say, 'I need five units of 2x4s. I will offer you print,' and depending on where we are at, we could say, 'Yeah, we will take your offer of print,' or we are going to say, 'Nah. We don't think print is right. Things are tighter than that. We want print plus $10."

8.4 Capacity Utilization

This section contains evidence that the capacity utilization decisions of commodity manufacturers are consistent with their factories having marginal variable costs that remain constant or decline as output increases until it is near capacity. The evidence is that mills that produce commodity plywood, oriented strand board, and lumber tend to run at full capacity or to shut down. Shutting down often does not save much money, because a large share of the costs or running a mill are fixed. The President of the Building Products Division (the distributor) for a huge lumber company said:

> "Both in structural panels, plywood OSB combined, and lumber, there is significant excess capacity ... You still get the price runs. [Because they cannot change their output that fast?] Well, they tend to run full out. [Plywood mills do too?] Yeah. Or they tend to be shut down ... There is too much capacity to meet a steady demand, but there is not enough capacity to meet an inventory – [Hoarding.] Hoarding, yeah."[3]

The President of a large lumber and plywood brokerage said:

> "As we become more automated, it is harder to shut down, because your fixed costs become a bigger and bigger percentage of your costs. So if you shut the mill down and you only let two people go, well what is the point? I mean, we can go into OSB mills, oriented strand board mills, and it is uncanny. A production facility of 500,000 square feet making 10 boxcars a day of oriented strand board and there is one engineer on the line and there is two guys driving a forklift and a supervisor, and that is the plant. I suppose you have got a maintenance crew. [So it would only be worthwhile to shut down if the price goes below the materials cost.] Right."

The owner of northeastern lumber producer A said:

> "In 1981, nobody wanted to buy ... [So what happened? Did you cut back on production because of that?] No. I can't do that, because if you cut back production, then your unit production costs go right through the roof. [Because there are so many fixed costs.] Yeah."

Shut down decisions can depend on whether the mill is big enough that by reducing output it could cause the market prices of its products to rise. The Marketing Director for Dimension Lumber for western lumber company B said:

> "There is a lot of different mills ... It makes it very competitive, and people want to keep running to keep their costs down ... [So a lot of mills are shut down?] Yeah. [So you have not shut down

yours?] We finally did in September. We took a shift off. But up until last year, we were running full out three shifts . . . [Did you take account of the impact that that might have on the price of 2x4s?] Yeah. That is what we look at and hope to do, when we do it. [Because it supports the price?] It supports the price, yeah, and it did. It worked."

Some mills increase output when lumber prices fall, believing that a larger output makes it easier to remain solvent by reducing costs per unit. The owner of northeastern lumber producer C, which produces white pine lumber, said:

"One of the jokes, and it was a joke because it was half true in the lumber business, in the mill business, was when prices went down you had to make more lumber . . . The content was that you could just keep lowering your unit cost. That would be your best path to keep up with low prices. So when prices go down, make more lumber to drive your unit cost down and see if you can survive that way. [Does anybody actually do that?] Yeah. We have tried it quite a few times actually. It does not really work . . . We actually found . . . we could actually keep our unit costs at the same level with a third less production . . . It has given us a lot more control over maintaining stable prices. We just dialed back production."

The mill of the man just quoted is such a large producer of white pine lumber that the mill's output has an impact on its market price.

8.5 Price Behavior

All respondents in the lumber business said that industry prices are volatile. Although the general trend of prices moves in synchrony with the level of housing construction, prices have sharp short-term peaks and valleys, perhaps due to price-inventory cycles. This instability does not apply to all types of lumber. It applies to douglas fir and spruce, but not to white pine, which is a more specialized wood sold in smaller volume. The President of the Building Products Division (the distributor) for a huge lumber company said:

"For something like lumber or plywood, the price changes with each transaction . . . Right now we have – we could buy wood today and get it shipped this week. In a normal situation, you can buy wood and get it shipped in three weeks . . . If the market were to start moving upward, order files would start lengthening. As soon as order files start lengthening, mills – that is their signal to increase their price. Customers then believe prices are going up, so they start ordering and decide prices are going up, I had better lock in these old prices. The mill extends their order file. They raise their price. The customers get even more intent on building inventory . . . You create a shortage. It is not real, if the shortage is people want to put it in inventory, because they believe prices are going up . . . What we have to be careful of is not getting caught up in this dynamic . . . Get overstocked, because that obviously hits some point to where you hit a peak. When that peak hits, everybody decides, all the buyers decide prices are coming down. So they don't buy anything. They start liquidating their own inventory. Mills start cutting prices, because their order files are shrinking. Availability increases, convinces all the buyers that well why would I buy it if availability is good. I don't need to have it in inventory, and besides the price is falling. And so we just run through this cycle, and we run through that maybe three or four times a year. [Of what magnitude are the fluctuations from top to bottom?] From the bottom to the top, you are probably looking at 100 percent. [This is lumber and plywood?] Yeah."

The Vice President of Sales of northeastern lumber producer C said:

"[Do you get these spontaneous huge fluctuations in pricing, like with plywood and studs?] No. Eastern white pine and boards in general do not move like studs and plywood . . . (The price) tends to grow . . . What I consider a commodity is a roller coaster."

There follow graphs showing softwood lumber and plywood monthly price indices for the United States from January 1947 to March 2021. I also show weekly data for Southern pine 2x4s created by an industry market-reporting company. These graphs give some idea of the volatility of lumber and plywood prices. The volatility is not as extreme as respondents reported.[4,5,6]

Commodity Lumber, Plywood, and Oriented Strand Board 181

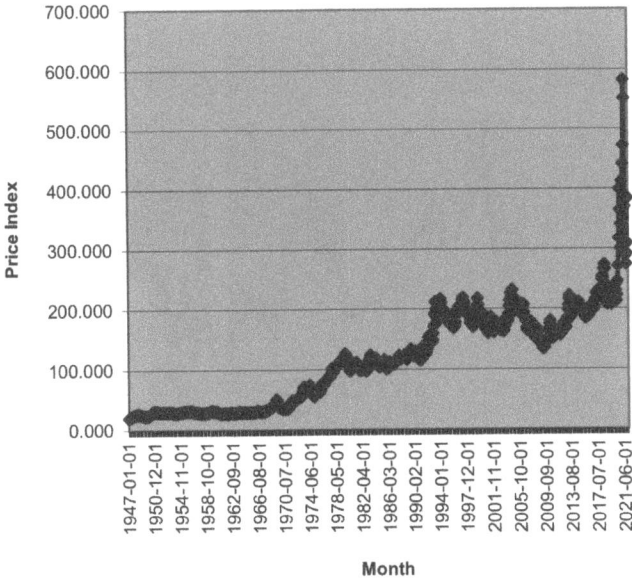

Figure 8.5.1 Producer Price Index for Softwood Lumber, Monthly Data, Not Seasonally Adjusted, January 1947–December 2021

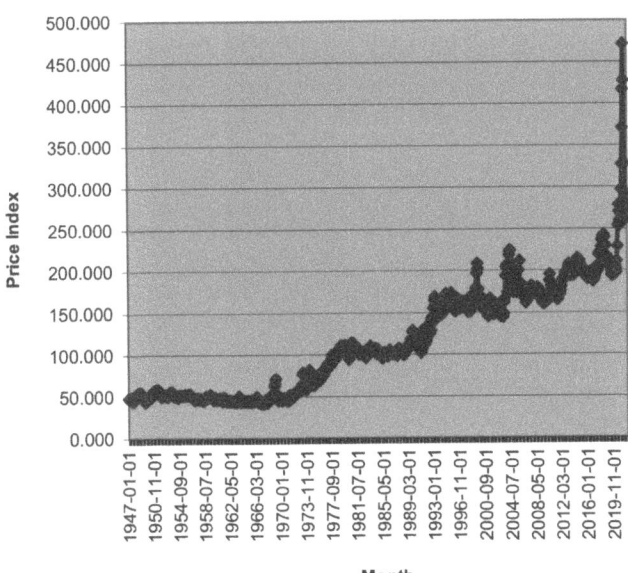

Figure 8.5.2 Producer Price Index for Plywood, Monthly Data, Not Seasonally Adjusted, January 1947–December 2021

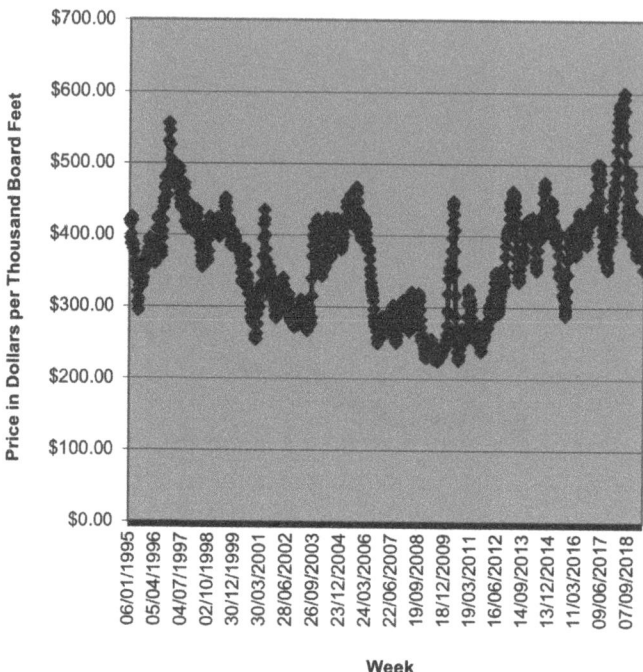

Figure 8.5.3 Prices of Southern Pine 2x4s in Dollars per Thousand Board Feet, Weekly Data, June 1995–May 2019

9

The Pricing of Midwestern Food and Feed Grains[1]

Buyers and sellers of grains quote prices either as dollar amounts, called flat prices, or as formula-based prices that are a futures price for the grain plus a differential. The differential is called a basis, where "basis" is a word for the difference between two prices. The formula-based prices are said to float. Prices of this sort are appropriate for commodities with volatile flat spot market prices that are highly correlated with a futures price for the same commodity. In the floating price, the basis is normally smaller and more stable than the futures price. Floating prices are useful when the price in a transaction is agreed to a significant amount of time before consummation of the transaction. In this situation, buyer and seller may believe that the floating price is more likely to be close to the market value of the commodity when it is delivered and paid for than would be any flat spot price chosen when the deal was arranged. Hence buyer and seller agree that the price the buyer pays is the floating price's value at the time of payment. Another advantage of floating prices is that they facilitate hedging, which in the context of futures trading means the use of transactions in futures to offset risk created by fluctuations in a commodity price.

9.1 Futures[2]

I present simplified explanations of grain futures and their use for hedging. A grain futures contract is an agreement to buy or sell a specific quantity of grain at a specific price, to be delivered or received at a specific location, in a specific future month, called the settlement month. A contract to buy is called a long contract and is a one-sided obligation in that it does not specify a particular seller from whom grain will be purchased. A contract to sell is called a short contract and is also a one-sided obligation in that it does not specify a particular buyer to whom grain will be sold. No money or grain changes hands until the settlement month. When a trader agrees to sell later, she or he has a short position and owns one or more short contracts. When a trader agrees to buy later, she or he has a long position and owns one or more long contracts.[3] A trader is said to buy when she or he makes an agreement to buy later and a trader is said to sell when she or he makes an agreement to sell later.

Trading in futures is organized by an exchange, which has rules that specify the quantity of grain to be purchased or sold by the holder of one contract. In addition, the rules require that the grain be of a standard quality and specify the delivery location and the settlement months. The purpose of the standardization is to encourage a large volume of trade in each futures contract. The advantage of a large volume is that it makes markets liquid, where a market is liquid if large transactions have little impact on the price.

Associated with every futures market is a clearinghouse firm, which is independent of the exchange. When traders buy or sell futures contracts, they pay the clearinghouse, or are paid by it, though the clearinghouse does not buy or sell grain but acts as an intermediary. Buyers and sellers of futures "contracts do not create financial obligations to one another, but, rather, to the clearinghouses."[4] The owner of a long contract who takes delivery of grain in a settlement month pays the clearinghouse and pays the price at which the owner originally purchased the long contract. The clearinghouse pays the owner of a short contract who delivers grain in a settlement month and pays the price at which the owner originally sold the short contract.

The sale of a grain futures contract may be thought of as accomplished in two to four stages. At stage one, the buyer B and the seller S or their agents agree on a price P, where, let us say, the units for the price are dollars per contract. At stage two, the clearinghouse creates a short contract and assigns it to S and creates a long contract and assigns it to B. The short contract obliges S to sell one contract of grain at the delivery location, during the settlement month, at the price P. The long contract obliges B to buy one contract of grain at the delivery location, during the settlement month, at the price P. More happens at stage three, if at stage one S held a long contract (for the same commodity, delivery month, and delivery location and on the same exchange) and purchased earlier at some price p. In this situation at the end of stage two, S holds a long contract that obliges S to buy one contract of grain at the price p and S holds a short contract that obliges S to sell one contract of grain at the price P. If S were to carry out both these obligations, S would deliver and receive one contract of grain and earn a profit of P − p dollars. The exchange rules handle this circumstance by requiring that at stage three the clearinghouse cancel the long and short contracts held by S and commit to paying S the profit P − p. Since S held a long contract at stage one, we see that the holder of a long contract gains from a sale, if the price of a futures contract has risen, that is, if P − p > 0. More happens at stage four, if at stage one B held a short contract (for the same commodity, delivery month, and delivery location and on the same exchange) sold earlier at some price q. If this is so, then at the end of stage three, B holds a long contract that obliges B to buy one contract of grain at price P and B holds a short contract that obliges B to sell one contract of grain at the price q. If B were to carry out both these obligations, B would both deliver and receive one contract of grain and would earn a profit of q − P. The exchange rules handle this situation by requiring that at stage four the clearinghouse cancel the short and long contracts held by B and commit to paying B the profit q − P. Since B sold a short contract before the purchase from S, we see that the holder of a short contract gains from a purchase, if the futures price of grain has fallen, that is, if q − P > 0.

Step two in the sale of a contract creates a short and a long contract, and this is the only way to create contracts. The only ways a short or long contract can be eliminated are by delivery of grain during the settlement month or by cancellation following a purchase or sale of a contract. In traders' jargon, contracts are settled, when they are eliminated, and contracts that have not been settled are open.

Trade in contracts for a given settlement month begins at a time determined by the exchange's rules. There is more than one exchange for grain futures, and the rules vary. Typical times are thirty months and three years before the settlement month. Trade in contracts for a given settlement month ends at a time determined by the exchange's rules. A typical time is seven business days before the end of the settlement month. All contracts that are open after the end of trading are settled by delivery. Traders with open short positions can initiate delivery during a settlement month but before the cessation of trading. Traders with open long positions can force delivery on their positions by retaining them until after trading ends. A trader who wants to deliver on an open short contract notifies the clearinghouse of her or his intention to deliver. The clearinghouse then matches the seller to a trader with an open long position using a system described in the exchange's rules.[5] The clearinghouse notifies the designated buyer that she or he will be called on to accept delivery. The buyer then prepares to accept delivery or immediately sells her or his long position, and the clearinghouse chooses another buyer. The seller delivers grain to a grain elevator at the delivery location specified by the exchange, receives a warehouse receipt for the grain, and gives the receipt to the clearinghouse. The clearinghouse transfers the receipt to the buyer, who can then use it to obtain grain from the elevator. The grain received is not likely to be the grain the seller delivered, but this does not matter because grain quality is standardized.

I show that a futures market for one settlement month clears at all times from the moment trading for the month begins until it ends. I also show that trading in futures for the settlement month is at all times a zero-sum game for the traders, provided traders pay no commissions to brokers and no fees to the clearinghouse, and provided all payments by the clearinghouse to traders and by traders to the clearinghouse are made simultaneously at some time after trading for the settlement month ends.[6] If these conditions do not apply, and if the interest rate on cash balances is positive, then trading may be neither a zero-sum nor a constant sum game for the traders, as is shown by an example in the Appendix. Stated more precisely, I show that if the conditions apply, then at all times from the moment trading in futures for the settlement month begins until trading ends, the following two balance equations hold: (1) the total number of open long contracts equals the total number of open short contracts and (2) the total amount of money the clearinghouse has committed to paying traders equals the total amount of money traders have committed to paying the clearinghouse. These assertions are well known,[7] though I have been unable to find formal proofs in the literature. A common informal argument is that trading in futures is a zero-sum game, because any change in a futures price has equal and opposite effects on the wealth of holders of long and short positions.[8] That this argument is incomplete is shown by the example in the Appendix. I give formal proofs to help readers new to the subject grasp how futures markets work.

Verification of the balance equations goes as follows. At the moment trading in futures for a settlement month begins, there are no open short or long contracts, and the traders and the clearinghouse have not made any payment commitments. Therefore both balance equations apply at that time. Thereafter, changes affecting the balance equations occur only when contracts are bought and sold, or when a seller and buyer deliver and take delivery on a contract.

Consider the changes affecting contracts and payments that occur during the sale of one contract by trader S to trader B. At stage one, there are no changes. At stage two, the clearinghouse creates two contracts with the same price P, an open short contract for trader S and an open long contract for trader B. Hence, at the end of stage two the total numbers of open short and long contracts are equal, if they were equal before stage two. During stage two, the clearinghouse commits to paying P dollars to S on S's newly created open short contract, and B commits to paying P dollars to the clearinghouse on B's newly created open long contract. Hence, there is no change during stage two in the difference between the total payment commitments by the clearinghouse to traders and the total payment commitments by traders to the clearinghouse. At stage three, S's newly created open short contract cancels his or her open long contract for the purchase of one contract of grain at a price p. Hence, the total numbers of open short and long contracts remain equal at the end of that stage, if they were equal at the beginning of stage three. Because of the cancellation, the clearinghouse is no longer committed to paying P dollars to S and S is no longer committed to paying p dollars to the clearinghouse. The clearinghouse commits to paying $P - p$ dollars in profits to S. Hence at stage three, there is no change in the net amount the clearinghouse has committed to paying traders. The same arguments apply to stage four. Therefore if the balance equations were true before the sale of a contract, they are true after its sale.

Consider what happens when traders deliver on and take delivery of a single open short contract. Delivery on one contract eliminates one open short contract and one open long contract. Hence, delivery does not change the difference between the number of open short and open long contracts. Therefore, if the number of open short contracts equaled the number of open long contracts before delivery, the numbers of open short and long contracts remain equal after delivery. Suppose that the short contract eliminated by delivery was a committment to sell at a price P per contract, and suppose that the long contract eliminated by delivery was a committment to buy at a price p per contract. Then, the clearinghouse was committed to paying the seller the amount P before delivery, and continues after delivery to be committed to paying the seller that amount, until all payments are made after trading ends. Similarly, the buyer was committed to paying the clearinghouse p before delivery, and continues afterwards to be committed to paying the clearinghouse that amount until trading ends and payments are made. Hence, delivery has no effect on the total amount owed by the clearinghouse to traders or the total amount owed by traders to the clearinghouse. Therefore, if before delivery, the clearinghouse owed as much to traders as traders owed to the clearinghouse, then the same is true after delivery.

In summary, if the two balance equations held before a contract's sale or before delivery on a contract, the equations hold afterwards. Since these equations applied when trading for the settlement month began, they apply at all times until trading for the settlement month ceases and payments are made. By the second balance equation, when payments are made, the total amount paid by the clearinghouse to traders equals the total amount paid by traders to the clearinghouse. Hence, the total of all the changes in wealth of the traders is zero, so that trading in contracts for one settlement month is a zero-sum game for traders.

During the settlement month and before the end of trading in futures contracts for that month, a long contract purchased at price p is a nearly perfect substitute for a spot purchase made during this period of one contract of grain at the flat price p and delivered at the exchange's delivery location. This is so, because the flat spot price of grain at a location is the price for immediate delivery. Hence the flat spot price of grain delivered at the location specified by the exchange should converge to the futures price for that location as the date of the spot transaction approaches the exchange's settlement month, and the two prices should be nearly equal during the settlement month before trading ends.

Another way to grasp the reason for the convergence just described is to imagine that during the settlement month, and before futures trading for that month ends, the flat spot price of the grain at the delivery location exceeds the futures price. Then, an investor can make a profit during the settlement month by buying futures contracts for the settlement month, taking or forcing delivery on the futures, and immediately selling the delivered grain on the spot market. Similarly, if the flat spot price at the delivery location is less than the futures price during the settlement month and before trading ends, an investor can make money by selling futures and using grain purchased on the spot market at the flat price to deliver on the futures contracts sold. These operations are forms of arbitrage and should make the spot price during the settlement month nearly equal the futures price, until trading in the futures contracts ends.

In practice, convergence does not always occur, and the possibility of non-convergence is sometimes referred to as basis risk. Near convergence normally does occur, however. If flat spot market prices reflect the supply of and demand for grain by those who produce and use it, then convergence connects futures prices, which are financial prices, to prices generated by the economy's real side.

Important bits of terminology are that the next settlement month for futures contracts is called the prompt month and the futures for the prompt month is called the nearby futures. Another bit of terminology is a futures contract's settlement price for a day. This is roughly the price at which the last trade of the day was made. Each exchange has its own rules for determining this price. When I visited the Kansas City wheat market in 2009, the settlement price was the weighted average of the prices of all the trades that took place in the last 30 seconds of trading before the market closed at 1:15 pm.

Grain traders speak of the cash price or spot price of a grain at a particular time and location as equal to the floating price d + q, where the differential d is the basis and q is the settlement futures price of the previous business day for grain to be delivered in the prompt month to the futures exchange. The units are cents per bushel. In traders' jargon, the basis d is said to be d over the sell, or –d under the sell if d is negative.

In the expression d + q for the cash price, the futures price q is for a contract to be delivered in a certain month and at a location specified by a futures exchange. A spot sale's delivery date and location need not be the same as those specified by the exchange. Hence the basis d depends on the delivery date and location specified in the spot transaction with price d + q. If the futures price converges to the spot during the settlement month, then the basis d is near zero if the spot price is for delivery in the same month and at the same location as those of the futures contract with price q. Delivery date and location influence the basis, because it is the difference between the value of the grain at the date and location specified in the spot contract and the value of the grain in the month and at the location specified in a futures contract. For this reason, abundance of a grain in a geographic area is likely to lower the grain's basis in that area. The basis d could depend on the quality of the grain purchased, though I have never heard about a specific instance of this dependence. Buyers and sellers of grain may negotiate the basis d, though large buyers and sellers of grain with facilities for handling and storing it normally choose and post their own bases, and adjust them to achieve desired levels of grain purchases or sales. Even large buyers and sellers who post bases may negotiate bases for exceptionally large transactions. Basis selection is constrained by market forces, since a basis is the difference between two market prices.

One of the main functions of futures contracts is to serve as a vehicle for hedging. By focusing on simple examples, it is easy to grasp the nature of hedging and the importance to it of convergence of futures prices to settlement month spot prices.

Suppose you are a wheat merchant with a grain elevator. It is harvest time in August, and you buy wheat from local farmers at the current spot price with the intention of selling it to flourmills in December, which we assume is a settlement month for the wheat futures market. Since the flourmills must be competitive, in December they will not pay more than the then current spot price, which is p cents per bushel.

The price p is not known in August and, because the mills are risk averse, they will not agree in August to a price to be paid in December, unless it is ridiculously low. In August, the December futures price of wheat is P cents per bushel, and given the August spot prices of wheat you know that you could make a good profit if you bought wheat in August at August spot prices, and sold it in December at the price P. Since the flourmills refuse to commit to buying wheat in December at the price P, you sell for the price P per bushel a quantity of December wheat futures equal to the quantity of wheat you accumulate in August. If we assume perfect convergence, then the price in December of the December futures contract will equal the December spot price p. In December, you buy back at the price p the December futures contracts you have sold, so that your profit from transactions in futures is $P - p$ per bushel. This profit is negative if p exceeds P but, since you sell the wheat on the December spot market at the price p, your total revenue per bushel is $P - p + p = P$. This level is profitable, given the prices you paid for wheat in August. By selling December wheat futures, you have in effect fixed the December price you receive for wheat to be P. This is a hypothetical example of what is called a short hedge or a selling hedge.

I describe an example of a long or buying hedge. Suppose you operate a flourmill, it is August, and you must arrange a supply of wheat for the month of December, to be converted to flour in that month, and sold to bakers for making Christmas cakes. The bakers must prepare advertising for their cakes well in advance, and so need to decide in August on the December prices for the cakes. Hence, the bakers want the flourmills that supply them to give them – in August – firm prices for the flour the bakers will buy in December. In order for the mills to offer such prices, they must know what wheat will cost them in December. Suppose that the price in August of a December futures contract for wheat is P cents per bushel. Let the December spot price of wheat be p cents per bushel, where the price p is not known in August. A flourmill can guarantee in August that it will pay P cents per bushel for wheat in December by proceeding as follows. In August, it buys December futures contracts for the amount of wheat it will need in December, and pays P cents per bushel. It sells these contracts in December at the then current futures price. If we assume perfect convergence, the current futures price equals the current spot price of p cents per bushel. In December, the mill buys the wheat it needs on the spot market at the spot price p. The mill's total cost per bushel is $P - p + p = P$ cents. In August, it has fixed its cost of wheat purchased in December to be P cents per bushel.

Often, spot grain buyers and sellers hedge their positions before trading. Sellers sell nearby futures to offset the price risk on their grain holdings, and buyers buy nearby futures to hedge the price risk on anticipated purchases. When a fully hedged buyer buys from a fully hedged seller, the buyer and seller agree on a basis and the futures exchange cancels the futures positions of the two sides at the same current futures price, in a special transaction called an ex-pit transaction. Each side then pays for its loss or is paid its profit from the cancellation of its futures position, and the buyer pays the seller for the grain at a price equal to the basis, plus the futures price at which the futures exchange canceled the buyer's and seller's futures positions. Informally, the transaction is called swapping futures. More formally, the transaction is called an exchange for physicals, or an EFP.

Not all trading in futures contracts is done for hedging, since speculators also buy and sell futures. Assume that all trades in futures are done either for speculation or hedging. Since the second balance equation implies that at all times the total profit from all trades that have been made is zero, it follows that at all times the total profit from all trades that have been made for speculation is equal and opposite in sign to the total profit from all trades that have been made for hedging. In this sense, the futures market may be viewed as a mechanism for transferring price risk from hedgers to speculators.

Speculators play an important role in futures markets. For instance, their expectations about flat spot prices of a grain in a contract's settlement month help connect futures prices to future flat spot market prices, and hence to the future real side of the economy. If speculators count on convergence, then they believe that the futures price and flat spot price of a grain at the futures exchange delivery location will be nearly equal in the settlement month. If, at a time prior to the settlement month, the futures price is below the flat spot price speculators expect in the settlement month, then speculators expect the futures price to rise, and so will buy futures contracts, increasing their price. Similarly, if the futures price exceeds the expected flat spot price in the settlement month, then speculators will sell futures contracts, reducing their price.

It is tempting to assume that trade in futures contracts is equivalent to forward trading in the underlying commodity, where forward trading is the sale and purchase of future output by producers and end users. Futures markets can be used in this way. For instance, farmers can sell their expected future wheat crop as futures, and millers can buy as futures the wheat they expect to use to produce flour. In reality, however, only a part of future demands and supplies are expressed on futures markets. Farmers are said to be reluctant to sell their entire expected grain crops in advance on futures markets, though some do sell part of their crops forward. Millers do hedge by buying wheat futures contracts, but normally only when filling firm orders for flour. Hence, even if the use of futures markets in forward trading fully determines futures prices, there is no guarantee that futures prices are close to what they would be if end users and producers fully expressed forward demands and supplies on futures markets.

One of the uses of hedging is to protect the value of stored grain. Buyers of large quantities of grain, who intend to store and sell it later, normally immediately sell futures contracts for roughly the quantity of grain they purchased. They then buy the contracts back when selling the grain. These transactions are profitable, because the person who stores the grain charges a fee for storing and caring for it, or because the person can do something with the grain that yields a profit. In this sense, the ultimate goal of protecting the stored grain's value is to protect a profit margin. The President and CEO of price consulting company A said:

> "I think hedging is a less than full answer, mainly because it is not about locking in an input price. It is about achieving a margin. And unless you can simultaneously lock in an output price and have some control over that relative to the input price, all you have done with hedging is gone from one form of risk to a new form of risk, and most firms truly don't understand that."

Floating prices exist for most commodities with futures markets, and a natural question is – Why? One benefit of floating prices is that they make it easy to calculate hedging strategies. This advantage encourages people to participate in hedging, and increased participation increases the liquidity of futures contracts. The interview quoted next was about petroleum pricing. A Managing Director of New York investment bank B said:

> "[One of the major questions is why you have floating prices.] . . . So the reason for all these floating prices, it is a practical issue. It separates out the actual selling of the physical from the hedging . . . It means that the hedging contracts can be financial

contracts (i.e. futures contracts). Financial contracts have much more liquidity than physical contracts, and the reason for that is almost anyone can participate in something financially. You need a computer. To do something physically, you need a storage facility or you need to be able to do something with that oil."

In describing futures trading, I have omitted a great deal of detail, including margin requirements, and fees associated with futures trading. These expenses do not, I believe, have much effect on the economic role of futures. I have neglected an important point, however. Hedging can offset price risk, but not risk due to variation in the quantity sold, purchased, or stored. For instance, futures trading cannot offset the risk to a spot buyer that the spot seller fails to deliver all the promised quantity of grain. For this reason, grain business deals that are to be hedged usually specify precise quantities of grain, and penalties for violation of the quantity requirements.

9.2 Grain Pricing

The main food and feed grains I learned about in Kansas, where I did most of the interviews on grain pricing, are wheat, corn, soybeans, and milo, which is a kind of grain sorghum. The grain traders discussed here are farmers, farmer cooperatives, grain brokers, commercial grain companies, grain end users, and terminals. The farmers I interviewed had large farms.

Cooperatives are farmer owned businesses, where a member's share of the profits depends on the amount of business she or he does with the cooperative. Grain cooperatives own elevators, where they store and care for grain. Members can store their grain at their cooperative in exchange for a fee of roughly a mill a day per bushel. A cooperative keeps track of how much grain each farmer stores in its elevators, but does not keep grain from different farmers separate. Farmers must pay a significant in-and-out fee for removing grain from storage, unless it is for a sale arranged by the cooperative. The cooperative posts a price for each kind of grain it trades and is always ready to purchase a member's grain at the posted price. The cooperative also helps members merchandise their grain, acting as advisor and broker and arranging or providing transport of the grain. The cooperative provides hedging services to members and sells them technical advice and farm supplies.

Grain brokerages do more than act as brokers. They buy and sell grain and transport it in trucks. A broker's role is to have contacts with people who have grain and with people who need it and to be able to arrange transport quickly. Like cooperatives, they provide marketing services to farmers, and some own elevators. There are elevators scattered through the countryside and owned by cooperatives, grain brokerages, and commercial grain companies. These are called country elevators and are convenient for farmers who do not have on farm storage.

Grain end users are companies that export grain or transform it into other products. Ones I have heard the most about were flourmills, soybean crushing plants, feed mills, feedlots, large dairy farms, ethanol plants, biodiesel plants, and a dog food factory that used corn.

A terminal is a collection of closely spaced grain elevators situated next to a railroad line. Terminals are capable of loading a hundred-car train with grain. The delivery points for grain futures exchanges are terminals.

9.2.1 Sale Prices of Grain

The four grains considered in this chapter have futures markets in Chicago, Minneapolis, and Kansas City, Kansas. I asked whomever I could what determines futures prices, and the following answer is typical. A Vice President of a grain-trading firm said:

> "Basically the price is determined by anyone who has got an interest in that market (the Kansas City wheat market) ... They are all voting with their dollars as to what they think that stuff is worth ... So to say who determines the prices, nobody in particular but everybody in general ... At the end, the fundamentals of supply and demand, in my opinion, always are the final determinant ... But in the meantime, there is a lot of things that go on from psychology to emotion ... that will tend to skew it too hard in one direction or another."

In the expression $d + q$ of the cash price of a grain, the basis d is normally small relative to the futures price q. A Manager of soybean crushing plants said:

> "The Chicago Board of Trade price is, say, $12 a bushel, and our basis will be, say, anywhere from 50¢ (to minus 50¢) ... In relevance to the overall price of the soybean, the basis is not a large component of that."

Helmuth (1977) provides statistical evidence of the relative size of the basis. In his Table 1, he gives the average absolute value of the basis for winter wheat at Kansas City as a percent of the average cash price for the months from July 1970 to June 1975. The average of the 60 percentages he calculates is 3.75 percent.

At the end of every business day, most of the large grain businesses post prices at which they will purchase grains during the following business day, where the purchase prices are for grain delivered to the bid poster's plant or elevator. Those who post prices include cooperatives, terminals, country elevators, and end users, such as flourmills, ethanol plants, and soybean crushing plants. Those who post bids announce a basis and a cash price. A cooperative in choosing a posted price and basis collects bids for its grain from its customers, such as end users and terminals. It subtracts from each of these the cost per bushel of transporting the grain from its elevator to the bidder and a margin for the cooperative's services. Using this information on the value of its grain, the cooperative then makes a judgment as to what its basis should be. Normally the cooperative increases its basis if it is not attracting enough grain and reduces it in the contrary case. In making its calculations, the cooperative takes into account that it has to compete for grain with, for instance, futures exchanges, country elevators, terminals, and end users. All the entities posting bids make similar calculations. Any of these entities might pay slightly more than its posted bid for large quantities. Such elevated prices are not posted but are negotiated. A Location Manager for Midwestern agricultural cooperative and grain elevator A said:

> "Basically what we do, we have several end users, larger grain companies that we have done business with for years, and we get bids from them everyday and we will record those and then we have to subtract what we want for margins and we usually work on 20 cents a bushel. If it is a product we are going to have to deliver, we take our freight costs off . . . That is our daily bid . . . to the farmers that we post everyday."

Since grain flows to an elevator from nearby farms and elevators, those choosing posted bids for grain may explore the local market by contacting farmers and nearby elevators and soliciting offers of grain. A Manager of soybean crushing plants said:

> "What we will do is we will also call around and look at the local supply, if there are farmer customers or our commercial elevator customers, the country elevators around the area, and we will ask them to propose an offer, so we have a bid offer situation

... We are bidding everybody, and then we are calling people to get offers, if they have soybeans ... And they call us. So we develop pretty close relationships with our supply base, both on the commercial side and on the producer side."

9.2.2 Hedging by Elevator Owners

A standard practice of companies with grain elevators is to hedge the grain they own. This they do by selling futures contracts for the prompt month for a quantity close to the number of bushels they own. Because elevators have short futures positions and because the price of the nearby futures contract moves in tandem with the cash price, if the cash price falls, the company gains approximately as much money on its short futures position as it loses on the value of the physical bushels it owns. As an elevator sells grain, it buys futures contracts it had previously sold to hedge the grain that has disappeared from its holdings. Elevator owners hedge their grain holdings, because they are in business to earn a profit by providing storage services rather than to speculate.[9]

Because grain futures markets are volatile, hedging is important. A Manager of soybean crushing plants said:

> "What we will do is the minute that we buy soybeans in a hedgeable quantity, we will sell a futures contract on the Chicago Board of Trade to protect ourselves from any movement in the futures price. [In units of a thousand bushels?] 5,000 bushels ... The volatility in the market makes execution of our hedging even more important. You can lose a lot of money if you make a mistake."

9.2.3 Brokers

Grain brokers play an important role in arranging movement of grain from those who possess it to those who need it. The owner of a cash grain-trading firm (grain brokerage) said:

> "Basically our niche in the market is we are small time, even though we do a lot. The guy that his train cars didn't show because of a rail derailment or engine shortages or something and he has got to make dog food tomorrow and he needs 20 loads of corn, and the railroads tell him it ain't going to be there till Friday. So he is suddenly in the market for corn today, and they call us. Then it is our job to go and find where he is at and where

is the closest corn to him and the freight lines and bid it into him. But he wants it tomorrow."

Some farmers market their grain through brokers. Brokers charge roughly the same fees that cooperatives do. The owner of a Midwestern grain farm A said:

"We sell through brokers generally, grain brokers . . . Grain brokers work for 3 to 4.5, 3, 4, 5 cents (per bushel) and up . . . They are basically, what would you say, accumulating or commingling – I mean, they are gathering a volume of grain in from a lot of different directions and then they go out to the market."

Farmers feel free to bargain with brokers and make them compete with each other. Owner 1 of Midwestern grain farm B said:

"We actually go through brokers . . . There is a deal through one of the brokers. He supplies a dog food plant with corn, and there is times that they won't get a trainload in on time and he will call me up and say, 'I need a load now. I have got a truck sitting in Wichita. I will have him up there in 30 minutes. I need it.' And let's say I was getting $3.50 for the last two loads of corn, I can sometimes tell him, 'Hey, let's make this one $3.65.'"

9.2.4 Farmers' Marketing of Grain

An important decision for farmers when considering how to market their harvest is whether to invest in farm grain storage. Grain stored on the farm can be sold without any time pressure from storage fees, and without any penalty from in-and-out fees for withdrawing grain from storage.

Another important decision that affects farmers' economic behavior is whether to participate in the federal government's subsidized crop insurance program. Most farmers participate. The federal crop insurance program allows farmers to insure crops up to what is termed the average proven yield, which is roughly the average crop in the previous five years. The federal subsidy of the insurance premium diminishes rapidly as the insured crop level increases beyond 75 percent of the average proven yield. Consequently few farmers insure more than 75 percent of their average proven yield.

A way for farmers to protect their revenues is to sell part of their expected crop forward, where sometimes the sale is arranged even before the crop is planted. Such sales are seldom made on a futures market, but are made to cooperatives, grain brokers, and grain merchandisers. Since farmers who cannot deliver the quantity agreed on must buy and deliver the missing quantity, farmers usually agree to deliver only quantities guaranteed by the federal crop insurance program. Typically farmers who sell forward sell 75 percent of their average proven yield. In setting the forward price, the buyer fixes a basis and the farmer has a set period of time in which to take the futures price for the grain. After the farmer takes the futures price, the price is the fixed basis plus the futures price taken. The buyer bears the risk of the fixed basis and compensates for that risk by diminishing what she or he pays the farmer. The buyer can offset the risk from fluctuations in the futures part of the price by buying futures contracts before the farmer takes the futures price and selling futures contracts after the farmer takes the futures price. Because forward sales of grain are normally hedged on the futures market, the sales are for precisely specified quantities of grain. Sales of futures contracts that hedge forward contracts with farmers transfer the farmers' forward supply to the futures market.

According to people at the two farmer cooperatives where I interviewed, it can be difficult to persuade farmers to sell grain forward. They are often suspicious of futures contracts and tend to be overly optimistic about future grain prices. Of the five grain farmers I talked to, two refused to sell forward. A Location Manager for a Midwestern agricultural cooperative and grain elevator A said:

> "[Do you make contracts with farmers?] We will. We don't do it too much. Farmers are – they don't really understand a lot of things like that, and commodities markets kind of scare them, because they hear of people losing so much money on them and stuff. Even cash contracts, they back off of those, because they want to be sure they are going to raise the grain. They don't want to commit to sell us grain at a flat rate."

A cattle farmer who also raised grain expressed farmers' attitude toward selling grain. The owner of a cattle farm[10] said:

> "As far as grain, we don't do a good job of marketing our grains. I don't know why. Because farmers are too much optimists, and we never did do much with forward pricing of our product. We would say, 'Well, the good Lord will send us some rain. We will always have a crop. Let's sell half of it, when the Board of Trade

gets up high.' . . . When we gathered the crop in, we would take it and put it in the bin or put it in our bins here or take it to the elevator and say, 'Well, let's keep it a little while. It will surely get higher than it is now. It is harvest time' (when grain prices tend to be low). Then you start selling some you need to pay this and pay that."

Helmuth (1977) provides statistical evidence of grain farmers' aversion to forward sales and to trading in futures, though his information may be outdated. According to his Table 13, about 10 percent of grain farmers in the United States sold grain crops forward in 1976. According to his Table 6, less than ten percent of U.S. farmers bought or sold futures in 1976, even in the main grain growing regions of the country.

Farmers' reluctance to use futures markets makes it somewhat difficult for grain traders to deal with them. If farmers are not hedged, their grain trading decisions tend to be more sensitive to futures price gyrations than are the decisions of professional grain traders. Professionals fully hedge their positions, and fully hedged traders should be indifferent to the grain's futures price when deciding when to sell. The owner of a cash grain-trading firm said:

"They (farmers) are kind of a pain to deal with. That is another story, but they are a different breed, the farmer. So that is why I deal with very few of them, because it is so much easier to deal with an elevator professional, who trades grain and has got it hedged. The farmer will be calling, 'Hey, I want to sell grain. I want to sell grain.' 'Well, the market is not going up, so what do you want?' Well, the day the market heads up to what you want – what he wanted – you call him to buy the grain. It is, 'Well, the market is going up. I don't want to sell now.' . . . The professional guy, the elevator guy has hedged it to the market, because they are required to lock in a hedge . . . They are required to hedge everything . . . So they are a more willing seller."

A Location Manager for Midwestern agricultural cooperative and grain elevator A said:

"[And these end users, are they hedging too?] Yeah. They will usually hedge on the other side, lock in their buy price. So when I sell to them, for example, and I like those because it is easy. You know what your margin is going to be – I will have futures on one side and I will have futures on the other and I say, 'Okay, I am going to sell to you 20 (cents) over' – the basis will be 20 over the sell. We just swap futures. So it doesn't matter from the time I talk to them and call my broker that the market goes down a dime or up a dime. It doesn't matter, because we have set the price we are going to swap at. And if it is a truck broker that doesn't hedge, he will call me and I will sell him 5,000 bushels. 'Okay, here is a price.' I pick up the phone. I have got to wait for that order to fill and I may make 21 cents. I may make 18 cents. [Because the price can change.] Can change. When you are exchanging futures with a large end user, then that risk is gone, because you set the price."

In order to give an idea of how hedging is used, I present two examples explained to me by respondents who worked for manufacturers of food products. The examples illustrate the point made earlier that the main purpose of hedging is to protect profit margins.

9.2.5 Pricing of Flour and Hedging by Flourmills and Bakeries[11]

Flourmills transform wheat into flour and millfeed or midds, which is mostly bran and is used to feed animals. Most flour is sold to baking companies, since the retail demand for flour is small in comparison with that of bakers. A mill uses about 133 pounds of wheat to produce 100 pounds of flour, and the rest is the byproduct midds that generally goes to the feed mill that bids the most for it. The price of flour is the cost of wheat used to produce it minus the value of the midds produced plus a processing margin of 50¢ to $1 per hundred-weight of wheat. The processing margin varies with the competitive environment where the mill is located and depends on the season. The price of bulk flour is $200 to $250 per ton and the price of midds is roughly $70 per ton. A baker needing flour is likely to call four or five mills to get prices, so that each mill has to be competitive everyday with its price. The mill typically has prices for the next month, three months, six months, and year, because customers often buy forward. Because the price of wheat can fluctuate dramatically, the forward prices derive from futures prices of wheat plus the wheat basis plus transport costs. Consider three contrasting cases.

In the first case, a flourmill agrees in July to sell a specified quantity of flour to a baker in the following December. The sequence of events is that the baker agrees in July to buy flour in December at a price fixed in July but to be paid in December and then in December the mill acquires the wheat and produces the flour. The price of the flour is based on the formula described verbally in the previous paragraph, where the price of wheat is the price in July of December wheat futures plus an agreed on basis for December wheat, where both the basis and the futures price are payable in December. The risk to the mill is that the price of wheat rises before the mill acquires the wheat in December. The mill hedges this risk in July by buying December futures contracts for the amount of wheat needed to produce the amount of flour the baker ordered. In this example, the mill reacts to the baker's order by buying wheat futures, futures that it sells as it buys wheat.

In the second case, the flourmill does not know exactly when the baker is going to buy the flour it orders and the baker is not obliged to take delivery. The baker places its order in July but does not specify when in August through December it will take delivery. The mill then buys and stores wheat in July to have it on hand to be turned into flour when the baker asks for it. The mill's risk is that the price of wheat falls and the mill is undersold by competitors who bought wheat later than the mill did. The mill can hedge this risk by immediately selling futures contracts for the quantity of wheat it bought in July with the settlement month of the futures sold being the prompt month. Every time a settlement month arrives, the mill buys back the futures it sold and sells new ones for the subsequent prompt month. If the mill hedges its stock of wheat in this way, the net cost of the stored wheat to the mill always equals the current cash price of wheat minus any basis gain. The price the mill charges when the baker requests flour is derived from the net cost of the wheat and the price of mill feed when the mill delivers flour to the baker, in the manner described above. In this example, the mill reacts to the baker's order by buying and storing wheat and selling wheat futures, futures that it will buy back as it sells flour to the baker.

In the third case, the mill produces flour on speculation and stores it, waiting for a buyer. In this case, the mill's risk is again that the price of wheat falls, bringing down the market price of flour. The mill can protect itself from this risk by selling the appropriate number of wheat futures contracts. All three cases can occur simultaneously with different customers, so that the appropriate net hedging position of the mill may require careful accounting.

Since the price of flour is volatile, some bakers hedge its cost. Since bakers sell to retailers and restaurants who abhor price increases, bakers wish to guard against cost increases. Since the price of flour is closely tied to the price of wheat, bakers may protect themselves from increases in the cost of flour by buying wheat futures. Sometimes a bakery's customers buy the futures for it. The VP of Supply Chain Management for large bakery A serving restaurant chains said:

> "If the bottom falls out of the wheat market and prices go way down, yeah, we are going to be paying more because we locked in at a higher price, but we have traded away that upside risk . . . Flour for the bakery is our biggest raw material input. So we are vulnerable to the price of wheat, and that became abundantly clear over the last couple of years when commodity markets got a little crazy. Wheat had traded in the three to four dollar (per bushel) range for a decade and then suddenly it shot up into double digits . . . So thank goodness we had begun a hedging program by then. So we were locked in at lower prices than that, because we had looked out into the future. [You just bought futures?] Yes. And the other beauty of our business is that with our big stable customer base that doesn't have a lot of fluctuation . . . I can guess pretty close to how much flour we are going to use within a 5 to 10 percent band for all of next year (which increases the effectiveness of hedging)."

9.2.6 Hedging by Soybean Crushing Plants[12]

Soybean crushing plants transform soybeans into soybean meal, crude soybean oil, and soybean hulls. Soybean meal is a protein rich pulp fed to animals. Refining plants transform crude soybean oil into a clear vegetable oil used for human consumption. Hulls are the exterior of soybeans and are a good source of fiber in animal feed. There are futures markets for soybeans, soybean meal, and crude soybean oil, but there are no futures markets for hulls or for refined soybean oil.

I describe the marketing of crude soybean oil. Crude oil refiners sell their product to manufacturers of cooking oil, salad dressings, and mayonnaise. Since these products are sold to grocery stores and restaurants that resist price increases, refiners are under pressure to avoid increasing the price of their product and so want to buy crude soybean oil at prices that are constant for a fairly long period, say eight months. A fixed price sale to a refinery might be arranged in October roughly in the following manner for the eight months January through August of the following year. Of these eight months, the five months January, March, May, July, and August are settlement months for soybean crude oil futures. The oil refiner orders from the soybean crushing plant a precise amount of crude oil for each of the delivery periods January to February, March to April, May to June, July, and August in the following year. Each of these quantities divided by the total quantity gives a weight for the corresponding period, call it a delivery weight, where the weights sum to one. For each of the periods, there is a futures price in October for crude oil delivered in the lead month of the period. That is, the futures prices are those for January, March, May, July, and August. The constant price for crude oil delivered to the refinery is a basis declared by the crushing plant plus the weighted average of the five futures prices, where the weights are the corresponding delivery weights. The soybean crushing plant hedges its sale by buying in October crude soybean oil futures contracts for each of the five settlement months, where the quantity purchased for each month is as close as possible to the quantity ordered by the refinery for the corresponding period. When a settlement month arrives, the crushing plant sells the futures contracts expiring in that month. This hedge protects the crushing plant against surges in the cost of crude soybean oil. This protection would be especially important if the crushing plant had a fire and had to buy the crude soybean oil it could not produce.

9.2.7 Price Behavior

According to respondents, the prices of corn, milo, soybeans, wheat, and their products are volatile. The following graphs illustrate the volatility of the prices of wheat and wheat flour. The graphs for corn, milo, and soybeans are similar.[13,14]

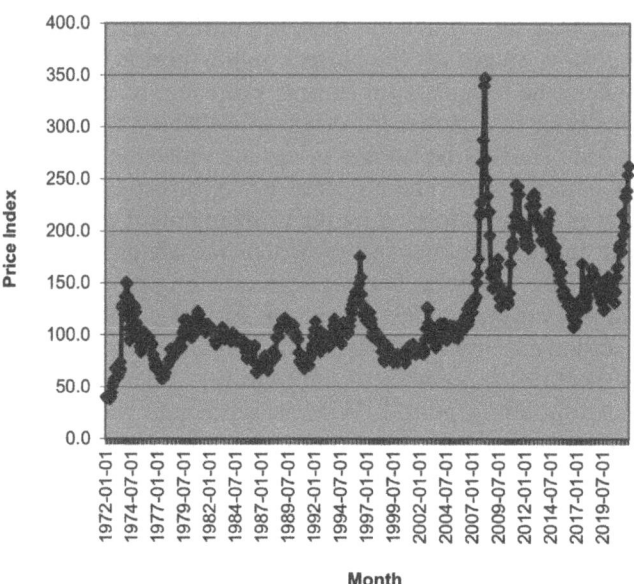

Figure 9.2.1 Price Index for Wheat, Monthly Data, Not Seasonally Adjusted, January 1972–December 2021

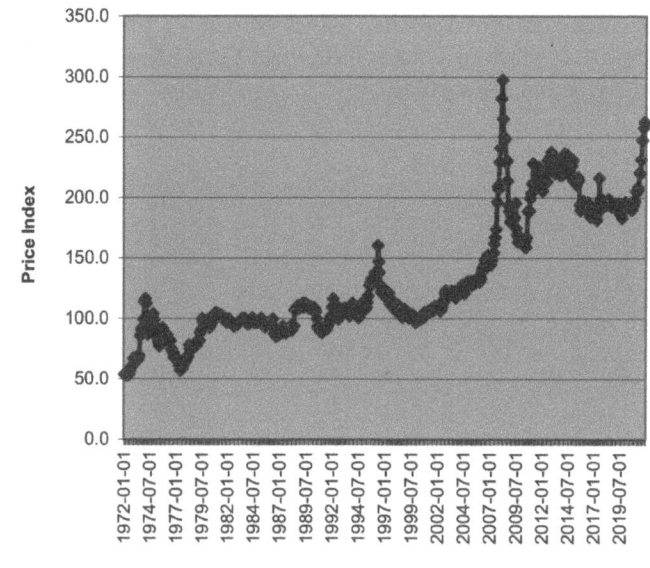

Figure 9.2.2 Producer Price Index for Wheat Flour, Monthly Data, Not Seasonally Adjusted, January 1972–December 2021

10

Conclusion

I have focused on the extremes of product differentiation in order to make clear the role it plays in price stickiness. I provide an explanation of why some prices react strongly to the business cycle and others react little. A part of the explanation requires acceptance of price setters' assertions that final demand for highly differentiated products responds little to price reductions during periods of low demand. These assertions could be tested by locating estimates of demand elasticities made by companies. If the assertions seem valid, the reasons for the demand inelasticity could be explored by detailed study of the demand for a few highly differentiated goods during a recession and done with the cooperation of the goods' producers or vendors.

Another project is to try to learn how those who choose wages, salaries, and prices think about and react to inflation. Such an undertaking should probably be done by a group, since it would require a great deal of interviewing during an inflationary period, and such periods can be brief.

Appendix

Example 1: Demand for a Single Input into Production

Consider the demand for the first input in a Leontief production function for a single output. Let the production function be

$$y = \min(a_1^{-1}x_1, a_2^{-1}x_2, \ldots, a_N^{-1}x_N),$$

where y is output, x_n is the input of the nth productive factor, and the constant coefficients a_n are positive numbers. If p_n is the price of the nth productive factor, for each n, then the total cost of producing y units of output is

$$C = y(p_1a_1 + p_2a_2 + \ldots + p_Na_N).$$

Suppose that the demand for the output y is the differentiable function D(c) of the unit cost, c, of producing the output, where $c = p_1a_1 + p_2a_2 + \ldots + p_Na_N$. Then the demand for input 1 is

$$x_1 = a_1y = a_1D(p_1a_1 + p_2a_2 + \ldots + p_Na_N)$$

and the sales revenue of the supplier of input 1 is

$$p_1x_1 = p_1a_1D(p_1a_1 + p_2a_2 + \ldots + p_Na_N).$$

The derivative of the sales revenue with respect to p_1 is

$$d(p_1x_1)/dp_1 = x_1 + p_1a_1^2 dD(c)/dc$$

$$= x_1 + p_1a_1(p_1a_1 + p_2a_2 + \ldots + p_Na_N)^{-1}a_1[cdD(c)/dc].$$

Although we should expect $cdD(c)/dc$ to be negative, $d(p_1x_1)/dp_1$ is positive if the cost p_1a_1 of the first factor is a sufficiently small fraction of the total unit cost of production. In this case, increasing the price of good 1 increases the revenue of the supplier of good 1, so that the supplier has an incentive to increase its price. Presumably, buyer opposition would prevent such an increase, but if the price of good 1 were raised too far, we can imagine that good 1 would be replaced by a substitute. Similarly, if p_1 were reduced far enough, we can imagine that good 1 might replace some other input used to produce another product perhaps in another firm. Thus we imagine that the demand curve for good 1 would look something like the heavy line in Figure A.1. If the seller of good 1 raised its price above P^U, demand for it as a factor of production would disappear. If the price were reduced below P_L, demand would expand. At the current price P, the supplier of good 1 has an incentive to increase its price, if the cost of the first factor is a sufficiently small fraction of the total costs of production. Any switching cost of replacing input 1 by a substitute input would increase P^U. Any switching cost of replacing another input with input 1 would decrease P_L. Hence the distance between P^U and P_L may be thought of as a measure of the differentiation of input 1. In this sense, we can say that the greater the differentiation of the productive input, the larger is the interval for the price of the input over which the revenue from its sale may increase as its price is increased.

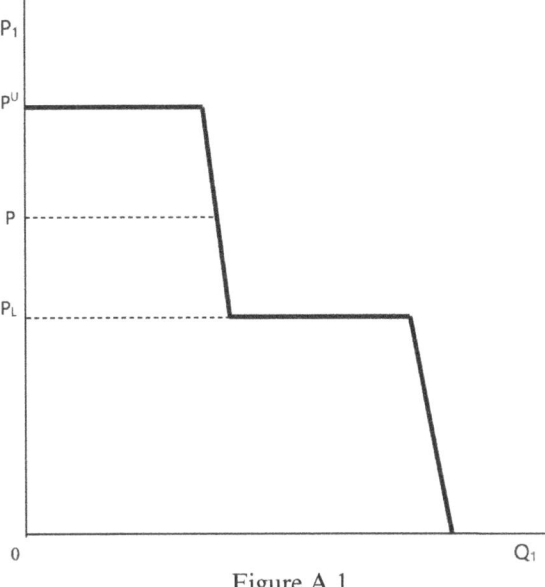

Figure A.1

Example 2: Demand for a Consumption Good

I go to an extreme of non-substitutability by assuming that all consumers have the same Leontief utility function

$$u(x_1, \ldots, x_N) = v(\min(a_1^{-1}x_1, a_2^{-1}x_2, \ldots, a_N^{-1}x_N)),$$

where there are N highly differentiated goods, x_n is the non-negative consumption of the nth such good, the coefficients a_n are positive numbers, and v is a strictly increasing function from the real numbers to the real numbers. Let p_n be the price of good n, for all n, and let w be the wealth a consumer has available for expenditure on highly differentiated goods. The demand for good 1 is found by maximizing the utility function subject to the budget constraint

$$p_1 x_1 + \ldots + p_N x_N \leq w.$$

The solution is

$$x_1 = (a_1 w)(p_1 a_1 + p_2 a_2 + \ldots + p_N a_N)^{-1},$$

which is a decreasing function of p_1. The sales revenue of the supplier of good 1 is

$$p_1 x_1 = (p_1 a_1 w)(p_1 a_1 + p_2 a_2 + \ldots + p_N a_N)^{-1},$$

which is an increasing function of p_1. That is, the elasticity of demand for good 1 is less than 1. Reducing the price of good 1 increases the demand for the good but decreases the supplier's total sales revenue and hence its profits.

Example 3: Futures Trading

The example is of a grain futures market, where payment for delivered grain is made immediately. There are four traders, B_1, S_1, B_2, and S_2, and these are the only traders in the market. The settlement month is August 2021. Trading begins on August 1, 2020 and ends on August 20, 2021. In September of 2020, S_1 sells one short futures contract and B_1 buys one long contract at a price of P_1 dollars per contract. In October of 2020, S_2 sells one short futures contract and B_2 buys one long contract at a price of P_2 dollars per contract, where $P_2 < P_1$. There are no other trades. On August 1, 2021, S_2 announces that she or he wishes to deliver on her or his short contract, and the clearinghouse matches S_2 to B_1. The delivery to B_1 is made on August 2, 2021, at which time B_1 pays P_1 dollars to the clearinghouse and the clearinghouse pays P_2 dollars to S_2. Hence at the end of August 2, the clearinghouse has a positive money balance of $P_1 - P_2$ dollars. Since neither S_1 nor B_2 makes another transaction on or before the deadline of August 20, 2021, on August 21, 2021, S_1 is obliged to deliver one contract of grain to B_2. On that day, the clearinghouse pays P_1 dollars to S_1 and B_2 pays P_2 dollars to the clearinghouse. At the end of August 21, 2021, the clearinghouse has a balance of $(1 + r)(P_1 - P_2) + (P_2 - P_1) = r(P_1 - P_2)$ dollars, where r is the rate of interest on money balances held by the clearinghouse or by traders from August 2, 2021 to August 21, 2021. If r is positive, the clearinghouse ends up with a positive balance, so that the four traders end up with a negative total balance of $r(P_2 - P_1)$. That is, at the end of August 21, 2021, the total wealth of the four traders would have been greater by the amount $r(P_1 - P_2)$ if they had not traded in futures and had left their money in an interest bearing bank account. In this sense, trading in futures was not a zero-sum or constant sum game for the four traders.

Notes

1 Introduction

1 My colleague Professor William Brainard participated in nineteen of the interviews. The interviews took place throughout the contiguous United States, two in Canada, one in Germany, and one in the United Kingdom. I ended up doing 563 interviews from June 1999 to June 2015 in over 500 companies or government agencies.
2 I had not thought of this explanation either, but pieced it together from what respondents told me.
3 Although there were well-publicized pay cuts in the U.S. during the recession of 2008–9, economy wide average pay rates continued to rise. There was a brief decline in average pay rates in 2020, apparently due to a composition effect caused by the reemployment of relatively low paid restaurant workers as the pandemic ended. See Federal Reserve Economic Data, Research Division, Federal Reserve Bank of St. Louis, data series AHETPI.
4 See Blinder et al. (1998, ch. 12).
5 A spot transaction is a purchase or sale for delivery at a specific location and date in the near future.
6 Bewley (1999) describes the behavior of the wages and salaries of temporary and regular employees and reasons why employers hesitate to cut pay.
7 There is a large economics literature on the dependence of price on "full costs." Three references are Hall and Hitch (1939); Coutts, Godley, and Nordhaus (1978); and Okun (1981, pp. 160–4).

2 The Pricing of Manufactured Goods

1 Since this company was a distributor, it was strictly speaking not a manufacturer. However it did the price setting and marketing for a few client manufacturing companies who produced what this company told them to produce. Hence the company acted as a manufacturer in its product pricing.
2 Because of my style of interviewing, I could not oblige respondents to address the question of why they did not reduce prices when demand sagged.
3 This quotation is from notes handwritten during the interview. Although I

have labeled this company as a machine shop, I have included it in the set of companies selling highly differentiated products, because it produced proprietary products for its retail business.
4 This quotation is from notes handwritten during the interview.
5 This quotation is from notes handwritten during the interview.
6 "OEM" means "Original Equipment Manufacturer."
7 In the automobile industry, reductions in sticker prices during a model year are called repositioning.
8 This quotation is from notes handwritten during the interview.
9 This list includes only the papers that seemed the most relevant.
10 The surveys that include Blinder style questions are Amirault, Kwan, and Wilkinson (2004–2005); Apel, Friberg, and Hallsten (2005); Correa, Petrassi, and Santos (2018); Greenslade and Parker (2012); Hall, Walsh, and Yates (2000); Hoeberichts and Stokman (2010); Kwapil, Scharler, and Baumgartner (2007, 2010); Loupias and Ricart (2006); Stahl (2010). The paper of Amirault, Kwan, and Wilkinson (2004–2005) is especially interesting because the authors excluded firms that produce commodities.
11 From Federal Reserve Economic Data, Research Division, Federal Reserve Bank of St. Louis, data series CUUR0000SETA0.
12 From Federal Reserve Economic Data, Research Division, Federal Reserve Bank of St. Louis, data series TOTALSA.
13 From Federal Reserve Economic Data, Research Division, Federal Reserve Bank of St. Louis, data series WPU1241.
14 From Federal Reserve Economic Data, Research Division, Federal Reserve Bank of St. Louis, data series IPG33522S.
15 These twenty firms included companies operating oil refineries, aluminum smelters, blast furnaces, paper mills, cement mills, and petrochemical plants.
16 Different respondents from the same company did not always have the same assessment of the relation of average variable cost to output. In case of conflict, I assigned to the firm the majority view or, in the case of a tie, I chose the view most favorable to the conclusion that increased output increases average variable costs.
17 SG&A is an abbreviation for Selling, General, and Administrative expenses and is an important component of the fixed costs of many firms.
18 The eleven respondents include the person quoted at the end of Section 2.6.7 below.

3 Retail Pricing

1 This chapter is based on 95 interviews. These included 22 with retail grocers, two with officials of large home improvement retail chains, three with officials of large chains selling office supplies and household appliances, six with retailers selling sporting goods and clothes, eleven with diverse other retailers, two with large grocery wholesalers, three with specialized food wholesalers, two with large non-food wholesalers, 33 with food manufacturers, five with non-food manufacturers that sell to grocery stores, three with food brokers, and three with food pricing consultants. The 22 with retail grocers included interviews with officials in nine large supermarket chains.
2 Food brokers are paid by manufacturers to act as their agents in dealing with grocers.

3 Respondents' arithmetic is often approximate.
4 From Federal Reserve Economic Data, Research Division, Federal Reserve Bank of St. Louis, data series APU0000712211.
5 This quotation is from notes handwritten during the interview.
6 The reasons are explained in the first paragraph of Section 2.7 and in Section 2.7.3 of Chapter 2.
7 This quotation is from notes handwritten during the interview.
8 This quotation is from notes handwritten during the interview.
9 I am grateful to Professor William Brainard for suggesting that I graph data on total grocery store sales.
10 From Federal Reserve Economic Data, Research Division, Federal Reserve Bank of St. Louis, data series RSGC.
11 From Federal Reserve Economic Data, Research Division, Federal Reserve Bank of St. Louis, data series MRTSSM7225USN.
12 Private or store brands are products whose production is commissioned by retail companies to be sold in their stores. The producers are usually chosen by competitive bidding, and the products are normally cheaper than the branded equivalents because the producers have no marketing or advertising expenses. This quotation is from notes handwritten during the interview.
13 This quotation is from notes handwritten during the interview.

4 Restaurant Pricing

1 This chapter is based on thirty interviews, twelve with restaurant managers or owners, one with a pricing consultant for restaurant chains, ten with manufacturers supplying food to restaurants and supermarkets, five with food service distributors, and two with pricing consultants for the meat industry.
2 It is a common practice in the restaurant industry to refer to individual restaurants as stores.
3 This respondent claimed that desserts were low margin items, whereas others made the opposite claim. In this chain, desserts were treated as central items that should carry low margins in order to attract customers.
4 In business jargon, "food service" refers to the restaurant industry.
5 From Section 3.6 of Chapter 3.
6 From Federal Reserve Economic Data, Research Division, Federal Reserve Bank of St. Louis, data series CUUR0000SEFV.

5 Pricing by Contract Manufacturers

1 This chapter is based on 36 interviews in 35 companies. Of these companies, seven manufacture folding cartons, three are aluminum extruders, one makes zinc-aluminum castings, two are plating companies, one is a heat treating company, five are injection molding companies, three are machine shops, five manufacture parts from compressed and sintered powdered metal, three are stamping companies, three are contract manufacturers of electronic devices, and two are general contract manufacturers.
2 An interesting question is whether capital goods manufacturers and contract manufacturers, because they often bid for work, are like construction firms in

that they have a greater tendency than most other firms to reduce wages and salaries during a recession. I do not know whether they do.
3 From Section 2.6.3 of Chapter 2.

6 Pricing in the Construction Industry

1 This chapter is based on 43 interviews, four with construction contractors or construction managers, thirteen with construction subcontractors, three with wholesalers of building materials sold to construction professionals, twelve with building material manufacturers, three with lumber wholesalers, four with lumber manufacturers, one with a company that both produces lumber and retails building materials to construction professionals, one with the manager of a plywood mill, one with the manager of a factory that produces laminated veneer lumber, and one with a price reporting company that covers lumber, plywood, and oriented strand board.
2 This quotation is from a conversation about construction managers rather than general contractors.
3 Drywall is a term for gypsum wallboard.

7 The Pricing of Cement

1 This chapter is based on eleven interviews, four with officials in cement manufacturing companies, four with officials in ready mix companies, two with officials in companies that produce pre-stressed concrete parts for buildings and bridges, and one with the owner and president of a cement block company.
2 FOB, Free On Board, means the price includes transportation to a specified location and no further (Wikipedia).
3 Competitive situation is a technical term that refers to a provision of the Robinson–Patman Act of 1936. This Act is described briefly in Section 2.2.5 of Chapter 2.
4 From Federal Reserve Economic Data, Research Division, Federal Reserve Bank of St. Louis, data series PCU3273132731.
5 From Federal Reserve Economic Data, Research Division, Federal Reserve Bank of St. Louis, data series IPN32731S.

8 The Pricing of Commodity Lumber, Plywood, and Oriented Strand Board

1 This chapter is based on eighteen interviews, thirteen from the lumber industry, two with respondents from lumber yards serving contractors, two with respondents from home improvement retail chains, and one with the President and Publisher of a lumber price-reporting company.
2 In Section 2.2.7 of Chapter 2.
3 The respondent means that although the industry has more than enough capacity to meet the regular flow of demand, it does not have enough capacity to meet demand created by rapid inventory accumulation.
4 From Federal Reserve Economic Data, Research Division, Federal Reserve Bank of St. Louis, data series WPU0811.

214 Notes to pages 180–203

5 From Federal Reserve Economic Data, Research Division, Federal Reserve Bank of St. Louis, data series WPU083.
6 I am grateful to the lumber market-reporting company Random Lengths for the data displayed in this figure.

9 The Pricing of Midwestern Food and Feed Grains

1 This chapter is based on seventeen interviews, two with officials of New York investment banks who were experts on petroleum pricing and hence the use of futures for hedging, five with Kansas grain farmers, two with officials of grain cooperatives that had country elevators, four with officials of three large grain-trading and processing companies, one with a grain broker, one with two officials of a large commercial bakery, one with a commodity market consultant, and one with the general manager of a feedlot.
2 Excellent references on futures are: Bernstein (1989); Hieronymus (1971); Kolb (1997); Stebbins (1989); and Stein (1986).
3 The wording of these definitions is close to that of Hieronymus (1971, pp. 28, 39).
4 Stebbins (1989, p. 15).
5 According to Stebbins (1989, p. 69), clearinghouses associated with the Chicago Board of Trade match the seller to the buyer with the oldest reported open long position.
6 In reality, traders pay commissions to brokers and clearinghouses collect small clearance fees. See Hieronymus (1971, p. 43).
7 For the assertion that futures trading is a zero-sum game see, for example, the second paragraph on p. 43 of Hieronymus (1971).
8 See, for instance, Crowder, Schneeweis, and Kazemi (2011, bottom of p. 101).
9 This explanation of hedging behavior may be found in Helmuth (1977, p. 15).
10 I do not count this farmer as one of the five grain farmers I interviewed.
11 This section is based on an interview with a vice president of a huge food manufacturing company.
12 This section is based on an interview with the manager of soybean crushing plants owned by a large food products manufacturer.
13 From Federal Reserve Economic Data, Research Division, Federal Reserve Bank of St. Louis, data series WPU0121.
14 From Federal Reserve Economic Data, Research Division, Federal Reserve Bank of St. Louis, data series PCU3112113112111.

References

Abreu, D., D. Pearce, and E. Stacchetti (1986) Optimal Cartel Equilibria with Imperfect Monitoring. *Journal of Economic Theory*, 39(1).

Adelman, M. (1959) Pricing Objectives in Large Companies: Comment. *American Economic Review*, 49(4).

Akerlof, G. and J. Yellen (1985) A Near-Rational Model of the Business Cycle with Wage and Price Inertia. *Quarterly Journal of Economics*, 100 (Supplement).

Alvarez, L., P. Burriel, and I. Hernando (2010) Price-setting Behaviour in Spain: Evidence from Micro PPI Data. *Managerial and Decision Economics*, 31(2–3).

Amirault, D., C. Kwan, and G. Wilkinson (2004–2005) A Survey of the Price-Setting Behavior of Canadian Companies. *Bank of Canada Review*, 12(Winter).

Andrews, P. (1949) *Manufacturing Business*. Macmillan.

Apel, M., R. Friberg, and K. Hallsten (2005) Micro Foundations of Macroeconomic Price Adjustment: Survey Evidence from Swedish Firms. *Journal of Money, Credit, and Banking*, 37(2).

Balkin, N. (1956) Prices in the Clothing Industry. *Journal of Industrial Economics*, 5(1).

Barback, R. (1964) *The Pricing of Manufactures*. Macmillan.

Beggs, A. and P. Klemperer (1992) Multi-Period Competition with Switching Costs. *Econometrica*, 60(3).

Bernstein, J. (1989) *How the Futures Markets Work*. New York Institute of Finance.

Bewley, T. (1999) *Why Wages Don't Fall During a Recession*. Harvard University Press.

Bils, M. and P. Klenow (2004) Some Evidence on the Importance of Sticky Prices. *Journal of Political Economics*, 112(5).

Blinder, A., E. Canetti, D. Lebow, and J. Rudd (1998) *Asking About Prices*. Russell Sage Foundation.

Caplin, A. and J. Leahy (1997) Aggregation and Optimization with State-Dependent Pricing. *Econometrica*, 65(3).

Carlsson, M. and O. Skans (2012) Evaluating Microfoundations for Aggregate Price Rigidities: Evidence from Matched Firm-Level Data on Product Prices and Unit Labor Costs. *American Economic Review*, 102(4).

Carson, D., A. Gilmore, D. Cummins, A. O'Donnell, and K. Grant (1998) Prices in SMEs: Some Empirical Findings. *Journal of Product and Brand Management*, 7(1).

Chevalier, J., A. Kashyap, and P. Rossi (2003) Why Don't Prices Rise during Peak Demand Periods? Evidence from Scanner Data. *American Economic Review*, 93(1).

Correa, A., M. Petrassi, and R. Santos (2018) Price Setting Beharior in Brazil: Survey Evidence. *Journal of Business Cycle Research*, 14(2).

Costa Dias, M., D. Dias, and P. Duarte Neves (2008) Stylised Features of Consumer Price Setting Behaviour in Portugal: 1992–2001. *Portuguese Economic Journal*, 7(2).

Coutts, K., W. Godley, and W. Nordhaus (1978) *Industrial Pricing in United Kingdom*. Cambridge University Press.

Crowder, G., T. Schneeweis, and H. Kazemi (2011) *Postmodern Investment*. John Wiley & Sons.

Dhyne, E., L. Bihan, H. Le, G. Veronese, D. Dias, J. Hoffmann, N. Jonker, P. Lünnemann, F. Rumier, and J. Viimunen (2006) Price Changes in the Euro Area and the United States: Some Facts from Individual Consumer Prices. *Journal of Economic Perspectives*, 20(2).

Druant, M., S. Fabiani, G. Kezdi, A. Lamo, F. Martins, and R. Sabbatini (2012) Firms' Price and Wage Adjustment in Europe: Survey Evidence on Nominal Stickiness. *Labour Economics*, 19(5).

Dutta, S., M. Bergen, D. Levy, and R. Venable (1999) Menu Costs, Posted Prices, and Multiproduct Retailers. *Journal of Money Credit, and Banking*, 31(4).

Earley, J. (1956) Marginal Policies of Excellently Managed Companies. *American Economic Review*, 46(1).

Edwards, R. S. (1952) The Pricing of Manufactured Products. *Economica*, 19(75).

Fabiani, S., A. Gattulli, G. Veronese, and R. Sabbatini (2010) Price Adjustment in Italy: Evidence from Micro Producer and Consumer Prices. *Managerial and Decision Economics*, 31(2–3).

Fog, B. (1960) *Industrial Pricing Policies: An Analysis of Pricing Policies of Danish Manufacturers*. North Holland.

Golosov, M. and R. Lucas (2007) Menu Costs and Phillips Curves. *Journal of Political Economy*, 115(2).

Gordon, R. (1948) Short-Period Price Determination in Theory and Practice. *American Economic Review*, 38(3).

Greenslade, J. and M. Parker (2012) New Insights into Price-Setting Behaviour in the UK: Introduction and Survey Results. *Economic Journal*, 122(558).

Guimaraes, B. and K. Sheedy (2011) Sales and Monetary Policy. *American Economic Review*, 101(2).

Hague, D. (1971) *Pricing in Business*. George Allen and Unwin.

Hall, R. (1986) Market Structure and Macroeconomic Fluctuations. *Brookings Papers on Economic Activity* (2).

Hall, R. and C. Hitch (1939) Price Theory and Business Behaviour. *Oxford Economic Papers*, os-2(1).

Hall, S., M. Walsh, and A. Yates (2000) Are UK Companies' Prices Sticky?. *Oxford Economic Papers*, 52(3).
Haynes, W. (1973) *Pricing Decisions in Small Business*. Greenwood Press.
Helmuth, J. (1977) *Grain Pricing*. Commodity Futures Trading Commission.
Hieronymus, T. (1971) *Economics of Futures Trading, for Commercial and Personal Profit*. Commodity Research Bureau.
Hoeberichts, M. and A. Stokman (2010) Price Setting Behaviour in the Netherlands: Results of a Survey. *Managerial and Decision Economics*, 31 (2–3).
Kackmeister, A (2007) Yesterday's Bad Times Are Today's Good Old Times: Retail Price Changes are More Frequent Today than in the 1890s. *Journal of Money, Credit and Banking*, 39(8).
Kahn, A. (1959) Pricing Objectives in Large Companies: Comment. *American Economic Review*, 49(4).
Kaplan, A., J. Dirlam, and R. Lanzillotti (1958) *Pricing in Big Business, A Case Approach*. The Brookings Institution.
Kashyap, A. (1995) Sticky Prices: New Evidence from Retail Catalogues. *Quarterly Journal of Economics*, 110(1).
Klemperer, P. (1987a) The Competitiveness of Markets with Switching Costs. *The RAND Journal of Economics*, 18(1).
_____ (1987b) Markets with Consumer Switching Costs. *Quarterly Journal of Economics*, 102(2).
_____ (1987c) Entry Deterrence in Markets with Consumer Switching Costs. *Economic Journal*, 97(Suppl).
_____ (1989) Price Wars Caused by Switching Costs. *Review of Economic Studies*, 56(3).
_____ (1995) Competition when Consumers Have Switching Costs: An Overview with Applications to Industrial Organization, Macroeconomics, and International Trade. *Review of Economic Studies*, 62(4).
Klenow, P. and O. Kryvtsov (2008) State-Dependent or Time-Dependent Pricing: Does It Matter for Recent U.S. Inflation?. *Quarterly Journal of Eonomics*, 123(3).
Kolb, R. (1997) *Understanding Futures Markets*. Blackwell Publishers, Inc.
Kwapil, C., J. Scharler, and J. Baumgartner (2007) Price-Setting Behavior of Austrian Firms. *Empirica*, 34(5).
_____ (2010) How Are Prices Adjusted in Response to Shocks? Survey Evidence from Austrian Firms. *Managerial and Decision Economics*, 31(2–3).
Lanzillotti, R. (1958) Pricing Objectives in Large Companies. *American Economic Review*, 48(5).
_____ (1959) Pricing Objectives in Large Companies: Reply. *American Economic Review*, 49(4).
_____ (1964) *Pricing, Production and Marketing Policies of Small Manufacturers*. University of Washington Press.
Lazear, Edward P. (1986) Retail Pricing and Clearance Sales. *American Economic Review*, 76(1).
Lester, R. A. (1946) Shortcomings of Marginal Analysis for Wage-Employment Problems. *American Economic Review*, 36(1).

Levy, D., M. Bergen, S. Dutta, and R. Venable (1997) The Magnitude of Menu Costs: Direct Evidence from Large US Supermarket Chains. *Quarterly Hournal of Economics*, 112(3).

____ (1998) Price Adjustment at Multiproduct Retailers. *Managerial and Decision Economics*, 19(2).

Levy, D. and A. Young (2004) The Real Thing: Nominal Price Rigidity of the Nickel Coke, 1886–1959. *Journal of Money, Credit, and Banking*, 36(4).

Loupias, C. and R. Ricart (2006) Price-Setting in the French Manufacturing Sector: New Evidence from Survey Data. *Revue d'economie politique*, 116(4).

Machlup, F. (1946) Marginal Analysis and Empirical Research. *American Economic Review*, 36(4).

Mankiw, N. G. (1985) Small Menu Costs and Large Business Cycles: A Macroeconomic Model of Monopoly. *Quarterly Journal of Econnomics*, 100(2).

Means, G. (1935) Industrial Prices and Their Relative Inflexibility. U. S. Senate Document 13. 24th Congress. First Session. Washington D. C.

_____ (1962) *Pricing Power and the Public Interest, A Study Based on Steel.* Harper Brothers.

____ (1972) The Administered-Price Thesis Reconfirmed. *American Economic Review*, 62(3).

Moura, M. and J. Rossi Jr. (2010) Price-Setting Policy Determinants: Micro-Evidence from Brazil. *Economia Aplicada*, 14(2).

Nakamura, E. and J. Steinsson (2008) Five Facts about Prices: A Reevaluation of Menu Cost Models. *Quarterly Journal of Economics*, 123(4).

____ (2011) Price Setting in Forward-Looking Customer Markets. *Journal of Monetary Economics*, 58(3).

____ (2013) Price Rigidity: Microeconomic Evidence and Macroeconomic Implications. *Annual Review of Economics*, 5(1).

Narasimhan, C. (1988) Competitive Promotional Strategies. *Journal of Business*, 61(4).

Okun, A. (1981) *Prices and Quantities: A Macroeconomic Analysis*. The Brookings Institution.

Parkin, M. (1986) The Output-Inflation Trade-Off When Prices Are Costly to Change. *Journal of Political Economy*, 94(1).

Pashigian, B. P. (1988) Demand Uncertainty and Sales: A Study of Fashion and Markdown Pricing. *American Economic Review*, 78(5).

Pashigian, B. P. and B. Bowen (1991) Why Are Products Sold on Sales? Explanation of Pricing Regularities. *Quarterly Journal of Economics*, 106(4).

Pearce, I. F. (1956) A Study in Price Policy. *Economica*, 23(90).

Pearce, I. F. and L. Amey (1956–1957) Price Policy with a Branded Product. *Review of Economic Studies*, 24(1).

Ramey, V. (1991) Nonconvex Costs and the Behavior of Inventories. *Journal of Political Economy*, 99(2).

Simester, D. (1997) Note. Optimal Promotion Strategies: A Demand-Sided Characterization. *Management Science*, 43(2).

Sobel, J. (1984) The Timing of Sales. *Review of Economic Studies*, 51(3).

Stahl, H. (2010) Price Adjustment in German Manufacturing: Evidence from Two Merged Surveys. *Managerial and Decision Economics*, 31(2–3).

Stebbins, C. (editor) (1989) *Commodity Trading Manual*. Education and Marketing Services Department of the Chicago Board of Trade.

Stein, J. (1986) *The Economics of Futures Markets*. Basil Blackwell.

Sweezy, P. (1939) Demand under Conditions of Oligopoly. *Journal of Political Economy*, 47(4).

Varian, H. (1980) A Model of Sales. *American Economic Review*, 70(4).

Vermeulen, P., D. Dias, M. Dossche, E. Gautier, I. Hernando, R. Sabbatini, and H. Stahl (2012) Price Setting in the Euro Area: Some Stylized Facts from Individual Producer Price Data. *Journal of Money, Credit, and Banking*, 44(8).

von Weizsäcker, C. (1984) The Costs of Substitution. *Econometrica*, 52(5).

Zbaracki, M., M. Ritson, D. Levy, S. Dutta, and M. Bergen (2004) Managerial and Customer Costs of Price Adjustment: Direct Evidence from Industrial Markets. *Review of Economics and Statistics*, 86(2).

Index

administrative costs of price change
  See menu costs and price change

basis 183
Blinder, Alan 1–2, 4
broad line distributor 136

cash price 189
cement pricing 163–173
  how prices decrease 169–170
clearinghouse 184
commoditize 7
commodity 5
competitive situation 38
construction company pricing 152–160
  influence of fixed and overhead costs 152, 156–157
  instances of downward rigidity of 159–160
contract manufacturer pricing 145–148
  downward price rigidity of 144, 149–151
  influence of fixed and overhead costs 144, 147–148
  use of contribution margin pricing 149
contract manufacturing 10–11, 144–151
contribution margin pricing 4, 63, 69–71, 149
convergence of futures to spot prices 188
customer markets 14

delivery on futures contracts 185–186
distributors *See* wholesalers

everyday low pricing (EDLP) 14, 90
exchange for physicals (EFP) 191

fixed costs can affect prices 63–65, 71–72, 126–127, 144, 147–148
  impact of product development costs on prices 72–75
flat price 183
floor stock protection 46
food broker 90, n.2
food costs and food and paper costs 122
formula-based pricing 4–6, 10, 17, 76–86
  drawbacks of 85–86
forward buying 11
  by restaurant chains 11, 136–140
  by supermarket chains 95–101
forward guidance 3
forward trading and futures 191–192
fully absorbing costs 4, 60–62
  attitudes toward 67–68
  effects of 63–67
  use of may indicate constant or declining marginal variable costs 60–61
futures contracts 183–184
  delivery on 185–186
  long futures contracts 183
  nearby futures contracts 189
  open futures contracts 185
  prompt month of 188–189
  sale of 184–185
  settlement of 185
  settlement month of 183

settlement price of 189
short futures contracts 183–184
futures exchange 184
futures trading is a zero-sum game 186–187

hedging 183
  long hedge or buying hedge 190–191
  short hedge or selling hedge 189–190
highly differentiated product 3

incremental business 65
inflation targeting 3

kinked demand curve theory 13–14, 46–47

line pricing 91–92
liquid market 184
lumber, plywood, and oriented strand board pricing 176–177
  and capacity utilization 177–179

MAP *See* minimum advertised price
marginal variable cost and output 15–16, 53–59, 122
  and capacity utilization 16–17
market reporter 77–79
market risk (of fixed prices) 77
market price surveys 77–80
Means, Gardiner 20
meet comp situation 38
menu costs and price change 7, 11, 51–53, 134–136
  effect on retail prices 108–112
  effect on retail prices for expensive goods 111–112
  effect on prices paid by retailers 110–112
method of research 1–2
  confidentiality 2
  interviewing 1–2
  sampling 2
  transcription 2
minimum advertised price 36–37

Okun, Arthur 14
overhead costs 61

price discovery 77

price downward rigidity of, for highly differentiated products 6–11, 37–47
  and floor stock protection 46
  and switching costs 7, 13, 42–44
  and value pricing 44–45
  in contract manufacturing 10–11, 144, 149–151
  in restaurants 10, 130–134
  market power as a cause of 10
price instability of commodities 93–95
price reduction of highly differentiated products 29–32, 41–42
price stability of highly differentiated products 48–50
pricing of highly differentiated products 22–27
promotional discounts 8–9, 89–90, 127–130
  strongly increase sales 38–40, 91

recessions' impact on retailers 112–116
  on grocery stores 112–113
  on restaurants 141–142
regular price 90
resistance to price increases of highly differentiated products 9, 12, 32–36, 39–40, 105–108, 130–134
  by restaurants 130–134
restaurant pricing 122–130
  efforts to stabilize food costs 136–140
  franchisee pricing 119–120
  influence of fixed costs 126–127
  labor costs are fixed 121–122
  menu costs and price change 134–136
  promotions and specials 127–130
  reluctance to increase prices 130–134
  reluctance to reduce prices 130–134, 141–142
  restaurant industry competitiveness 117–119
  variable costs 121–126
retailers' efforts to stabilize commodity prices 95–99
retailers' methods for setting promotional prices for commodities in advance 99–101
retailers' pricing strategy 88–92

retailers secure supplies of branded products by using contracts with fixed or formula-based prices 101–103
Robinson–Patman Act 37–38

spot transaction 5, n.5

systems distributor 136

value pricing 9

wage rigidity 4, n.3
wholesalers 87–88